STORRS LECTURES ON JURISPRUDENCE

YALE LAW SCHOOL, 1963

Location of African nations and tribes

THE IDEAS IN

BAROTSE JURISPRUDENCE

MAX GLUCKMAN

NEW HAVEN AND LONDON, YALE UNIVERSITY PRESS, 1965

To

The Jurists of Barotseland and of the

Yale Law School

Who welcomed a stranger and made him

feel one of them

Contents

FOREWORD

by Charles L. Black, Jr.

ONE WHO SAW a lot of Max Gluckman during the weeks when he was at Yale in April 1963 to deliver his Storrs Lectures can never separate the book from the man as he then showed himself—a great chief in the dispersed but self-recognizing tribe "di color che sanno." He opened the windows to my office to admit the bracing early spring air, and he hooked open the door so that all might come and talk to him. Nearly all did—law professors, colleagues in anthropology, students from as near as the *Law Journal* and from the farthest corners of Yale. In that office or down in the smaller but more used of the student lounges, seated at lunch or walking a bit too fast even for a pretty well-seasoned walker, Wordsworthian through the days or a tenth part Porsonian by night, he was copious of apt and accurate citation, flowing with ideas, the thorough-paced academic humanist whose command of his own specialty was evidently the fulcrum of a lever aspiring toward the length of Archimedean dream and solidly reaching a very long way. It is to be doubted that anybody else ever made such an impression on the Yale Law School in two weeks. He left behind a buzz of talk as to when we might get him to come back.

Yet the book stands by itself. It stands, above all, as a unity. In its unity, its most immediately impressive feature, and the one of most crucial importance to both parties in the law–anthropology relation, is its courageous and uncompromising insistence on applying the best in modern jurisprudential analysis to the Barotse material. The title is not a paradox; its promise is sustained, and this method is explicitly and skillfully defended (pp. 254 f.). It is unlikely that Gluckman would claim finality for his present application of this means to conceptual unification. But it seems certain that the road he takes is one that must be followed if the most is to be said that can be said about meaningful relations among all the systems of law we can know about.

When Sir Arthur Goodhart wrote the foreword to Gluckman's earlier and now classic *Judicial Process among the Barotse,* the assumption seems to have been that the chief relation was between the "early" and the "late." One who is nothing but a "late" lawyer may be permitted to query whether the Barotse law of 1947 is any "earlier" than the law of the Portal-to-Portal Pay Cases. What is independently interesting, at least, is that the ideas and techniques applied, say, to the solution of the fishing-net case cited and set out herein (pp. 178 f.) seem about as intricate as those applied to the Portal-to-Portal Pay Cases. Economic and social life tender us, to be sure, many more complex problems than the Barotse are conscious of facing, but "primitive" law, as here illustrated in one of its systems, seems just about as intricate, as intellectual, as "civilized" law through much of the latter's range. There is overlap, not stellar distance; stone is still used for building, though iron has been refined.

One of the insights unifying the book is the point that we must not look for conceptual differentiation only where our system exhibits it. Gluckman is able to show that the seeming paucity of "ownership" and "title" terminology in Barotse means no more than that the task of making necessary distinctions, and these quite fine, is transposed, projected onto the status system, which dominates the land system: "the rights of Barotse in land and chattels . . . were contained in the Law of Persons" (p. 170).

It is certain that different legal specialists will find special interest in different parts of the book. The commercial lawyer will be interested in the Barotse rule *caveat vendor,* extending unto the hidden defect discovered long after sale, or even sometimes to the misfortune; we may think this bizarre, until we happen to recall how certain transactions are treated by our better department stores. With the Barotse, as with us, the Law of Damages searches the theory of liability; the explicitness of this in Barotse might lead us to remember it more often ourselves. A near stranger to modern land law hazards the guess that specialists in that field may find a wealth of insightful comparison in Gluckman's treatment.

A constitutional lawyer naturally reports most eagerly on another part of the elephant. The Barotse have a highly developed theory of power, much like our own in its distrust of that tricky substance. The most interesting aspect of their theory, one repeatedly insisted on by Gluckman, is the one seemingly compacted in the term

Ngambela, the name of the king's chief councillor and of figures standing in the same kind of relation to other powerful persons—including
the King's Ngambela, who has an Ngambela of his own. The Ngambela seems to be at once an executant and a thwarter or softener of
the will of his principal. With the Barotse, this ambivalence is con-
sciously acknowledged and seems natural. We are not as aware of it,
but surely the Barotse are right. The bureaucracy exists, in our theory,
to execute policy, yet (not just once in a while, but always, as a part
of its factually accepted if not of its explicitly recognized function)
it alters, deflects, changes policy given from above. In good part, the
ostensible office of the British and of our federal judiciary is the application, the execution of Acts of Parliament and Acts of Congress respectively; need one say more? In America, we have added the explicitly checking function of judicial review for constitutionality, but
it may be that the braking force of a judiciary that must, using its
own men and methods, individuate the general command, is greater
than any special device that could be added. Freeman's *Lee's Lieuten-
ants,* and probably every other military history, shows the same phenomenon in the military. I can remember only one occasion on which I
enjoyed political power. I was Chairman of the Charter Revision Com-
mission in New Haven, and we held a public hearing. In the back of
the hall there stood a policeman, and it suddenly came to me that I
was in charge, and that if someone became disorderly I could tell that
policeman, with the ultimate power of the State in his hands, to throw
the disturber out. I felt a certain thrill at this, and thought I understood what it was that could drive men to seek the command of armies
and peoples. Then I was checked (as commanders of armies and peoples
must often have been checked, *parvis sic componere magna*) by the
sure knowledge that that policeman would not do just anything I told
him to—far from it—and that what he did he would do in his own
manner. If nothing else stands in the way of absolute power, it is made
impossible by the fact that it has to work through human beings, and
that they have an inertia of their own, and even their own counteraction. The most natural limitation on power builds on this, as the Barotse seem to understand.

The Barotse know that the obligation of allegiance may be not the
less intense for its being precisely defined. Gluckman finds a parallel
in the English Middle Ages. There, as among the Barotse, he finds
treason was to the *kingship;* one could make war on the king, with

the aim of replacing him, without being a traitor. More, such rebellion or insurrection "has to be related to more than resentment of injustice; it can be connected with the total political process" (p. 57). Though the structural problem is not the same, it may not be long before we in the United States have to consider similarly searching questions about the exact direction of allegiance, for the Negro community in one or more of our states may be driven into total civil disobedience to state authority, while seeking no quarrel with the nation, and the rest of us will have to consider whether such an act is a rupture of the essential allegiance that binds us all together, or a mere "rebellion," albeit peaceful, to rid the state of an unjust rule, and the nation of a state rule defiant of national order.

At the end of our Civil War the nation faced a question in the same field of reference, when it had to decide whether the Southern people were to be looked upon as rebels or as traitors. Surely the right choice was made, for the Southern rebellion, ironically enough but very truly, was undertaken under a claim of legal right asserted under the federal Constitution itself.

As one final reflection, the constitutionalist who knows nothing of Africa must ask himself why it is that well-developed political structures such as the one Gluckman here describes seem to have been so little employed in building the modern governments of the new African states.

Such a book as this starts countless thoughts and queries. But one must return to the first point; Gluckman's account of Barotse is a thing in itself, and it is a unity. Sir Arthur Goodhart concluded his foreword to Gluckman's *Judicial Process* with the words: "It will be many years before a more interesting and a more path-breaking book is published in this field of political science." Literally, this has to stand, for the present book is in the path first broken by the other. But one may say now that it has been a long time since legal anthropology has seen a book so thorough, so learned, so rich in thesis and allusion as *The Ideas in Barotse Jurisprudence*.

THIS BOOK is the outcome of field research on the law and social life of the Barotse of Northern Rhodesia. It is a sequel to my study, *The Judicial Process among the Barotse of Northern Rhodesia*, which was published in 1955. When I wrote that book I was thinking about why the Barotse had certain ideas on constitutional matters, contract, injury, landholding, property, and so on. Other commitments prevented me from completing a book on this theme, but I read around it and drafted a few analyses. In October 1960 I was honored by an invitation to deliver the Storrs Lectures in the Yale Law School, and decided that this subject, in "the sociology of legal ideas," would be appropriate. The lectures were delivered at Yale in April 1963. I am deeply grateful to the members of the Yale Law School for the high honor they accorded me, for the warmth and the criticisms with which they received the lectures, and for their personal friendliness and hospitality. I mention especially Dean Eugene V. Rostow and Mrs. Rostow, and Professor Charles L. Black, Jr., and Mrs. Black, but all members of the school faculty and many students made my whole visit most memorable. Charles Black gave me his room, all his time, and his full intellectual help for a fortnight.

When A. E. Housman was appointed to the Chair in Latin at the University of Cambridge, Trinity College staged a dinner in his honor. It is said that he began his reply to the toasting of his health thus: "I am told that in these halls Porson was once seen sober, and Wordsworth was once seen drunk. A finer poet than Porson, a better scholar than Wordsworth, I stand before you tonight betwixt and between." In this book I too stand betwixt and between—a better anthropologist than some lawyers, a finer lawyer than some anthropologists; if I stagger somewhat in the attempt to acquit myself, I plead for your forbearance. Yet perhaps I may draw solace from the manner in which Dean Rostow introduced his William W. Cook Lectures at the University of Michigan (*Planning for Freedom*,

1959). He said: "I have long been engaged in trying to expound economic problems to lawyers, and legal problems to economists—a task yielding unexpected comfort since some members of each group tend to accept my credentials in the other without the usual tests." My own plea therefore is that none of you tests my credentials in the field in which he is himself expert. If the lawyers concentrate on my anthropology, and the anthropologists on my law, I may possibly say something new to everyone.

I write as a social anthropologist who has had only too little training in law, but I propose to discuss some of the principal ideas involved in the law of a particular African tribe, to examine the implications of these ideas, and to try to explain why these kinds of ideas are held, by relating them to other aspects of economic and social life. I spent some thirty months studying this tribe, which rules a large kingdom in Northern Rhodesia. I am concentrating mainly on my own research instead of making a general analysis of the law of what I call the tribal societies because I am, as far as I know, the first anthropologist to tackle this specific set of problems: the relation of legal ideas to the general social system of a tribe. Some of my colleagues have touched on these problems incidentally, in the course of pursuing other analyses, and so far as space allows me I shall indicate whether or not their evidence supports my conclusions.

My compelled dependence on my own field research in this way gives me a great advantage, balanced by a major disadvantage. My advantage is that since I am the first anthropologist to adopt this specific approach to an analysis of the legal ideas of a tribal people, anything I say may be new and to some extent illuminating. The corresponding disadvantage is that I bear responsibility not only for my analysis but also for the data on which I work. I cannot plead that gaps in interpretation are due to "most important links . . . [which] are missing through the caprice of time [because] indeed whole periods and whole problems are plunged in entire darkness," to quote Vinogradoff [1] on early European law. These gaps exist because I did not think of the problems when I was working among the Barotse and hence did not collect the information I might have. If I point out

1. "The Teachings of Sir Henry Maine," Inaugural Lecture in the University of Oxford, reprinted from *Law Quarterly Review*, April 1904, in *The Collected Papers of Paul Vinogradoff*, 2 (1928), 173 f.

these gaps, other anthropologists may collect the appropriate data before the radical changes which are occurring in the developing countries obscure from us forever their indigenous legal ideas.

The advantage—that I bring fresh data from an unstudied system of law to the attention of jurists—has so far served me well. I owed the invitation to deliver a series of Storrs lectures, as the first anthropologist in a line of jurists and philosophers, to my book, *The Judicial Process among the Barotse*. This was the first book to analyze in detail the judicial reasoning of an African people. In making this analysis I cited the whole course, as far as I could record it in the Barotse language, of a number of cases. I was able to show that the reasoning of Barotse judges had much in common with the reasoning of Western judges. I also found significant differences in the aims and logic of Western and Barotse judges, and I tried to relate these to the general social and economic background of the nation.

I follow here a similar procedure in describing a number of Barotse jurisprudential ideas. These ideas are found in most systems of jurisprudence: the law of the constitution and the theory of power; treason and royal succession; the nature of rights in land; the different laws applying to immovable and movable property; concepts of property, of contract, of wrong and injury, and of debt. I shall try to relate similarities and differences between these ideas and our own to the social and economic conditions of Barotse life. The Barotse ideas are, in brief, the legal ideas of a people who had relatively few contracts, though those few were important in enabling them to attain their economic goals. But on the whole, most men acquired access to the use of land through status, and most of their transactions with material goods were part of claims and obligations arising from pre-established status relationships. These relationships were largely familial or kinship; and even political status, which also controlled access to land and transactions with goods, was couched in a kinship idiom. The effect of this situation, I shall argue, is that there is a stress on duty or liability, rather than on right or immunity, and we can best understand both the law of contract and the law of wrongs in terms of this stress. Property is an inherent attribute of all relationships, and law is cast generally in terms of owing debts, whether these arise from obligations of status, from contract, or from injury and tort. Since I was not fully aware of the implications of some of these problems when I was in Barotseland, the separate chapters vary somewhat in the level of their analysis and their dependence on data from other tribes.

The Barotse is a society dominated by status and hence covered by Sir Henry Maine's most sweeping generalization: "If then we employ status, agreeably with the usage of the best writers (to designate the powers and privileges anciently residing in the Family), and avoid applying the term to such conditions as are the immediate or remote result of agreement, we may say that the movement of the progressive societies has hitherto been a movement *from Status to Contract*." [2] The Barotse, in fact, in terms of technology and commerce stand, so to speak, farther back on the scale by which Maine measured the movement of progressive societies than do most of the peoples whose law he analyzed. Observations on their life therefore enable us to test some of his pregnant generalizations, as whether in the early stages of law the Law of Persons and the Law of Things are inextricably intertwined (and I would add to this tangle the Law of Obligations), whether the individual is submerged in the *familia*, whether contracts are incomplete conveyances so that executory contracts do not found obligations, whether substantive law is secreted in the interstices of procedure, to what extent religion, magic, and ritual dominate the law, and whether fictions are important in the development of the law. Since Maine had to work from remnants of Roman, Germanic, and Celtic law, as these survived in a few documents, and from relatively poor records on the practice of Hindu law, my detailed records of cases may help correct judgments on the way jurisprudential ideas and ideals operated in practice. Particularly, I may state at once, I believe that my cases, like other records of tribal law, dispose of theories that early legal procedures were highly formal. Otherwise, modern anthropological research, in my opinion, validates the chief outlines of Maine's analysis, once we recognize that he was in fact analyzing relatively advanced types of legal systems. I am not sure but that "Footnotes to Sir Henry Maine's *Ancient Law*" would be a more accurate title for this book than *The Ideas in Barotse Jurisprudence*, a more grandiloquent title which is adapted from Gibbon's first subtitle

2. *Ancient Law* (1861), final sentence of Chap. 5 (from the 1909 ed.). If we take this statement of progression as classifying two contrasted types of society, and omit any implication of unilinear evolution (see Stone, *The Province and Function of Law*, 1946, pp. 461–62) it sorts with a similar contrast, though made in different terms, by sociologists like Durkheim, Von Wiese, and Max Weber, and almost all anthropologists, notably Redfield.

to Chapter XLIX—"Idea of the Roman Jurisprudence"—in *The Decline and Fall of the Roman Empire*. I may say for the benefit of law students that when a learned South African judge found me wrestling with the *Institutes* and the *Digest,* with Sohm and Savigny, he told me that I could pass a first examination in Roman law on Gibbon alone, and I am emboldened to hope that invoking Gibbon's spirit will sustain me through my present greater task.

For frankly it is a task. Presenting my Barotse data is relatively easy, and I hope they have intrinsic value. But I essay in addition to point to parallels in the history of early English legal ideas. I do so to focus the attention of anthropological colleagues on pertinent similarities and problems, knowledge of which may improve field research in the tribal societies. But I have gone farther. I have tried to indicate to lawyers where I think the kind of data I have collected might illuminate, to quote Vinogradoff again, "the entire darkness" into which "whole periods and whole problems are plunged" through "the caprice of time." I might have managed more easily had I compared Barotse law with Roman–Dutch law, which I studied in South Africa some thirty years ago; but I felt that comparison with English law would be more appropriate. I inevitably found it too tricky to work out the main principles from specific studies, so I have drawn on the generalizations of Maitland, of Holmes, of Seagle, and of Stone.

When I planned the lectures, my model was Mr. Justice Benjamin N. Cardozo's *The Nature of the Judicial Process* (1921) which had been of the utmost help to me in my own analysis of the Barotse judicial process. It was so full of ideas that I thought it contained at least eight lectures, and I designed my own series at similar length, though with little hope of approaching my exemplar in quality. In practice the program of work in the Yale Law School allowed for only four lectures to be delivered, and I selected for this purpose those on the constitution, landholding, ideas of property, and contract (chapters 2, 3, 5, and 6). I had already drafted the other four lectures, and I completed them for publication in order to deal with the whole field on which I had data. The written lectures were overlong for delivery: I did not inflict all that appears here on my audiences.

Certain names are difficult. The Barotse are a nation of at least twenty-five tribes, with one tribe dominant. By convention I have decided that, since their homeland is marked as Barotseland on maps and they are thus referred to in the press and official documents, I would apply "Barotse" to the nation as a whole, and reserve the vernacular "Malozi," in the form "Lozi" (without the plural prefix), for the dominant tribe. But I ask readers to remember that when I use Barotse my statements apply to the several sections of the nation I studied (I am not sure if this is true of all sections), while statements about Lozi mean that the facts apply only to the Lozi dominant group or that I have information on them only on that point. For similar reasons I have referred to the Kololo (temporary conquerors of Barotseland) as Basuto, since their dominant core came from Basutoland. I have also referred to the Tswana, whose law was studied by Professor I. Schapera, as Bechuana, because they are best known by that name. Finally, I have mentioned throughout the British Government, although for many years the British protecting power was in fact the British South Africa Company. It was not relevant for me to specify more precisely at any point. Since my last tour in Barotseland was in 1947, the present tense refers to the 1940s, in contrast with the past tense which refers to earlier periods.

I note further that the general development of African nationalism throughout the continent, and the specific development of Northern Rhodesian (now Zambian) nationalism in reaction to the imposition of the Central African Federation on the two Rhodesias and Nyasaland (now Malawi), seem to have radically altered the relations of the Barotse king and his council with their subjects. To protect his own position the king at least flirted with the federal authorities, and for a long time he refused to allow Mr. Kenneth Kaunda, leader of the United National Independence Party, to visit Barotseland. In 1964 he agreed to this visit, and in the elections in that year Kaunda's party won all the Barotse seats. Since I was last in Barotseland in 1947, the firm allegiance of most Barotse, and particularly Lozi, to their monarchy may have been seriously disturbed.

I have thanked the people who helped me in my field research, both Barotse and British, in the Preface to my book on the Barotse judicial process. But I again express here my deep gratitude to the Barotse people for their friendliness and for their aid in my studies, especially my assistants, Davidson S. Sianga and Mwanamulena Mwendawelie Lewanika, and to the Trustees of the Rhodes-Livingstone Institute in which I worked for several happy years. The Trustees have kindly allowed me to publish the lectures, as in duty-bound to my hosts at

Yale, outside of the Rhodes-Livingstone series of books. Professor M. Fortes of Cambridge discussed many ideas with me. Professor Harry Street, Professor of Common Law at Manchester University, encouraged and helped me by reading the lectures, as did my colleague Dr. A. L. Epstein. My wife helped gather material in the field, read and criticized the lectures, and above all pursued for me points in English history as new problems arose when I tried to compare Barotse with early English law. Dr. M. Tyson, Librarian at Manchester University, provided me with peace to work at Manchester; Dr. Margaret Mead and Dr. Rhoda Metraux extended that peace for final revision in New York before I went to Yale and after I returned. Miss E. Borer, Miss S. Perrin, Miss S. M. Davis, and Mrs. D. Sansom coped with the manuscript. Prof. I. Schapera and Mr. T. Evens helped proof and index.

When one moves into a field where one is very inexpert, certain books are a great inspiration. Dr. W. Seagle's *The Quest for Law* (1941, republished as *The History of Law* in 1946) proved to be such an inspiration when I read it between my two major tours in Barotseland and in subsequent years when I was trying to analyze Barotse law. Later, unfortunately after writing on the Barotse judicial process, I came upon Professor Julius Stone's *The Province and Function of Law* (1947); and I then had the good fortune to meet him in Australia and discuss problems with him. When one's indebtedness is very great, one seems to make inadequate acknowledgment in detailed references, and I am very conscious that this has happened to me. References to Seagle and Stone should spatter my pages, and there are but few. I make my acknowledgment here.

I also acknowledge gladly the stimulus to my studies of tribal law given me by the writings and the friendship of Professor E. Adamson Hoebel. I agree with him on almost every point; and perhaps therefore I take that agreement for granted, and write only about our points of difference.

A generous grant for my personal research from the Ford Foundation has enabled me to secure various kinds of help for this work. It greatly eased my task, and I am most grateful to the Foundation's Trustees for this aid.

MAX GLUCKMAN

University of Manchester
June 1964

Chapter 1

INTRODUCTION: THE PROCESS OF TRIBAL LAW

I HAVE SAID in the Preface that my study of the Barotse judicial process was the first of its kind in Africa. It had, however, been preceded by earlier studies of tribal juridical method, carried out by Americans. I start from their studies for two reasons. First, I wish to acknowledge the value of these studies; second, I want to emphasize that the rule *ubi remedium, ibi jus,* which is so significant in Roman, early English, and other archaic law, represents a late development. In tribal law the principle is *ubi jus, ibi remedium.* These studies also illuminate the social background of disputes.

Up to the year 1940, reports on the settlement of disputes among tribal peoples were relatively meager, and few of them worked out a detailed analysis of how mediating, arbitral, or judicial procedure and logic were applied to a series of cases. In 1940 an anthropologist, E. A. Hoebel, published *The Political Organization and Law-ways of the Comanche Indians.* He acknowledges there the influence of his "stimulating association" with one of the most creative modern American jurists, Karl N. Llewellyn, whose recent death we mourn. In the following year they published in collaboration *The Cheyenne Way,* a study of how the Cheyenne handled what the authors called "trouble cases." They therein raised new problems and set new standards in the analysis of tribal law.[1] These monographs, and particularly the one on the Cheyenne, traced the course of each of over a hundred disputes from its inception, through its crisis and the reaction of tribal leaders both in terms of action and reasoning, to its settlement or petering out. The Cheyenne had the beginnings of the development of governmental authority, and both their chiefs and the six Soldier Societies in which men were grouped were able to seize jurisdiction in some disputes and compel the parties to submit to their adjudication and

---

1. Among American anthropologists who have worked in the same way are Richardson on the Kiowa (1940), Lips on the Naskapi (1947), W. Smith and Roberts on the Zuni (1954), and Pospisil on the Kapauku (1958). Hoebel also wrote a general book, *The Law of Primitive Man* (1954), which concentrates largely on juristic method.

abide by their judgment. I cannot here do justice to the richness of the data or the stimulating penetration of this work as it exhibits the increasing juristic skill of Cheyenne leaders, while emphasizing the extent to which they suffered under an "absence of legal form." In the authors' own concluding words,

> For all the prodigality of juristic ingenuity, not enough of its results were cumulated into easily accessible patterns to draw minor trouble-festers to a head, and so to get them settled. This shows again and again in smouldering irritations over points of fact. It shows in the hanging-on of minor grievances. It shows in protest suicides which had too little reason. It shows in the non-development of pipe-settlement into all the cases where pipe-settlement with its power of true appeasement would have been good to have. Had the chiefs of their own initiative, for instance, picked up pipe-carrying as a usual matter, the efficiency of the whole legal system would have been stepped up immeasureably.

In result, Llewellyn and Hoebel see Cheyenne juristic method just before the tribe lost its independence as poised between a stage when individual litigants suffered because there were not adequate legal forms, and a stage when legalism might creep in "to obscure the fundamental juristic task, that of getting the right answer with the tools at hand." Instead of having authorities secure in their powers of jurisdiction, the Cheyenne had "pleading-by-action, with a spectator waiting tensely for the apt moment to step in." Overall they graphically conclude that the Cheyenne system was "in full flux—while the buffalo vanish[ed] and the white man move[d] inexorably in. Cheyenne law leaped to its glory as it set." [2]

I may perhaps be interpreting into this analysis the implication that in the simplest legal systems proceedings are informal, and it is not necessary for plaintiffs to prosecute their suits in set forms. There is not yet a restriction imposed by rules like *ubi remedium, ibi jus*, such as existed in the early Roman and Anglo-Saxon law, which influenced Maine's analysis. If Llewellyn and Hoebel in fact meant to state this as a general, though as yet unsubstantiated, generalization, my own view is that they were correct.[3]

In most of the tribes of Africa, procedure is not trammeled by

2. *The Cheyenne Way* (1941), pp. 339–40.
3. Professor Hoebel informs me that this interpretation of their thesis is correct.

forms of pleading. Even among the nations of West Africa, whose economies approached those of the states of the Western Mediterranean in that slave labor was employed on plantations, there were no specific procedures or writs for bringing suit in court. One went to court and reported one's distress.[4] The Ashanti of Ghana had a specific procedure, but it was a device to found jurisdiction, not a mode of pleading. Ashanti was a federation of smaller federations. If two persons in discrete political groups came into dispute they took an oath by the name of the chief under whose common authority they both fell, and this empowered him with authority to inquire into who was the ritual offender and incidentally give judgment on the substantive issue.[5]

The procedure seems similar to that in early Roman times when suit was brought before the praetor by the *legis actio per sacramentum*. Of this Jolowicz states that since *sacramentum*, which denoted the stake forfeited by the loser, "literally means 'oath' it is supposed that, originally at any rate, the parties each made an oath as to the justice of their claims, and that what the judge had to decide was which oath was justified, the loser forfeiting a certain sum as penalty for his false oath." [6]

In Ashanti and other tribal law this kind of ritual formalism is characteristic of an uncertain jurisdiction, and the ritual element in it cannot be taken to show that early law was, or tribal law is, dominated by magic and religion.[7] The kind of formalism which demanded that action be brought in set words and forms, if it is general, apparently develops on the other hand only with writing, in the hands of a trained bureaucracy.[8] I have not found indications, in what I would call the true tribal societies, that any action has been ruled out of court because it did not accord with some formality. I venture to

4. See, e.g., Herskovits, *Dahomey*, 2 (1938), 16 ff. (bare information), and Nadel, *A Black Byzantium* (on the Nupe Kingdom) (1942), p. 57.

5. As Rattray pointed out in *Ashanti* (1923), p. 124 n., and in *Ashanti Law and Constitution* (1929); and also Busia, *The Position of the Chief in the Modern Political System of Ashanti* (1951), p. 69. Hoebel's interpretation in *The Law of Primitive Man* (1954), pp. 245–46, seems to me askew on this point. Correct interpretations are in Diamond, *Primitive Law* (1935), p. 338, and Seagle, *The Quest for Law* (1941), p. 94.

6. *Historical Introduction to Roman Law* (1939), pp. 182 f. See also Maine, *Ancient Law* (1861, 1909 ed.), pp. 384–85.

7. For sound criticism of Maine on this point see Seagle, *The Quest for Law* (1941), Chap. 10.

8. This is clearly stated by Seagle as generally true, ibid., Chap. 8; Diamond, *Primitive Law* (1935), Chap. 30, 31.

suggest that had the Cheyenne authorities developed a more complete jurisdiction over disputes, they would not have been restricted by any straitjacket of legal forms. Among the Barotse we are dealing with a powerful kingship exercising its authority through a hierarchy of councils which acted as parliaments, executives, and courts of justice; yet their proceedings in court, while highly marked by a distinctive etiquette, had no special procedures to restrict the search for redress by the allegedly aggrieved. Anyone could plead any suit in whatever words he himself pleased.

I do not think that the festering troubles, the smoldering irritations over points of fact, and the hanging-on of minor grievances, or even perhaps the suicides committed in protest among the Cheyenne, can be entirely ascribed to what Llewellyn and Hoebel call "absence of legal form." Minor grievances hang on, and irritation over points of fact rankles in all small-scale fields of social relations, such as characterize tribal societies. I distinguish a society as "tribal" by several interrelated characteristics: there are only relatively simple tools, so that each worker produces little beyond what he can himself consume of the basic primary goods; since a wealthy man cannot eat more than a certain amount of food, wear luxurious clothes when only materials like skin, barkcloth, and a little cotton are available, or live in a palace when habitations are made of skin, grass, mud, and similar materials, these societies are marked by a basically egalitarian standard of living; trade goods may travel from hand to hand in a series of exchanges over distances, but the total volume of trade is limited.

Two important general results flow from this situation. First, the wealthy and powerful do not form what might be called a separate "class," cut off from the poor by a quite different style of life. Those of varying power and riches mix fairly freely with one another, and intermarriage can occur between their families without provoking a public scandal. They can thus be kin to one another. In fact, the powerful and wealthy use the lands and goods they control to attract followers, and a man's prestige is determined by the number of dependents or subjects he has, much more than by mere possession and use of goods. Prestige and power are important in all these societies and enable a man to control the actions of others; but he gains that control through establishing relationships of personal dependence with as many others as he can.

Second, the usual settlements of these societies are camps, hamlets, or villages of a number of closely related families—what Ehrlich called "genetic associations." The core of organization of these settlements may be a number of men related to one another by descent through the agnatic line, or in other tribes through the matrilineal line; or the core may be in yet other tribes a number of females related to one another by descent through the female line. These are the most clearly defined possibilities. But extremely complex situations are also found, in which men and women may choose to live with any kinsfolk, as among the Barotse, so that families within a settlement are related to one another in a most complex pattern.

Despite these variations, in all societies of this type a grouping of some kind of kinsmen and/or kinswomen, with their spouses and usually their children, tends to live together. As a group, sometimes through particular representatives, they own certain rights (which I shall later discuss) of access to land, in which they have other rights as members of smaller units and as individuals. As we shall see, goods are appropriated by the individual who produces them, despite some collaboration in productive activities, but consumption involves considerable and constant sharing.[9] Since there are no specialized priests, these groups also form congregations, worshiping the spirits of their dead kin or supplicating at common land shrines or other ritual objects. There are no schools, and children are educated as well as reared in the settlement. The settlement also tends to form a political unit for important purposes, whether or not the tribe be organized under a chief. Relations among the members of these groups are thus directed to a multiplicity of purposes, and I have therefore named them *multiplex*.[10] It is this situation that I describe continuously as one "dominated by status."

These ties establish the most important sets of obligations between persons, and hence transactions between persons are determined by their status (in Maine's sense) relative to one another. The relations involved stand in sharp contrast with the relations, arising out of single interests, in which we nowadays become associated with other persons through the many contracts into which we enter throughout our daily lives. Even relations with chiefs in tribal society take on

9. I have analyzed a whole series of studies which support and fill in this brief summary in my *Politics, Law and Ritual in Tribal Society* (1965), Chap. 2.

10. Talcott Parsons (*The Social System*, 1952) named them *particularistic*, to emphasize a different aspect.

this multiplex form, since each man is entitled to claim land from the chief in virtue of his citizenship and to solicit gifts directly from the chief in return for the tribute he personally gives to the chief. The chief is expected to succor directly all in need, in a way very different from the impersonal help that may be given by our state welfare agencies.

I remember sitting conversing with a number of my own followers round a campfire in the cold of a winter night just outside the Barotse capital, when a ragged, middle-aged woman came out of the darkness and crouched beside us. We found it impossible to get any coherent information about herself from her, and my people concluded that she was mad. Eventually they told her that she could not stay with us, since there were only men in our camp. She asked us: "Is there a chief who drives the poor away from his fire?" My men remarked: "She is not mad. She has sense [or reason—it is the same word in Barotse]." After feeding her and taking her to her true chief's protection in the capital, they sadly shook their heads over her and said she must have become a wanderer, driven somewhat, but only somewhat, out of her senses by trying to use magic to make her fellow-wife lose the affection of their common husband—magic which had turned against its user.

This story brings home the emphatically personal nature of the relationships in these societies and their stress on the obligations of generosity and hospitality, as well as on liability and responsibility, rather than on immunity and power. The situation is magnificently illustrated by one of the Cheyenne cases cited by Llewellyn and Hoebel. When the Cheyenne launched their attacks on the herds of buffalo, one of the six Soldier Societies to which all men belonged, acted as policemen for the hunt. No one was supposed to charge upon a herd until they gave a signal, in order that all members of the tribe might have an equal chance to hunt successfully. Two young men once violated the rule. When the Soldier Society chief saw them riding down on the buffalo, he ordered his soldiers to pursue and whip them. The first men to reach them shot their horses, and others smashed their guns, while all whipped them. Their father and the chiefs reprimanded them. Then the chiefs relented and said to their men: "Look how these two boys are here in our midst. Now they have no horses and no weapons. What do you want to do about it?" The police, out of their own resources, thereupon re-equipped the wrongdoers.[11]

11. *The Cheyenne Way* (1941), pp. 112–13.

Spencer says of the North Alaskan Eskimo that in time of food shortage it was the successful hunter and his family who might go hungry, since "in his generosity he gave away whatever he had in hand." The lazy and shiftless could beg their way through life.[12] This kind of practical forgivingness exhibits the obligatory ethos of generosity in tribal society. We can also understand a Barotse tradition that their great chief Mulambwa, known as the lawgiver, promulgated: "A thief is a brave man and must not therefore be put to death but he must be brought to the chief who will give him a village or cattle or make him a tribute collector. People will then see if he will thieve again or become a good citizen." It is not, alas! recorded if any men sought through thievery a short cut to power.

Since most people in any tribe live in a complex of social relations of this kind, a large number of the disputes arising over both property and the fulfillment of obligations are between kinsmen, or at least between persons in a quasi-kinship with one another. These disputes are therefore inevitably very entangled. What appears to be a trifling dispute, to cite an example from my own experience, over the neglect of a woman to give her father a cup of beer may bring to a head a long record of festering troubles and produce recitals by both parties of grievances exacerbated by smoldering irritations over points of fact. I have here deliberately repeated the phrases of Llewellyn and Hoebel, for this must have been the situation among the Cheyenne, a tribe that numbered in all only some 4,000 people. Llewellyn and Hoebel's study was based on trouble cases which they drew out of older records, like Grinnell's *The Fighting Cheyennes*, or themselves collected from old Cheyenne who were living on a reservation. Their youngest informants were sixty years old and were describing cases of dispute in the distant past, in a life no longer lived—cases which are woefully lacking in information of the persons involved, when compared with the data collected by direct observation of tribes still living something of their old way of life. More honor, therefore, to the outstanding merit of *The Cheyenne Way*.

But it is specifically the interplay of social relations, focused temporarily on some dispute, which is required to illuminate the full mechanism of social control in so small a society. Judgments on the administration of law can go sadly astray in the absence of such information. And it is information on this interplay that is also left out in

12. Spencer, *The North Alaskan Eskimo* (1959), pp. 164–65.

historical records of judgments, once writing comes into use—espe-cially after writing also begins to restrict pleadings so that these pare down the elements that come before a tribunal.

Though the Barotse have highly organized courts with full powers to enforce their decisions, the settlement of the many disputes arising among kinsmen is in fact as difficult as among the Cheyenne. Far more is involved than the judgments of the court, both for the people and for the student. One might in fact say that disputes in these groups of kin can never be finally settled. Richard Werbner has recorded a Kalanga proverb from Southern Rhodesia, which pithily sums up the situation: "An old boil," they say, "is revived by a new boil." [13] That is, if a man forgives one offense and then is offended again, he can sue on the first case. The court can give a judgment at a particular mo-ment on a dispute that has flared up between a pair of kin, if one of them takes the issue to court. The verdict must be accepted by the quarreling kin, but for all save the most equable it only adds to the rankling accumulation of grievances.

These grievances ramify through the whole network of ties that bind various kin to one another in variegated patterns. During each dispute kin who are ostensibly outside the quarrel at issue side with one or the other litigant, and the way in which they take sides is influenced by degrees of kinship, by factional alignments within vil-lages, by past records of friendships and hostilities, and also—this is most important—by ideas of justice, judgments on which of the par-ties is in the right and which in the wrong.[14] Resentment is provoked to breed further disputes by the manner in which persons align them-selves in each quarrel. The festering troubles are exacerbated because in these societies it is believed that one's fellows are responsible not only for injuries patently inflicted on one, but maybe also for mishaps that we would describe as "natural misfortunes." Sickness, crop fail-ure, the illness of cattle, bad luck at fishing, death within the kin grouping, any of these may be ascribed to the witchcraft or sorcery of another. Breach of a taboo or omission of some appropriate offering to the spirits may cause affliction to someone other than the wrong-doer, or even to the community as a whole. A natural misfortune, so

13. Hoebel in this connection drew my attention to a smoldering grievance which broke out in a murder in *The Cheyenne Way* (1941): Case 8, p. 82, of Little Wolf.

14. See Evans-Pritchard on *The Nuer* (1940), a tribe whose ultimate enforcement of right relies on self-help (at pp. 164–65), and Howell, *Manual of Nuer Law* (1954), p. 28.

to speak, founds an action in tort. In this sort of situation, only the surface irruption out of a factional struggle bred by an increase in numbers of the kin grouping, which produces pressure on resources and competition for power, may be all that is before the court.[15]

I shall consider later how the law of wrongs is influenced by this background. Here I want to emphasize how difficult a task it lays upon those whose duty it is to settle disputes between kinsfolk. Many writers have discussed the process of law in tribal societies in such phrases as restoring the social balance or equilibrium, securing the agreement of both parties to a compromise judgment and, above all, reconciling the parties. This is the main aim of Barotse judges in all cases that arise between kin, for it is a dominant value of the society that villages should not break up and that kin should remain united.

In order to bring out all the facts that are relevant to this kind of dispute, the judges allow each party to recite the full tale of his grievances. The judges, who at the capital may number a score or more, helped by anyone else attending the session, cross-examine the parties as well as the witnesses these have brought. They may call for further evidence. There is no paring down of the facts in advance for presentation to court, and any judge who knows the parties may contribute that knowledge; the fiction of judicial ignorance is missing in all respects. Nor does a judge recuse himself if he is related to the parties; in fact if he is related to a wrongdoer he should emphasize the wrongdoing. But if he is a party to a case, he cannot sit as a judge.

Although the judges listen to all kinds of statements of fact, they do classify evidence as interested and disinterested, and direct or circumstantial or hearsay. They prefer disinterested and direct evidence, and may advise parties and witnesses not to repeat hearsay, particularly in cases not involving kinsmen. They look for corroboration, and they weigh evidence by several tests. Among the Barotse magical tests are used only in charges of witchcraft and sorcery that can be settled in no other way.[16] Ordeals, like licking the red-hot blade of a hoe or

15. Turner's *Schism and Continuity in an African Society* (1957) analyzes how dispute after dispute in a group is handled, and breaks out again, by treating a series of disputes in the history of a single village, to illuminate and develop principles established by other anthropologists. In my *Politics, Law and Ritual in Tribal Society* (1965) I discuss the deepening interpretation of anthropology through this form of analysis, and cite instances where failure by myself and others to appreciate this fact has misled or stultified analysis.

16. See Epstein, *Juridical Techniques and the Judicial Process* (1953), p. 2, citing Lindblom, *The Akamba* (1920), p. 165. I believe this is general in tribal society, where the

picking pebbles out of a pot of boiling water, were ordered in the past if the verdict on theft or adultery was "almost certainly guilty but not proven." In modern times, charges of witchcraft are not tried in officially established Barotse courts, and ordeals and torture are never used at capitals; if employed at district courts they are usually detected and punished.

After they have heard the evidence, the judges give judgment on the issue: they proceed in order from the most junior to the head of the court. This last, and not a majority of judgments, is what counts, but it is subject to the king's confirmation if the trial be at the capital.

Since the aim is to reconcile the litigants, the Barotse consider a judge to lack forensic wisdom if he rushes straight to the point at issue either in cross-examination or in judgment. The wise and skillful judge inquires into all the grievances that are brought up; he tries to bring into the open the whole record of quarrels and breaches of obligation on both sides. Yet a striking feature of this procedure is that judges during this cross-examination already begin to pass both legal and moral opinions on the actions of the parties and on the sentiments and motives that may be reasonably deduced to explain those actions. For though the judges are trying to reconcile the parties, in the hope that the threatened relationship may endure, they have to defend the law. Hence they state the law and attack any departure from its standards. Above all, in cross-examination the judges try to get the litigants themselves to admit where they have erred, by showing them how the evidence—either their own or that of witnesses—convicts them of breach.

Since Barotse is, or was, a homogeneous society, all of whose members accept the same standards of rightdoing and wrongdoing as the judges, litigants always cast their own stories in terms of these standards. This assists the judges to bring home to them their misdemeanors. Usually by the time the judgment begins, the judges have already made clear where they stand. As the Barotse and other tribes do not have lawyers to represent parties and to cross-examine opponents, this task falls on the judges. Questions in cross-examination are generally framed on the assumption that a person is lying, and it has therefore

---

presumption is innocence, and guilt must be established (see below). The existence of "trial by battle" is reported (Nadel, *The Nuba*, 1947, p. 506 and passim) but is rare, and its important position in early English law is no guide to the situation in tribal law.

been incorrectly alleged that in African courts an accused is assumed by the judges to be guilty and must prove his innocence.[17] In fact, in Barotse and all other African courts I know, guilt must be demonstrated. It seems to me that we can understand in similar terms an allegation made by some Anglo-Saxon lawyers, who are used to the judge as an umpire in the juridical contest between counsel, that the French court assumes guilt which the accused must rebut. Like the Barotse judge, the French judge is under duty to find out the truth himself and therefore he himself conducts much of the cross-examination, with the apparent implication that the accused is lying.

Before the Indians who rode selfishly into the buffalo herd were rehabilitated by the Soldier Society, they had to be punished in condign manner and the heinousness of their offense pointed out to them and to others, a lesson indeed remembered more than fifty years later. Similarly, Barotse judges not only have to try to reconcile the immediately disputing parties but also, since they are (as they themselves state) "the law" (*mulao*), they affirm that law against all parties and witnesses wherever the evidence shows default. Therefore they express strong approval or disapproval over many matters raised by the litigants. But they can give decisions that a person be punished or make restitution only on certain limited issues with which they are empowered to deal by accepted rule, and the issue before the court must be one over which the court has power. Occasionally, therefore, an aggrieved person who has been seriously affronted or neglected in terms of general moral norms by a kinsman or in-law, but lacks an issue on which he can sue, will himself commit an offense that forces the defaulter to prosecute him. He goes to court secure in the knowledge that though he may lose the case, the judges will publicly upbraid his opponent for all the latter's breaches of moral obligation.

It is therefore possible in general to distinguish some rules which Barotse value as rules whose breach raises issues that are adjudicated upon by their courts. Certain applications of the multivocal word "law" have proposed to restrict the word to "social control through the systematic application of the force of politically organized society" (in one of Pound's definitions widely adopted in anthropology). In these terms the Barotse then have a system of law. There are rules of law, most of which can be isolated from the rules of morals, of

17. E.g. even in Seagle's *The Quest for Law* (1941), p. 87.

etiquette, and so on. This formulation does scant justice to the complexity of the Barotse judicial process, a complexity that must be clarified for my later analyses.

It may well happen when the judges come to a decision on the issue before them that they take into account breaches of many other obligations. Let me make this clear by summarizing two cases which hinged on the same issue. Both cases involved the rule of law, in the usual sense of that phrase, that if a man leaves a village, he loses his rights to land attached to that village. In the first case [18] three nephews sued their father's brother, who was headman of their village, and his sons for the return of some gardens. They pleaded that when quarreling broke out between them and their cousins, the headman had not been impartial in adjudicating as he should have been, but had sided with his own eldest son against his nephews, who stood to him as sons (in fact, in Barotse they call him "father" and he calls them "my sons").

The headman's eldest son had committed adultery with the wife of one of his cousins; he admitted that this was true but retorted that previously another of his cousins had committed adultery with the wife of another kinsman. He then told a long tale of how his cousins had stinted his father by not giving him fish from their catches or money from their earnings in employment by Whites, had taken away from his father poles and thatching-grass which the old man had appropriated from one of them to build a hut, and so forth. The nephews replied that they had not stinted the old man until he had failed to reprimand his son for the adultery, but conceded that their uncle had provided cattle to obtain brides for them. They alleged that the headman told them to leave the village at night. They had gone to an old site, and thereupon their cousins began to work their old gardens, for which they were now suing, because, as they put it, "How can a man who has done no wrong lose his land?"

There were bewildering details of resentment and smoldering irritation concerning the actions of all the members of this village, including the attempts of the headman's sisters to evade questions so that they could avoid taking sides with either set of nephews. There was even a classical diatribe by the old man against the wickedness of youth. In this case in the end the judges decided that there was no point in trying to work out the exact truth of all these complaints and

18. "The Case of the Biassed Father" in my *Judicial Process among the Barotse* (1955), pp. 37–45.

counter-complaints, either through cross-examination of the parties or the witnesses. It became clear that the village and its associated kin groupings would break up unless they exerted pressure to induce the young men to return home and the headman to welcome them. Asked by a senior judge whether he wanted his nephews back, the old man replied that of course he did, they were his children though begotten by his brother; they might take better care of him than the sons he had himself begotten. The nephews told the judges they wished to return, if the matter of the gardens—here the judges interrupted to say they would settle the matter of the gardens. The adulterer also said he wanted his "brothers," i.e. his cousins, to come home. The judges then all concurred: the law was clear—if a man leaves a village he loses his rights to its lands, hence if the nephews refused to return home they had lost their gardens. But if they returned home, their gardens would be given back, and their cousins could not sue for any work they had done in these gardens. The old man was ordered to reinstate his nephews, and warned that he must be impartial in settling disputes between his own sons and other villagers. He was also told that when his son had seduced his nephew's wife he should have reprimanded his son and then sacrificed a beast to their ancestors so that all could eat in community and "wash away the offense."

Different judges rebuked the various parties for actions they considered to be wrongful. All the judges combined in warning the adulterer that he was making trouble and "dirtying the village"; he need not think because he was the eldest son of the present headman that he could act in the pride and conceit of his expectation to succeed his father as headman; he might not, for the kin and the court might choose one of his cousins. One of the nephews was castigated for inciting his brothers to leave in the alleged hope that he would become headman of an independent village. Finally, the court warned the parties that if they did not go home and live together amicably, but returned with fresh quarrels, they would all be fined. They went off in at least superficial amity.

We see here the court attempting to reconcile the parties, while at the same time stating the code by which kin should deal with one another and giving a clear judgment on the issue before it: who had rights to the gardens. The decision was predicated on alternatives in terms of which the consequences of ownership could accrue to one or the other of two sets of litigants. This final clear decision took account, however, of the whole tale of dispute between the parties. In terms of the rule of law, the court had to decide whether the headman had driven his nephews from the village by ordering them to leave or whether they had left the village without justification. In short, they were specifying the application of the phrase "leaves the village," to these particular circumstances. And to determine that controversial issue the judges inquired into whether the old man had behaved over a long period as a reasonable father-surrogate and impartial headman, whether his eldest son had behaved as a reasonable cousin to the others, and whether these had behaved as reasonable nephews to the old man. Most of the trial consisted therefore in determining whether the parties had behaved as reasonable incumbents of the social positions (to avoid the ugly plural "statuses") which they occupied in relation to one another. In short, the inquiry over rights to gardens turned into an inquiry into the fulfillment of status obligations.

I do not know what the court would have decided if the judges had become convinced that the headman had driven out his nephews—i.e. that they did not "leave" the village. From my knowledge of other cases I think they might have then condoned a temporary split into two villages, in the hope that the parties themselves, or their descendants, would later reunite. Or they may have decided that the case was hopeless, awarded the gardens to the headman as representative of the village on the grounds that all parties were in the wrong, and tried to find other land for the nephews or tried to induce another village to take them in; in this event the court would have been acting in another of its capacities, as distributor of the national land.

But I heard another case which illustrates particularly well these possibilities, and something more. A very bad-tempered headman named Mahalihali [19] quarreled with many of his kin (Fig. I). His younger brother, Sabangwa, and this brother's sons were allowed by the court to build a little distance away as a temporary solution to avoid fighting, with permission to work the land they had been given within the village's land. Without the knowledge of the court, the irascible headman drove out of the village a widowed daughter and her son, on the grounds that she had by sorcery killed a member of the village. Eventually the headman died and was succeeded by his son, who found himself head of a village without enough people in it.

19. "The Case of the Headman's Fish-dams" (also called "The Case of the Dog-in-the-Manger Headman"), ibid., pp. 178–87.

His expelled sister and her son were fishing a dam belonging to the village, although they lived at some distance in her mother's mother's village; another dam of the village was being fished by the sons of another sister, married into a nearby village. Their father had allowed his two daughters to fish the dams. The new headman therefore sued to have his sisters and their sons ordered to reside in his village or return the dams to him, under the rule just discussed that rights in land require residence. A local court found in his favor and his kin appealed to the court at the capital.

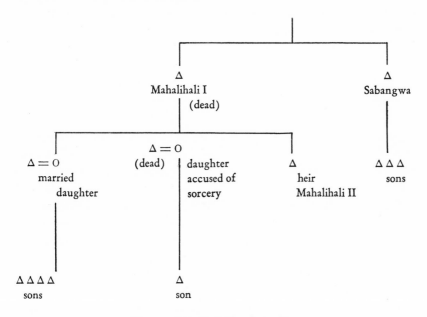

Figure 1. Mahalihali kin relationships

After the judges had inquired into the history of the dealings between the parties and the dead headman, they found themselves in a dilemma. The law states clearly that a man or woman must live in a village to gain rights in its lands; yet other kin have at least a moral right to use that land, if there is sufficient, even if they live elsewhere, unless they wrong the headman by not granting him respect or other obligations. The defendants had not wronged the headman. Were they to be expelled from the dams? No similar case had been brought before. Some of the judges bravely faced the issue and said the dams were the headman's unless his kin settled in his village for, as they put it, "We cannot change the law against Mahalihali." This was a decision under their maxim, "It is hard, but it is the law." But they all urged the headman to allow his kin to use the dams; being rich he ought to help them, not take their living from them. Other judges stated that he should not expel kin who had not wronged him—thus avoiding the well-known rule of law in what Barotse told me was a weak and cowardly way. But we must note that they made this decision for this case alone and might in cases with other merits have decided otherwise, since precedents, although they should be followed, are not recorded, and only their moral significance is remembered. A few of the final judges suddenly turned on the father's younger brother, who had been allowed to build on his own and who came to court to support his nephew, the new headman; they reprimanded him for not preventing his nephew from bringing this ungenerous suit and ordered him back into the main village to strengthen it.

Finally, the head of the court found a brilliant solution to the judicial dilemma. He told the headman that unless he were generous and allowed his kin to use the dams so that he drew them to his village by generosity and not by threats, the court would call on its powers to discharge unsatisfactory headmen and would find someone more generous to replace him. Under this solution, the court upheld the law that the land of a village is vested in the title of its headman and can only be used, save with his permission, by villagers themselves, while at the same time the defendants who had done no wrong were not penalized. Both justice and certainty of law were upheld. Shortly after this I left Barotseland, and I regret to say that on my final brief visit five years later I omitted to find out what had happened to these parties or those in the previous case.

In this case again the judges inquired carefully into the long history of interrelations of the parties. They set out to determine first who had, and who had not, behaved as a reasonable man or woman—or rather as a reasonable brother, sister, uncle, nephew, or general dependent of the new headman. In short, the judges considered the actions of the parties in terms of the several social positions each occupied in relation to others, in order to decide who was in the right and who in the wrong by the manner in which they had fulfilled the obligations of each status. Having heard this evidence, the judges decided that justice, fairness, truth—all these are Barotse concepts—lay with the defendants, and their problem was to reconcile this decision on the merits of the parties with the merits of the case, in terms of one of their dominant rules of land tenure. The final solution invoked a quite different rule—the power of the court to discharge an unsatisfactory headman. Thus the moral obligation of a headman to aid his kin wherever they dwell was potentially enforced. For Barotse law, like all bodies of law, consists of a large number of rules of different kinds, which are not necessarily related logically; and juristic skill, in the Barotse's estimation, consists in the ability to find and apply the rule that will most appropriately give justice in the case under trial.

The determination of which rule is appropriate, and how it shall be applied, in these cases between kinsfolk or other persons mutually obligated in terms of status, is markedly influenced by the extent to which the parties have fulfilled or broken moral obligations. In addition, the judges may be influenced, both in assessing evidence and in forming a conclusion on the merits of the case, by the manner in which the parties have respectively observed codes of etiquette or conformed to ritual prescriptions and other customary modes of behavior. I therefore found that I could not in practice write about the Barotse judicial process without using the word "law" to cover these kinds of rules and conventions, as well as the rules which the judges enforce more specifically. My feeling that I must use the word law loosely, to cover several ranges of rules and conventions as well as certain procedures to secure redress, was strengthened by the fact that the issue on which the judges were adjudicating was clearly not the narrow application of a single rule, or a small number of rules, to a set of facts. They were instead judging the general issue: whether particular people had behaved as reasonable incumbents of specified social positions.

Mr. Justice Holmes has said that "all rights are consequences attached to filling some situation of fact." [20] Barotse judges determine as the relevant facts in these cases the respective social positions of the parties and then how far each party has conformed to the obligations of his position. To these facts they then attach consequences, first in deciding which is more in the right, and second in deciding what rights they can enforce on his behalf. It seemed to me that I could not separate all these highly relevant judgments on facts, or the approval and disapproval evoked in the judges, from what might be called the final adjudicating ruling of the court over issues where they had the power to enforce action, and call the latter "law" and the former

20. *The Common Law* (1881), p. 340.

merely "moral." Moreover I found that the judges, in coming to a decision on the merits of the parties as reasonable incumbents of specific positions, were working with certain general presumptions about what is fair and proper, or just.

These conceptions, often unformulated, illuminated the course of trial and judgment. These equitable ideas also were so involved in adjudication that I felt they should be brought under the rubric of Barotse "law." But these general ideas were affected by the judges' presumptions about how men and women, chiefs and underlings, parents and children, and husbands and wives behave and reason, so that any unusual or unwarranted behavior provoked them to attack a party's whole version of affairs. Thus what one might call a Barotse "natural science of psychology," stating laws (the Barotse indeed use their equivalent word in this context) about the motives of people, was involved in assessing evidence and in judgment. The Barotse do not themselves work this out into a coherent theory; but there is a theory of motivation implicit in their judgments on people's actions.

Beyond this, the judges took note of what we would call other "natural laws": physiological laws, controlling the periods of gestation and rate of reproduction of women and cows; or botanical laws, controlling the rate of growth of crops; or pedological laws, controlling the manner of use and enrichment of soil. Hence the more or less regular operation of nature—its order—also influenced decisions on fact and hence final adjudication. The Barotse word *mulao* is used in these several contexts, as we use our own *law;* and to discuss the full problem of the judicial process among these people it seemed reasonable for me to stipulate that I would use law in all these senses, and try to specialize a series of other words from the riches of our language to cover phenomena to which some learned authorities had confined the word law. Thus words like "litigation" and "adjudication" and "legal or forensic procedures [21] and rules" could be applied to matters connected with established courts.

I felt that this use of the word law would simplify other issues. Both anthropologists and lawyers have filled pages with controversy over the issue whether there is law in tribes which lack courts-of-trial with

21. I now suggest "forensic" because Hoebel, in *The Law of Primitive Man* (1954), following his own and Llewellyn's earlier usage, has applied "legal" to so many sanctioning mechanisms. I cite various authorities in my "African Jurisprudence" (1961) and *Politics, Law and Ritual* (1965).

powers to summon parties and witnesses, to hear and assess evidence, and to take judgment and enforce that judgment. This controversy was clearly barren; it provoked argument about the meaning of words but not about facts and their interpretation, and thus held up rather than advanced understanding. The argument, for example, distracted attention from the substantive value of Malinowski's outstanding contribution to the study of social control, in his *Crime and Custom in Savage Society* (1926), because, in the Trobriand Islands where there were no indigenous courts, he defined "civil law" in terms of the pressure of reciprocal advantages and sanctions which induce parties in status relationships to fulfill their obligations. Too much criticism was directed to this definition.[22]

Argument over the application of the word law, which has so many meanings in our own language, caused another eminent anthropologist to struggle at length in order to persuade his government that a specific body of rules was recognized as law by the Nuba of the Anglo–Egyptian Sudan, since breach of these rules provoked some kind of forceful physical retaliation, although the Nuba had no courts. He then had to report that the newly established Nuba courts did not in practice enforce all or only these particular rules.[23] Above all, since in these kinds of societies there is a regular fulfillment of obligations according to a known code, and on the whole if facts are clear people can judge who was in the right and who in the wrong, it seemed inappropriate to me that Evans-Pritchard should state that "in the strict sense of the word law, the Nuer have no law," in an essay largely devoted to an analysis of regularity under rule in their lives. It was particularly inappropriate, since in another book he wrote about their law and their legal relations, and of "recognition by the one [losing] party of the justice of the other side's case." [24]

Clearly there is no single "strict sense" of the word law in our own language, or the equivalent word in other European languages. Schapera has set out fully the multiple meanings of the equivalent word in

22. But not by Pound, whose one definition ran counter to Malinowski's. See Pound's "Introduction" to Moll's translation (1936) of Ehrlich's *Fundamental Principles of the Sociology of Law* (1913), p. xxxiv, where he calls it "a fruitful idea from the sociological standpoint."

23. Nadel, *The Nuba* (1947), pp. 499 f. For a fuller discussion on this point see Gluckman, "African Jurisprudence" (1961) and *Politics, Law and Ritual in Tribal Society* (1964).

24. "The Nuer of the Anglo-Egyptian Sudan" (1940), pp. 293–96. Contrast *The Nuer* (1940), pp. 168, 164–65. He notes of course here that he uses "law" in a different sense.

Bechuanaland,[25] as has Bohannan for the Tiv of Nigeria.[26] This may be true of most or even all languages. The Barotse use *mulao*, which everyone including Barotse has translated as "law," to cover the following.

1. What in other contexts we might better translate as custom, traditional usage, manner, habit, innate propensity, or technical rule of craft.

2. Properly legislated statutes and orders of their councils.

3. Decisions of these councils acting as courts of trial on particular disputes.

4. Orders issued by anyone in authority to his subordinates.

5. Traditional rules and institutions found among many tribes, which they call "the laws of tribes" [or of nations].

6. Traditional rules and practices particular to a single tribe or group of tribes.

7. General ideas about justice, equity and fairness, equality, and truth, which they believe should inform governing and adjudicating and which they call "laws of humankind" or "laws of God."

8. Certain specific moral premises about the appropriate relations between categories of persons, some of which they believe to be general to all peoples and hence to be "laws of humankind" and some of which they consider particular to themselves; these are perhaps what Kohler would have called their "jural postulates."

9. Regularities in their environment and in the behavior of persons—our laws of nature—which they call also "laws of God"; for them these laws have a moral implication, since their operation can be disturbed by immoral action and even thought.

The word *mulao* is also used in a personified manner, as when a judge says, "The law binds me as well as you" [the accused]; or "I am here to speak the law," or "The law is greater than I am."

Characteristic of almost all these uses of the word among the Barotse is the general idea of regularity and order and of rightness—what ought to be—either existing or to be striven for. In addition, the idea of law always contains also for them the idea of reason and sense and principle, all of which they call *ngana*. The implications of this

25. *Handbook of Tswana Law and Custom* (1938), pp. 35–36.
26. *Justice and Judgment among the Tiv* (1957), passim.

idea are worked out in all their trials, where the standards by which
parties and witnesses frame evidence and by which judges cross-
examine and give judgment are the standards of "the reasonable man"
(*mutu yangana*), specified in particulars for incumbents of varied
positions in social life.

I have noted in the Preface that I had relatively little legal training;
this training was in a very narrow and orthodox jurisprudence. Since
then, for example, I have read that in his learned book *The Province
and Function of Law* (1947) Stone ended by refusing to define
law.[27] Stone himself has drawn my attention to Ehrlich, and again to
Savigny, in a friendly and encouraging commentary on my book. But
I am after all an anthropologist. Indeed when I began to find illumination in what I may call modern jurisprudence, and surrounded
myself with books to further my analysis, I had to be reminded that
my first duty was to analyze and present my field data, which I have
done. Perhaps with my minimal understanding of modern jurisprudential theories, I was not prevented from allowing Barotse lawyers to
speak for themselves. For this reason, I continue here unlearnedly to
summarize the Barotse process of law as I observed it.

I found a multiplicity of meanings and possibilities of application to
the facts of social life inherent in all the key terms of Barotse law.
Their word, which we might translate in its commonest usage as
"custom," covers many rules and items of behavior. Strikingly, in
view of Hohfeld's argument that the obligations covered in English
by the concepts of "right" and "duty" should be dissolved into eight
different concepts, in Barotse both right and duty are covered usually
by a single word, derived from a verbal form which we can translate
as "ought." There are, however, other words that can be specifically
applied to what we would call "power," "privilege," and "claim."
"Ownership" covers a variety of different situations. Anthropologists
are happily in the position where their only obligation is to study
social life. They are not called upon to improve it. Hence I was able to
accept that this multiplicity of meanings—what the philosophers call
"open texture"[28]—of terms was an inherent attribute of legal con-

27. See Chap. 25–27.

28. Hart, *The Concept of Law* (1961), passim. I repeat that Stone's most learned and
penetrating discussion of all these problems in *The Province and Function of Law* (1946) has
driven home to me my temerity in ever daring to write on the Barotse judicial process in such
general terms, and emphasized how much I would have profited from reading the studies of
Ehrlich and many other jurists I cannot cite.

cepts, and that my task was to study the range covered by each word and to investigate what the judges did with the word.[29] If I may use a metaphor, I tried to work out how the judges manipulated the uncertainty of words to give logical judgments in terms of general rules so as to achieve what they believed to be justice in individual cases, while maintaining the certainty of law and yet coping with the radical changes which Barotse life was undergoing as their country was absorbed into an alien polity and economy.

I believe that I was able to demonstrate through a series of cases that the judges in fact succeeded in both these aims. In consequence, even though the Barotse felt that the outcome of any piece of litigation might be uncertain, they also insisted that they lived by a code of law that was well known and certain. I have spoken of a paradox in which "the 'certainty' of law resides in the 'uncertainty' of its basic concepts."[30] Independently, therefore, I stated for the Barotse what Stone said of all law, when he considered what jurisprudents had worked out, and wrote:

> The defence of legal "certainty" insofar as it assumes that certainty can be attained by continuing to adhere closely to logical development of the "principles of law," is defending what has never existed. The appearance of certainty and stability in legal rules and principles conceals existing uncertainty.

Stone then quotes Cardozo, Ehrlich, and other jurists to the same effect.[31] My own discussion of how social conditions and changing interests, standards of morals, and measures of reasonableness in Barotseland controlled development of the law by judges had also been far better worked out by Western jurists.[32] Nevertheless I should like to continue presenting Barotse ideas as I saw them before I extended my learning a little.

At that time I was struck by a statement in an article, "Language and the Law," by Professor G. L. Williams, then of the University of London and now at Cambridge, that while lawyers on the whole "have appreciated the danger" of "the flatulencies that may gather round the unacknowledged puns of language," and "have been at

29. Turner has applied this argument to ritual symbols in "Symbols in Ndembu Ritual" (1964).

30. *Judicial Process among the Barotse* (1955), p. 326.

31. *Province and Function of Law* (1947), pp. 204–05.

32. Ibid., pp. 170–71, Chap. 21–23.

pains to construct a moderately precise technical language . . . oddly enough, it is least precise in its most fundamental parts." [33] This is exactly what I had found among the Barotse. It seemed to follow that the most important ideas of any legal system might be the least precise, in having the most open texture, precisely because they had to cover the widest range of rules and processes of social control. I therefore attempted to arrange Barotse legal analysis in a hierarchy ranging from simple determinations such as whether people had left a village or been driven from it, through decisions that they were therefore in the wrong or in the right (guilty or innocent), to the consequence that they possessed rights in the case, to the ultimate decision that "law" supported them. As I did so I found that the outstanding characteristic at the upper levels of this hierarchy was that the concepts of substantive law were multireferential: they were applicable to a variety of different rules, processes, and situations of fact.

On the other hand, the concepts low in the hierarchy were paired as opposites. At the lowest level these concepts involved specification of words describing actual behavior: leaving or not leaving a village, respecting or not respecting a headman. At a somewhat higher level these opposites consisted of pairs of more abstract concepts like wrongdoing and rightdoing or guilt and innocence, negligence and due care, breach of obligations and fulfillment of obligations. I called this attribute of concepts "elasticity" because they had to be stretched to cover actual situations. Hence I suggested that if we examine the reasoning of Barotse judges it consists in fitting in evidence along a line denoted by a pair of simple opposites defining the facts at issue, then stretching more abstract concepts like guilt and innocence to cover these facts, and then applying the multiple or multireferential concepts like "right–duty," "crime," "property," or "law" itself to cover the resulting situation. I may note here that this view of the changing nature of the concepts fitted with a statement by Professor Williams that "the difficulties discussed . . . under the heading of 'fringe-meaning' are very different from the difficulties caused by words of multiple meaning." [34] The Barotse do not themselves make this step-by-step analysis; the hierarchy of judgments has to be extracted from their judicial decisions.

I would add further that the concepts of Barotse law involved in

33. Williams, *Law Quarterly Review*, 61 (1945/46), 179.
34. Ibid., p. 301.

staging a trial, taking of evidence and cross-examination, and coming to judgment appear to me to be both multireferential and elastic. Hence they are more flexible still, and they cover what is obviously the most uncertain part of settling any case: the turning of disputed facts as reported by parties and witnesses into facts-in-law to which legal consequences can be attached. It is this process of the law which is also frequently described by Barotse, as by ourselves, in metaphorical, almost poetical, terms, like sifting and weighing evidence, shooting straight or missing the target in cross-examination, trapping a witness, cutting to the heart of an affair, or throwing it down as one drops a load.

I suggest also that legal concepts have two other attributes, whose importance has to be analyzed. Concepts are *absorbent* in that they can draw into themselves a variety of raw facts of very different kind. They are also *permeable*, in the sense that they are at any one time permeated by certain principles, presumptions, prejudices and postulates, which the judges hold to be beyond question. Many of our own legal concepts exist among the Barotse: law, property rights, marriage, and wrong, but they are permeated by quite different presumptions, derived from Barotse society as a whole. When the Barotse say, "If you are invited to a meal and a fish bone sticks in your throat, you cannot sue your host," their attitude agrees with that of the Romans, and ourselves, that *volenti non fit injuria*. But the situations to which they apply this doctrine differ widely from the situations to which we apply it, as ours differ from those of the Romans. Yet it is clear that common legal problems thus confront very different types of society. We shall see that the Barotse have also to consider the situations covered by the Roman maxims: *ex nuda pacta non oritur actio; ex turpi causa non oritur actio; in pari delicto potior est conditio defendentis; res judicata pro veritate accipitur.*

I am not sure whether the particular technical terms I suggested would be widely useful, or if I would now do better to adopt the terms proposed by philosophers and jurists. In *The Concept of Law* (1961), Hart has considered the functional operation of open-texture, vagueness, and indeterminacy of legal terms,[35] but with all respect these words do not seem sufficiently "functional" in their form

---

35. At pp. 124–32, 233, 249. Curtis used, as I did, "flexible" and "elastic," but thought "vague" was safer; see his *It's Your Law* (1954), passim, especially the section, " A Precise Degree of Imprecision."

to cover what the terms do. Stone's apparatus of concepts in *The Province and Function of Law* (1947) is far more complex and functional than anything I have attempted.[36] It would be valuable to try to apply his analysis to a fuller record of cases from Africa than I collected. My data could not sustain it. What my own concepts do enable me to do is to explain the cases I recorded.

When I was working in Barotseland, judges were still applying traditional general rules, defining the mutual obligations of kinsmen, to disputes, although the situation of the Barotse nation had changed radically. They could continue to apply their traditional rules because these are cast in elastic terms of respect and disrespect, help and failure to help, caring for and neglecting, and so forth, all of which were measured by what the judges considered to be reasonable in the present day. Judges specified those concepts in their application to particular issues by accepting that these concepts could be permeated by new standards.

The law applied was changing rapidly, but it was still formulated in terms of traditional legal propositions. This raised the whole problem of the attributes of different kinds of concepts of law and the question of how they were employed in the step-by-step logic of judgment. At critical points in the development of judicial argument, judges took certain leaps in selecting the rules to apply. They introduced new facets of social relations and hence new standards, and ultimately even new legal propositions, into the law. The Barotse judicial process in these respects did not differ from our own judicial process. In the absence of writing and of the paring down of issues by lawyers to fit special pleadings, certain problems seemed to me to emerge very sharply. Among the most important of these problems was the clear exhibition that errors in strict logic and use of the open texture of words might be a key to social analysis of judicial reasoning. I speak here of acceptable errors for, of course, the Barotse ascribe what they consider to be bad judgments to stupid, cowardly, or unjust judges.

The study of concepts in this sense raises issues different from the other problem on which I have touched: how we are to use our own concepts of law to further the comparatives study of law, including tribal law. Here I suggest that we must agree by mutual stipulation to draw on the riches of English and specialize a whole series of words in

36. Chap. 6, 7.

relation to one another. In Professor Williams' words, by accepting "the fact that words have no inherently proper meaning" (I would add *single* proper meaning) we could "write off almost the whole of the vast and futile controversy concerning the proper meaning of the word 'law.'" By applying different words to diverse phenomena, and the same word to similar phenomena, we can confine our own disputes to problems about facts and their interrelations. Whether or not this is necessary for lawyers, it is essential for anthropologists.

Chapter 2

THE BAROTSE CONSTITUTION AND THEIR THEORY OF POWER

THE BAROTSE political system is most complex, and I present only an outline of its structure.[1] I shall concentrate principally on three sets of ideas: first, how the Barotse formulate a theory of power providing for the representation of different elements of the state in their official organs; second, how far they consider their king and other officials to be bound by law; and third, what are the laws of succession to the throne and of treason.

The Lozi are the dominant tribe of Barotseland, and their king rules not only his own tribal people but also members of some twenty-five other tribal groups. The Barotse kingdom (Map 1) includes 250,000 to 300,000 people inhabiting some 80,000 square miles in northwestern Northern Rhodesia (now Zambia). The Lozi themselves live in the floodplain of the Upper Zambezi River, where it runs south from the Congo parallel to the border of Angola (Map 2). The plain is about 120 miles long and 25 to 35 miles wide. The Lozi build their villages on mounds in the plain, and each year when the Zambezi floods many of them have to live for a few months in a second set of villages on the margins of the plain. Other Lozi and some emigrants from other tribes dwell permanently on the margins, but most of the conquered and immigrant tribes of the kingdom dwell in the river valleys and small depressions that have water, and that are interspersed among the woodlands encircling the plain. The king maintains two capitals, one in the plain, the other at the margin.

The Lozi say that their royal family is descended from a daughter of their god Nyambe, whom he took to wife. The plain and its environs were then already inhabited by many tribes. A son of this daughter of God was out hunting, and members of a foreign tribe decided it would

---

1. Fuller details of the Barotse political and administrative systems are given in Gluckman, "The Lozi of Barotseland in North-Western Rhodesia" (1951) and *Administrative Organization of the Barotse Native Authorities* (1943).

Map 1. Distribution of the tribes of the Barotse kingdom

be polite to present him with part of their catch of fish. The local people were impressed by this propriety, when compared with their own practice of keeping all catches for themselves, so they chose this son of the queen to be their king and agreed to give him part of their produce.

God and his wife, whom he created to bear the mother of the first king, lie ten generations back from the present-day king. The Barotse

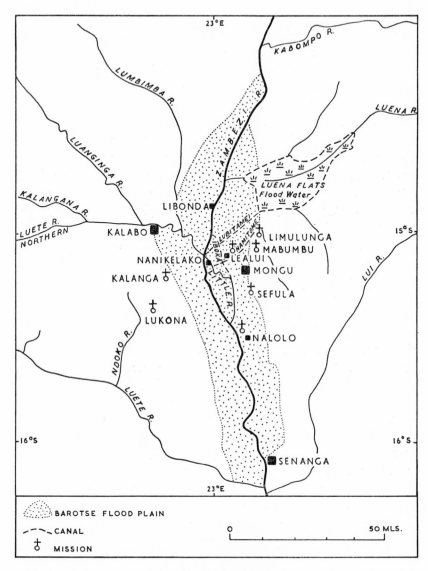

Map 2. Topography of Loziland

do not think of this as a limited number of generations—I doubt whether any of them has ever counted the generations, which for them would cover almost the whole of time. The events narrated in the myth occurred slightly later than the beginning of creation, and they emphasize that kingship was established by the people, who

themselves undertook the obligation to render tribute. There is an idea
of a contract between king and people here. The myth also hallows
the kingship, because the family that claims the kingship is doubly
descended from God. The myth thus establishes that no one outside
that family can be considered for the kingship. All eighteen of the
Barotse kings have come from the same family by agnatic descent,[2]
and it is inconceivable that someone not thus descended from the line
of kings should ascend the throne. During revolts by powerful councillors against a king and his favorites, the rebels have had to find an
ambitious prince, or even cajole a reluctant prince, into leading them.
Hence revolts attacked particular kings but not the kingship or the
rights of the royal family to it. They were emphatically rebellions and
not revolutions.[3]

The princes are very numerous for kings had many wives, though
princeliness is lost when a man's tie to a reigning king is more than
three or four generations away. Descent through a princess within this
range still transmits princeliness, but this female link bars a man from
the kingship. Among the agnatic descendants of kings anyone is eligi-
ble to be selected by the national council, but ideal candidates are sons
of a reigning king, born after he was enthroned, to a woman on whom
one of a number of queenly titles has been conferred, and after that
conferment. This is the Barotse definition of being born to the purple.
Barotse educated in English now define their kingship as "a constitutional monarchy." The king is supposed to legislate and judge only
with the consent of his councils, and to take action only through their
members. The councils are very complicated, but a simplified version
of them will elucidate Barotse ideas about the elements that make up
their state. When the king sits in full court, his magnates are disposed
in three divisions about his throne. On his right sit the most powerful
councillors, as well as a number of junior councillors. These councillors-
of-the-right are said by the Barotse to represent the common people
and their interests in the kingship, which are seen as distinct from the
interests of the royal family and the reigning king in that kingship.
The reigning king's interests are represented by councillors who sit on

2. The third king in modern versions was a son of God, own mother's brother to the first
king and a son of God. The first European records gave him as younger brother (see my
"The Lozi of Barotseland in North-Western Rhodesia," 1951, pp. 2–3).

3. The implications of this situation are examined in my *Order and Rebellion in Tribal
Africa* (1963) and more fully developed and differentiated in my *Politics, Law and Ritual in
Tribal Society* (1965).

his left. I shall refer to these men as the king's stewards because, besides acting as judges and national administrators, they, rather more than councillors-of-the-right, have the duty of looking after the king's property, his queens, and princes and princesses. The Barotse refer to the stewards as "wives" or "boys" of the king because they theoretically should look mainly to the reigning king's own interests: they represent him in the council. The king is politely addressed by the plural form of his senior steward's title, as he could not be by the title of a councillor-of-the-right.

A third group is constituted by the princes and the husbands of princesses. This group represents the interests of the royal family in the kingship, as against that of the reigning king; symbolically it sits in council facing the king.

The full court is thus seen as a balance around kingship of the interests of nation, reigning king, and royal family, somewhat in the way in which the British think of the sovereign in Parliament, which is broken into Lords and Commons, if Lords are equated with royal descent. And, like the British Parliament, the Barotse councils can act constitutionally only if all three elements are represented. In making up a delegation to report to, or discuss matters with, the British Government, or at another capital, care is always taken to see that it contains members of each set in the council. The senior councillor-of-the-right will always stop a trial if he sees that there are too few members of any set present at that moment.

Like the British, too, the Barotse think that membership of one part of the council is inimical to membership of another part, though many councillors-of-the-right and stewards are married to princesses and in another capacity are entitled to sit in the royal division. But princes by royal descent should not be appointed to councillorships-on-the-right or to stewardships (with one important exception). First, such appointment would vest more power in them to intrigue against the king, and second, Barotse believe that their interests as princes might conflict with the duty of councillors-of-the-right to represent the common people.

This applies particularly to the chief councillor-of-the-right, whose Barotse title, Ngambela, I must use for reasons that will become apparent. Each king is closely identified with this chief councillor, who sits at his right hand as his principal adviser and executive, and is yet the principal representative of the common people. Therefore the

Ngambela should never be a prince. It would of course be foolish of a king to grant so much power to a potential rival for the throne. And, say the people, how could a prince represent us against the king? Even when a prince barred from kingship by descent through a princess was appointed Ngambela in 1921, the common people predicted disaster; and they told me in 1940 that their predictions were fulfilled when eight years later he was deposed after being charged with murder and sedition. For though the king appoints his Ngambela, under duty to serve him, the Ngambela by his appointment moves into a titled position which is independent of the king, in that Barotse do not consider it possible for a king to abolish the Ngambelaship, though he can secure the deposition of a particular incumbent. Therefore Barotse speak of the Ngambela, in relation to the king, as "another chief or king." The Ngambela is thus seen by Barotse both as servant to the king and as independent of and opposed to the king.

Implicit in this discrimination of sets of roles is another Barotse rule, which states that "the king does nothing." By this they mean that the king should not personally try to implement any of his wishes or orders, because if in doing so he trespasses on the rights of a subject, it is impossible for that subject to seek redress in court.

Theoretically the king is a member of all courts, and in the capital he confirms all verdicts. Even in the district courts, which he does not visit, he is held to confirm the verdict if the losing party does not say he will appeal, and the successful litigant gives the royal salute to the court building. Hence the king cannot be tried by a court or bring suit in court for, in addition to such immunity as he possesses from his august status, Barotse hold that no man can be judge in his own suit. For this reason, treason cases, which I shall shortly discuss further, were not tried in court. The king acted outside the courts and ordered executions.

I shall be considering further parallels in these respects between the Barotse and the English medieval law of treason, but note here that according to Pollock and Maitland [4] when there was

> a charge of treason [in England], the king himself [was] the accuser, and life, limb and inheritance [were] at stake; it [was] not seemly that the king, either in person or by his justices, who represent[ed] his person, should be judge; so Bracton throws out

4. *History of English Law* (1923, 2d ed.), p. 410.

the suggestion that the cause should come before the "peers." We have here no privilege of peerage, but a special rule for all cases of high treason, based on the maxim that "no one should be judge in his own cause."

Vinogradoff [5] filled in this statement from his analysis of the Year Books. After the accession of Henry VII, various matters came up before, or were discussed by, the judges:

> Then came up the questions as to the rights of peers and commoners who had been attainted by Parliament under the late king, to sit and act in the present Parliament. It was resolved that they could do so after their attainders had been reversed. They had, however, to absent themselves from the sittings until this reversal had taken place. A similar problem arose in regard to the king himself: in the course of discussion, Townsend (Justice of the Common Pleas) recalled to mind the parallel case of King Henry VI, who, as he put it, had been attainted by Parliament (in 1461) and afterwards resumed his crown without any reversal of the attainder. It was pointed out to him by the other justices that Henry VI had not been attainted but *disabled* by Parliament in regard to his crown, kingdom, dignity, and estates, and by the very fact that he was able to resume his royal dignity and be king, all measures taken against him became void; in the same way the present king had no need for a reversal of his attainder. Chief Justice Hussey made a remark which, though not clearly connected with the foregoing discussion, deserves notice in itself, and has been received as authority. According to him, Sir John Markham, Chief Justice of the King's Bench in the time of Edward IV, had told this king that he could not personally arrest a subject on suspicion of treason, while one of his lieges could, and this for the reason that if the king did wrong, nobody could have an action against him.

The Barotse take very seriously the doctrine that the king must not himself act lest he bar a subject from suit in court. One of their kings, who ruled after the British Protectorate was established, disapproved strongly of beer drinking and passed laws to control it. He once discovered and broke the beer pots of some subjects in his capital. His

5. *Collected Papers,* 1 (1928), 196.

councillors made him vacate his chair on the dais in court and sit on the ground, where they harangued him severely and told him that if he wanted to be a policeman instead of a king they would dress him in uniform and send him around the country looking for malefactors. This happened many years before I myself was in Barotseland, and I was told that had it not been for the pleas of White officials and missionaries the king would have been deposed. I did not at the time check carefully enough the versions I was given of the king's threatened deposition. But the form of my notes indicates that he was not tried as ordinary malefactors are, since no case was made against him nor did he put forward a defense. He only pleaded for forgiveness, and I therefore have no record of a king being tried.

One of the early kings was a cannibal; the council discussed the villainous habit in secret and decided to kill him. Since he had been brought up in foreign parts and could not swim, holes were bored in his barge and he was taken out in the river and left to drown, since the blood of a king should not be shed. His escorting councillors swam ashore.

The king should take action only through his officials so that they can be sued by an aggrieved person. Although everyone knows that in many of these cases a trespassing official has done wrong under the instructions of the king, he cannot plead those instructions in his defense. If he does, he is accused of an offense, "working" or "spoiling" the king's name, for which he can be severely punished. If we were to put this doctrine into our own legal propositions, we could perhaps say that the king can do no wrong for which he can be tried, but if he himself commits an action that affects a subject, he is liable to deposition—which in the past possibly would have had to be carried out by open rebellion.

The king therefore should—and usually does—act through officials, all of whom can be sued in court. When an official is sued in this way he is made to leave his seat on one of the special mats for court members, as the king who broke the beer pots was made to leave his "throne." In a case where a foreigner from Tanganyika was accused of theft he complained that he stood alone against the whole Barotse nation. The judges replied that "the law does not choose," i.e. it is impartial, and a senior judge said that if any of the councillors did wrong, he too was "a slave of the law" and would be made to sit in the accused's position.[6]

6. My *The Judicial Process among the Barotse* (1955), pp. 203, 228–29.

The theory of Barotse law is clear on this point, but when I was in Barotseland the presence of the British protecting power and appeal to the Northern Rhodesian High Court had restricted the capacity of the king or his councillors to act arbitrarily. Before that, according to the records of missionaries, and according to Barotse tales, kings often committed arbitrary, tyrannical acts. Yet one record makes clear the position of the king in litigation. In 1899 Major St. Hill Gibbons was surveying Barotseland with the help of the then king, who gave him two councillors as guides. They subsequently refused to continue the march, and he was compelled to turn back. When he complained to the king they were tried in the court, with Gibbons as plaintiff, and the charge was leveled against them not by the king, but by a son-in-law of the king: "You . . . are accused of disobeying the king's orders, inasmuch as you made it impossible for the white man to continue his journey, and complete the work he had undertaken in the interests of the king. . . . What excuse for your conduct do you make?" The accused produced speciously reasonable pleas, which the judges demolished.[7] But the king himself apparently did not appear in court.

The king in theory rules therefore through the Ngambela and other councillors and officials. The councillors themselves have manifold functions although, as we shall see, they distinguish each type of function clearly. Yet the council not only judges disputes but also debates matters of national importance and legislates. It issues instructions on many matters; it distributes the national land for the king; it discusses national hunts (and in the past, wars); and it arranges for the appointment of priests and for the sacrifices at royal cenotaphs. These duties and responsibilities mean for the Barotse that the councillors are the state and its law; hence it is demanded of them that they be grave, judicious, impartial, brave. The Barotse see a basic incompatibility between these qualities and the use of violence. Therefore a councillor, like the king (and a Cheyenne tribal chief), must never himself use force—he must never act as if he were, in modern Barotse parlance, "a policeman." I recorded several cases of councillors who were tried and fined, and at least threatened with deposition, for using force.[8] I once asked a prince, who was my clerk, to use his prestige to control an unruly crowd who were preventing me from photographing a dance I was staging; he replied that he could not, because if the crowd

7. Cited ibid., pp. 161–62.
8. Ibid., pp. 83 f.

abused or maltreated him, the council would punish him for provoking their offense against his princeliness. For this reason, when the council sends one of its members to implement its orders or one of its judgments where it suspects there will be opposition, he should be accompanied by police to use any force that may be necessary.

The rule that a man cannot be tried in the court of which he is "owner," as the Barotse put it, is shown in a case in 1948 when the then ruling Ngambela was tried on a charge of neglecting the health of his king who had recently died.[9] The councillors held that he could not be tried in the highest court of the land since he was its head, and a special court was summoned of all the men of the nation to hear the case. In a sense, since the Ngambela represents the nation, the nation as a whole and it alone was superior to him.

This rule applied to the Ngambela only in his official capacity. In 1912 the cattle of the then Ngambela damaged crops of a policeman. The policeman hit and injured the Ngambela's son who was herding the cattle. The policeman also came into the council in war dress, with his shield and spears. The king declared that the policeman was making war and must not enter the council. The Ngambela was allowed to divest himself temporarily of his position—"he took off his Ngambelaship" said the Barotse to me—and he fought the policeman and choked him until he defecated. The Ngambela then resumed his Ngambelaship. Since the policeman had made war and had not sued, he was held to have lost his right to sue in court; but the Ngambela of his own free will paid a beast for the damage to the crops.[10] The description of this case as it was given to me makes clear that the Ngambela could have been sued by the policeman had he not taken to arms. This supports Barotse statements that, like any other councillor, the Ngambela when prosecuted privately is "a slave of the law" and abandons his office, though Barotse assured me that the Ngambela, like the king, far from resisting a valid complaint from a subordinate, will by grace give more redress than is due, as befits a great chief and as the Ngambela did after defeating the policeman in combat.

Where the Ngambela was tried as Ngambela, in his official capacity, the next senior commoner councillor insisted he could be tried only by the nation.[11] Clearly the constitutional decision may have been influ-

9. Important political changes and intrigues were involved in this charge.
10. Ibid., p. 89.
11. Commander T. S. L. Fox-Pitt, O.B.E., R.N., Acting Provincial Commissioner of Barotse, told me these details, among much other important information.

enced by the desire to assess public reaction; but this case brings out how precisely the Barotse distinguish between office and incumbent.

They also distinguish between the kingship and the king. As in medieval England,[12] the property the king acquired during his reign accrued to the kingship. But the village which he had held as a prince remained his private property, unless he selected it for his burial, whereupon it became a royal cenotaph. Otherwise the king's "village of princeship," as Barotse call it, might be inherited by his own son, even if this son did not become the next king.

I have stated that the Barotse conceive of the king and the Ngambela as "two different kinds of kings." They make the statement by using for king the word *mulena*, which can be translated as king, chief, lord, or sir. They have taken this word from the language of a group of Basuto (the Kololo), who fought their way northward out of Basutoland, 1,000 miles to the southeast, to conquer and rule Barotseland from 1838 to 1864. Barotse call their king "the great mulena." But in their original language they refer to the king as *Litunga*, which is one of a number of words restricted to "things of kingship." It means "the earth," and the king's full title is "Great One of the Earth," or even "Great-One-the-Earth." Litunga is applied also to the ruler of only one other capital, lying about 30 miles south of the king's capital. This ruler, who has always been a princess since the Barotse reconquered their homeland from the Basuto and re-established their system of rule, has a capital duplicating that of the king, and she is entitled to use certain royal emblems which are not permitted to royal rulers at other provincial capitals. She is the only other Litunga (in her case "Earth-of-the-South"). This restricted use of Litunga emphasizes the unique character of these two pre-eminent rulers and places them on a different plane from any other authority. It identifies them with the land itself.

A number of songs of praise containing historical lore and proverbial wisdom are attached to every Barotse title. One for the Ngambela states that "the king is owner of Loziland and its trees and his [own] servants, and its cattle [game, fish, birds]; the Ngambela is owner of the Lozi people." I shall discuss in chapter 5 the significance of the word "owner" in these contexts. Here I stress that this praise em-

12. "A distinction between the king's public capacity and his private capacity, a distinction between the king and the crown, is pretty modern and foreign to the Middle Ages. The royal revenue and the national revenue are all one; there is no such thing as national land, the king's lands are simply the king's lands, no matter by what title they became his" (Maitland, *The Constitutional History of England*, 1908, p. 303).

phasizes that the Ngambela as owner of the people is empowered to control their actions and has major responsibilities in representing them. The control is resented, say the Barotse, for in their political theory, all power is resented as well as appreciated by those subject to it: "Everyone loves a prince till he is made king; then everyone hates him." The king is contrasted with the Ngambela in the saying which states that he is removed from the actual exercise of rule, save over his own servants. But he alone is the owner of the land—his title means the earth—and of its riches: the trees, the wild creatures, and domesticated cattle. The people derive their subsistence from these and hence they are indebted to him for their lives. When I was in Barotseland, the right of the king to tribute had been long abolished by agreement with the British Government. The king's stewards had sent a request to the people of a certain district to bring in bark and roots to make the great fishing net of the king, and had told them they would be paid for their goods. When they brought these to the capital, they refused to be paid. They were summoned into council and the head councillor reminded them that tribute was abolished and they were entitled to payment. They insisted: "How can we take payment from the king, our father, for things which are his, when we live by his bounty?" At least until 1947, when I last visited Barotseland, this feeling was still strong. It was a principle insisted on by judges, both at the capital and in courts far in the bush, that the land was the king's and that every one of his subjects was entitled to gardens in it and to use its public pastures, woods, and waters.

This doctrine that the king owns the land, and that allegiance is due to him because he allows his subjects to use it, places him in an entirely different category from the Ngambela or any commoner councillor, however powerful. For the Barotse, it gives a unique element of continuity to the kingship. The nation depends for survival on the land, and the king is more than owner of the land: he *is* the land. When he is installed he spends a night in lonely vigil by a sacred pool, from which it is believed comes a monster, symbolizing the forces of nature, to lick and consecrate him. He is not a divine king in that the Barotse do not believe, as do some African tribes, that the fertility and prosperity of the land depend on the king's physical well-being, so that they require theoretically that he be slain ritually if his powers begin to fail. But Barotse do think of the king as embodying the well-being and the fertility of the nation. The spirits of ancestral kings are buried in cenotaphs, marked by specially planted trees so that they stand out on the treeless plain; and these spirits control the prosperity of the nation as a whole and of its individual members. Sacrifices and offerings were, and to a lesser extent still are, made at these cenotaphs. When he dies, the ruling king will have his own cenotaph. And when he dies, it is said that "the nation falls into a coma." All fires in the land should be extinguished, and fire should then be taken from the hearth of his successor and carried through the land to rekindle the fires so that the nation warms itself and cooks its food by the fires of the new king. In brief, the king is ritually installed and ritually buried, to continue to serve the nation as a spirit. The Ngambela is installed with ceremony but without ritual, and he is buried as a private citizen.

Through this element of continuity in the kingship the king is, in addition, associated with law and justice in a symbolical manner even more than is the council. The council in effect at least appears to do most of the ruling. Hence it is more likely to commit injustice than the king. The king can pardon by grace of mercy, despite the law, as council cannot. Therefore anything connected with the king is regarded as a sanctuary from execution of the council's punishments. If a condemned man can escape from the council and get to the royal palace or a royal cenotaph, to the courtyard of any of the queens, or to the private storehouse where the king keeps his personal property, he is temporarily reprieved. The king will himself hear the man's plea, instead of listening only to the council's report on the trial and confirming or rejecting their judgment. At the least he is likely to soften the punishment. The king's life is also symbolized in certain drums, which play periodically through the night and the day. Some of these drums and his bandsmen are always supposed to be in the council; if a convicted accused can seize hold of a drum or a bandsman, he is in sanctuary.

Most importantly, the sanctuary of mercy which resides in the king and royalty is represented by a councillor-of-the-right, who sits just beyond the Ngambela and is therefore second in seniority. He is the Natamoyo, Giver-of-Life or Mother-of-Life; and this is the only title (it exists at both northern and southern capitals) that must be filled by a senior prince.[13] Royalty is brought into the midst of the great

13. One other prince, Mboo Sipopa, sat fairly low among the councillors-of-the-right. He was extremely dissatisfied at being passed over for the kingship, since his father Sipopa had driven out the Basuto. He was given the eighteenth seat on the right (he sat third among the

commoners to represent mercy. If a suppliant can get to the Giver-of-Life in the council or if he can flee to this councillor's courtyard, he is reprieved. Even this is not enough for the Barotse: seventh on the right they have a title which is assistant to the Giver-of-Life as a sanctuary, and this title has to be occupied by a commoner relative of a prominent royal personage or by a prince so distant from the ruling line that he is beginning to merge into the commonalty. This assistant and his courtyard are also sanctuaries; but he has also to keep watch over his senior's discharge of his duties. The Barotse are apparently terrified of giving away power, even power to protect, for once a man is elevated, it is feared he will stand against those he ought to care for. They think always of the dual pressures of the ambivalence of power on an individual. If royalty is seated among commoners to protect the people, its bearer may become puffed with power and abuse it. He cannot be checked by another prince, since princes are in theory rivals for power; therefore when he has a deputy who restrains him and who acts in his absence (theoretically one or other must be present at every trial), this deputy is drawn from the ranks of those who interlink commoners and royalty. And both of these title holders must in judgment be soft and gentle, withal firm in supporting the law, even beyond what is demanded of other judges. Obtaining royal sanctuary founded a special jurisdiction, containing the royal prerogative of mercy.

This complicated Barotse theory of power is manifested in another way. The Giver-of-Life is placed among the great commoners to represent the king as the fountainhead of justice and mercy. Yet he there becomes associated with the commoners who should check the king if he abuses his power or plans unwise action. The late king told a senior British official that the Giver-of-Life must chide the king when he has done wrong, criticism which could not be tolerated from anyone but a relative, and this very special relative. No Giver-of-Life in the records I have of recent reigns has ever become king, although one Giver-of-Life became chief at a provincial capital. I did not inquire into this possibility that appointment to a position that allowed criticism of the king barred access to the kingship itself and therefore eliminated its princely occupant as a possible rival.

---

royals) as a solace. Among the councillors-of-the-right he represented his father, who did not form a political sector on the Barotse pattern, for he had ruled by Basuto custom (see below, pp. 41–42, 61 f.

The Barotse are hard-headed realists about power. Most sanctuaries are royal and exist to restrict oppression by the council. The king protects against the council. But kings also abuse their power, and against this abuse the council provides sanctuary. A man condemned by the king is temporarily reprieved, and his case will be examined, if he can get to the council house or to the royal storehouse, where the council keeps the national drums on which the king is seated at his coronation, or to the Ngambela or his courtyard. Yet even this is not enough for them. For king and council may combine to oppress a man. He can then flee and seek sanctuary with the princess who is Earth-of-the-South, and the northern capital should not bring pressure on her to repatriate him. Conversely, although exactly the same sanctuaries, including the Giver-of-Life and his royal/commoner assistant, exist in the southern capital, final sanctuary from the south lies in the northern capital.

When I was working in Barotseland, the main sanction on the abuse of power was provided by British authorities, and I could not observe the working of this elaborate set of sanctuaries. I was told many tales of how men sought sanctuary in different circumstances, and not one tale reported that those in power did not recognize the sanctuary. I was told, too, that the drums of all chiefs were sanctuaries for defeated enemies in battle: bandsmen were sacrosanct, and when an army broke in battle its warriors were reprieved from slaughter if they could get to the drummers of their own or the conquering chief. I met men who had been succored thus and then adopted into the Barotse nation.

I have already given enough data to show that the Barotse law embodies an elaboration of their theory that power may corrupt, and that those in power must be restrained from abusing it. This thesis is further elaborated in the concepts of the private Ngambela of the king and of the Ngambela of the Ngambela. I have described how the Ngambela is appointed by the king to serve the king, but that power to stand against the king on behalf of the commonalty is implicit in the appointment. Yet the Ngambela may turn against both the king and the people whose interests he represents. Therefore each king, aside from appointing a state Ngambela, also appoints "his own Ngambela." He does so by creating a new title, the holder of which sits on the right just beyond the Giver-of-Life. The king attaches a large number of men to this new private Ngambela, who thus becomes a powerful counterpoise to the state Ngambela, while almost all the king's stewards are put under the new title. As kings followed this practice the titles of the private Ngambelas of ancient kings have thus been moved farther and farther away from the royal throne, slowly losing secular power, but becoming more hallowed.

The state Ngambela also has his own "Ngambela," a councillor holding a permanent title (Imandi), who is specially charged, beyond other councillors, with restraining the state Ngambela should he abuse his power over the people whose interests he primarily represents. The title of this "Ngambela" of the Ngambela is placed high among the councillors-of-the-right—that is, near to the king. The Ngambela also has many followers who are attached to his title; and he has also, as Barotse put it, a "Ngambela" to represent him to them, and them to him, in the title of a junior councillor-of-the-right. Ngambelaship thus is a generic concept for the Barotse. It denotes assistant, deputy, and also protector against the represented superior; and it is applied to all situations in Barotse life which involve the delegating of power. The assistant sanctuary to the Giver-of-Life can thus be spoken of as the latter's Ngambela. I must stress yet again that each time power is delegated thus, the person who receives it from his superior is considered to hold powers in some sense in opposition to the giver and as a check upon him.

The idea of balancing powers in this way is carried a stage farther in the discussion by the council of all matters affecting national interests. I have described how the stewards represent the reigning king, while the princes and husbands of princesses represent the royal family, and the councillors-of-the-right represent the commonalty, as three basic elements in the structure of the state. But, according to Barotse theory, great councillors, stewards, and royals, as powerful persons, tend to look on problems similarly, and they cease to be aware of the manner in which ordinary folk are affected. Hence, they say, they divided their council horizontally along the middle to debate matters of national importance. All the senior councillors-of-the-right, the senior stewards, and the senior princes and husbands of senior princesses, were formed into a single chamber. The very large number of men holding junior titles-on-the-right or junior stewardships, and the less important royals, who sat behind the rows of senior men in full council, were formed into a second chamber. When legislation, or matters such as making war or accepting missionaries were debated, these two chambers separated. The chamber of senior men met in the courtyard of the Ngambela or in the council house; the chamber of juniors met in the courtyard of their leader, with a special title but known as their Ngambela, or in the council house. When they were separated, the junior chamber was equivalent to the senior chamber in status. They were called by a term meaning "men," "warriors," "veterans" and, in the words of the senior councillors to me, "They are another kind of chiefs." [14] In theory, and I think also in fact, they knew more of the people's wishes and feelings, since they spent more time away from the capital.

The system was not working while I was in Barotseland [15] but I was told that the senior chamber hesitated to force its will upon the other chamber, and that the king on occasion took the junior chamber's advice against the senior. The leader of the junior chamber sat also in the senior chamber; he moved between the two reporting the deliberations as they strove to reach unanimity. Barotse themselves say that the senior chamber represented the capital, whose interests on many matters diverged from those of the ordinary folk, so that the latter had to be represented by the junior chamber. It was as if in the British Parliament, leaders of Government and Opposition in both Lords and Commons were set against the backbenchers of both parties from both houses—those with power set against those without power or promise of power.

These two chambers met during the day; and they were jointly set against an evening council. The king met at night in his drummers' shed at the palace with the state Ngambela, the Giver-of-Life, the king's private Ngambela, the chief steward, and anyone else he chose to summon, to discuss in whispers news coming in from the country and to formulate policy to put before the chambers of the day or to consider their advice. And here the Barotse constitution established yet another check. All the councils and chambers so far considered were filled with men; but in the secrecy of the palace at night two women were drawn in to check the power elsewhere reserved to men. As the king debated matters with what literate Barotse describe—not inaptly —as his Privy Council, two officially appointed women, one a princess

14. See my *Administrative Organization of the Barotse Native Authorities* (1943).

15. A chamber with the same name was set up in 1947, to represent the mass of people. Its seats were filled by holders of old titles and some persons were elected to it. The vicissitudes it underwent lie beyond the scope of this analysis.

and the other a commoner, eavesdropped outside the shed. Their duty as women, sensitive to the tender feelings of the people, was to warn the king if his great magnates were giving him advice that would antagonize the people. They were known as Anatambumu, Mothers-of-the-King (i.e. of the Earth).

The division between the northern and southern capitals also complicated debate. In the past there was no appeal from the south to the north in suits at law; both rulers were Litunga (king) and, "How can you appeal from one king to another?" But on matters such as waging war, passing new laws, or agreements with the Whites, matters had to be referred from the northern to the southern capital, which had the same divisions and chambers within its council. In the end, northern opinion prevailed, but if there was radical disagreement the councillors of the south might come to the northern capital, where they interdigitated in their seating according to set seniority. First near the throne sat the Ngambela, then the husband of the princess-of-the-south since he represented a king, then the Giver-of-Life of the north, then the head of the southern capital, then the king's private Ngambela, then the Giver-of-Life of the south, and so on.

This summary has described only the constitution of the Barotse capital, and I have not yet outlined how people were attached to councillors and stewards. How did so complex a system of checks and balances, of devolutions of power and thus establishments of power, work in practice? The answer is that I do not know in detail. The system was not operating fully when I was studying it, for the British Government had imposed a new organization on top of it all.

This much I can say. Before the coming of the Whites, Barotse society was not faced with problems arising out of radical change. Matters for debate cannot often have provoked differences of opinion in terms of the differing status of the councillors. Problems were of this kind: Shall we wage war this year and, if so, against whom? Where shall we hunt? Have we enough food to dig another canal to carry canoes in the dry season, or a canal and feeding channels to drain the waterlogged peaty margins of the plain so as to provide gardens? If so, where shall we dig the canal? Occasionally, traditions show, there was legislation to change private law and much discussion, according to the tales, over the faults of various councillors. Once there was a long debate when, after the defeat of the Basuto conquerors, the king decided to reintroduce the ancient Barotse system of rule, which I have partly described, and revolt was provoked. Of this, more anon. Radical problems, on which points of view were sharply divided (but again across the sets and chambers), began to emerge with the coming of the Whites. When the council had to decide whether to accept the offer of the British South Africa Company's protection and an annual subsidy, in return for granting mineral rights, it finally summoned a meeting of all the men of the nation near the capital.[16] In olden times debate must have proceeded slowly, backward and forward, out of sheer enjoyment of debating.

Before I try to explain how the Barotse attitude toward power is related to their general social structure, I must assure you that it is their concept and not mine. If I may without undue presumption make the comparison, I have not arrived (as Ehrlich said Mommsen did for the Romans) at general legal propositions which, though drawn from the existence of the state, are the product of my own intellectual labor and are abstracted from the facts.[17] Since the Barotse lacked writing, none of them had been able to set out this theory as a full doctrine, but point by point, and with some interconnecting of various points, Barotse expounded these principles to me. If they did not surpass Dicey in the sophistication of their insight into political powers involved in the constitution, they certainly surpassed my own simplicity. They taught me more than I could teach them.

No one who has studied or worked in any political system can fail to be impressed by the Barotse's penetrating insight into relations of power. Yet it is curious that no other African society is yet reported to have so elaborate a theory. This may perhaps be because other students have not been interested in the problem. Yet, as I have said, the Barotse made clear their ideas to me. I am therefore led to ask why they should have developed these so far. For while I believe that these ideas do give us an objective, so-to-speak scientific understanding of relations of power, I think that there is a certain extravagant sophistication in the theory which is not warranted by how Barotse authorities actually exercised power or by how effective were restraints on that exercise of power. I do not imagine, of course, that they deliberately designed the state's organs to cope with anxieties created by the theory, as the founders of the United States designed the division of

16. See Coillard, *On the Threshold of Central Africa* (1904), pp. 356–57.
17. Ehrlich, *Fundamental Principles of the Sociology of Law* (1913: translation 1936), p. 31.

powers within the American constitution in reaction to a theory of how Britain was ruled. The Barotse system must have arrived at its complex elaboration over a long period of time, with more and more accretions of officers and institutions. The theory surely followed as an interpretation of the facts.

With the goods and technologies available to the Barotse economy, the rich and powerful could not live in much finer houses, surrounded by relatively luxurious furnishings, or bedeck themselves with fine clothes; there was therefore no point in attempting to exercise their power to profit from sweating the labor or to expropriate the goods of underlings. Instead, they used their control over land and goods to build up direct relationships with many followers. Men from distant tribes have described to me how the king would reward them, when they brought in their tribute, with gifts of other products which they lacked and which had been rendered to the king in tribute by others. These in their turn had been similarly rewarded. A British official of that period has described how the king, by drawing in tribute and then distributing it to others, acted as a kind of bank and market, achieving exchanges of goods between the various parts of Barotse-land.[18] From the crops produced by tribute labor in the king's many gardens, he fed his people. His cattle were distributed to be herded by people who lived off these cattle. The king could not draw on these herds without at least the formal permission of the herder, who could protest if too many were taken from him.[19] Even the first missionary in Barotseland, who regarded the king as a tyrant, has described how the king bought all the goods from caravans of traders from the south and from the West Coast and gave these out to his people.[20] When Portuguese traders and Arab slavers came to Barotse-land, both Basuto and Barotse kings sold only a few people to them in order to get guns, and then forbade trade in people, probably be-cause the Barotse had sufficient ivory and beeswax to obtain the goods they wanted and because they were themselves always short of labor to meet the demands of their productive system.[21]

18. Coryndon, first British Resident in Barotseland, cited in Gann, *The Birth of a Plural Society* (1958), p. 5.

19. See Chap. 5, p. 161.

20. Coillard, *On the Threshold of Central Africa* (1904), p. 301.

21. See Gann, "The End of the Slave-Trade in British Central Africa" (1954). For this productive system see my *Economy of the Central Barotse Plain* (1941), summarized in "The Lozi of Barotseland in North-Western Rhodesia" (1951).

In practice, then, the king and his councillors drew on the tribute of goods and labor from subjects to maintain the capital, but the inherent limitations of the technological and economic system, and their own interests in securing the allegiance of people, restricted exploitative actions. The divisions into sets of commoner councillors, stewards representing the reigning king, and royals, and the further division into the chambers of the capital and of the ordinary folk, which cut across these sets, did not therefore reflect deep and fundamental, or potentially revolutionary, cleavages in the nation. There were not such diverse and conflicting interests as lay behind the Houses of Lords and of Commons, at least in the later Parliaments of England. Some hostility between royalty and commoners was based on a conflict of interest. Some commoners were once explaining to me that they would never select a prince born or begotten in their family as main heir to their estate [22] because he would then draw the estate permanently away from them and vest it in the royal family. A son of a dead king who was sitting with us exclaimed ruefully: "We too had mothers." But though the king was ultimate owner of all land, I found no evidence to indicate that the many-wived and therefore prolific royal family was ousting commoners from their estates, as Evans-Pritchard reports the spreading noble class has done among the Anuak and the Shilluk of the Sudan [23] and as the cattle-keeping conquerors appropriated lands from the peasants they subjugated around what was to be named Lake Victoria.[24] In Barotseland, rather, the kings with the labor of their people built new mounds for royal villages and drained peaty land for gardens, to which princes and princesses had to attract followers.

Marc Bloch said that extensive land clearance in Europe from the beginning of the twelfth century resulted in the lords' offers of favorable conditions to attract pioneers, with at least the assurance that "they would not be subject to the arbitrary authority of the lord." Men could change their lords, and land was sought after in order to hold men.[25] So it was in Barotseland, where a high rate of infant

22. See below, Chap. 3, p. 93.

23. *Political System of the Anuak of the Anglo-Egyptian Sudan* (1940); *The Divine Kingship of the Shilluk* (1948).

24. See e.g. Maquet, *The Premiss of Inequality in Ruanda* (1961) and Oberg, "The Kingdom of Ankole in Uganda" (1940). There is a general discussion of these situations in my *Politics, Law and Ritual in Tribal Society* (1965), Chap. 4.

25. *Feudal Society* (1961), pp. 244, 251, 263, 276 (orig. French, 1939–40).

mortality and a low life expectancy meant a relatively slow, if any, increase in population. The Lozi kings even raided their own provinces for children to colonize the plain. These children, unlike serfs captured in war, had normal free status and were assimilated into the dominant Lozi tribe, among whom they came to represent relatives from other tribes.

Nevertheless, though the people seem at no point to have opposed the institutions of kingship and council, they did fear individual and arbitrary acts of tyranny by king or councillor. Africa has had its Caligulas and Neros, as well as its Aureliuses and Antonines. There was Shaka the Zulu king who ordered the execution of a warrior because the unfortunate fellow's face made him laugh and his sides to ache. According to Barotse traditions they had few such kings. I have already mentioned the early king, raised in foreign parts, who ate people and who was drowned by his councillors. Only one other of the other eight Barotse kings who ruled before the Basuto conquest is said to have been a general tyrant, although the fourth king killed all his sons until the people saved two to provide for the succession. This king also put certain bans on one of the neighboring tribes whom he conquered only after many defeats. Most kings are praised for their kindness to all people. The general tyrant was attacked unsuccessfully by the chief of the south. Because of his cruelty he was not mourned after his death.

The Barotse legends—we cannot tell whether they are accurate history but they may well be—of the early period report no general revolts against tyrants, but they emphasize that the king was bound by the law, and that if a king ruled cruelly his council and people were entitled to rebel against him and to try to dispose of him. But princes led rebellions even against good kings to gain the throne. The legends also report frequent attacks on the king by the ruler of the southern capital, attempting to gain the kingship, and occasions when the southern ruler disputed the succession with the prince chosen in the north as heir to a dead king. The idea of legitimated civil war waged by royal claimants is strongly entrenched in Lozi tradition. It is even validated by mythology, for they say that after the first king was installed, he and one of his younger brothers fell out with each other. The younger brother had miraculous power—a common attribute of the younger brother or sister in all mythology and folk tales. By virtue of these powers he outwitted the king, but he moved south, altering the landscape as he went. Here he established by conquest his own kingdom, where in time he was persistently attacked by the fourth king. This king too was outwitted by magical powers, till at last the king of the south, saying he was worn out, disappeared into the ground with his councillors, people, cattle, and possessions. Only the pegs and ropes with which his cattle were tethered and his porridge stirrers were left, and these grew into tall trees which still stand to mark the second most sacred and powerful royal cenotaph in the land.

I have not cited this myth just because myths are part of the stock-in-trade of anthropologists: it is relevant to our view of problems in tribal law. We are all acquainted with the considerable literature about the divine right of kings in the Middle Ages, and the right of subjects to rebel.[26] What this myth does is to hallow the right of princes to compete for the kingship, *vi et armis*. The myth thus legitimates civil war, and makes it part of the Barotse constitution. Tradition does not reproach the southern princes with breach of loyalty; it is in the nature and the accredited role of princes to struggle for the kingship. But Barotse blame their subjugation by the Basuto on division caused by civil war, and after they reconquered their homeland it became a convention that the chief of the south should always be a princess, barred from the kingship.

Princely attacks on the king were thus not considered treasonable in Barotse law, and though an unsuccessful attacker might be slain, he and his followers were not tried at law.

Evans-Pritchard and I have concentrated in our analysis of African states on this problem and I cannot, in the space I have, give all the evidence we have accumulated to illuminate the social arrangements and processes which are reflected in these laws.[27] Aristotle mentions the difference between plots to change incumbents of office and plots to change the structure of the state. Historians and constitutional lawyers, and some sociologists, have also treated of the difference between revolts to change office holders and revolts against the existing system. I believe that the African data have enabled us to push the analysis further so that we can see constant civil war and rebellion as

26. See e.g. Kern, *Kingship and the Law in the Middle Ages* (1939), and his citations.
27. I deal with this problem, citing Evans-Pritchard's and other anthropologists' work, as well as theories of other scholars from Aristotle onward, in my *Order and Rebellion in Tribal Africa* (1963) and *Politics, Law and Ritual in Tribal Africa* (1965).

inherent attributes of states with relatively simple technologies which necessitate widespread dispersal of the people for purposes of their husbandry. The thin spread of people over the land, where communications are poor and slow, requires that the ruler delegate power over territorial sections to magnates who help him hold his kingdom and administer it. Delegated power is power given away. In many Southern African tribes, but not among the Barotse, these posts of power become hereditary. The territorial sections are not held together by an integrating, differentiated economic system, though the sections all participate in the circulation of tribute through the king. These sections then develop strong loyalties to their own leaders, and also hostility against other sections and the central government itself. Since weapons are simple—spears, axes, clubs, bows and arrows, and shields [28] —and are owned by every man, each local authority has his own army to support his attempts at power, whether he be a prince trying to win the kingship or a local commoner leader trying to gain power and influence around the kingship, possibly by supporting as candidate for the throne a prince related to his own family. We have seen how the division of Barotseland into northern and southern capitals produced such civil wars.

The pressures of these forces produce the continuous segmentation of a number of African states and chiefdoms.[29] In others, the sections struggle for power around a kingship which, besides possibly organizing the state, is lifted onto a mystical plane where it is the symbol of unity. There is then recurrent civil war in which the sections by fighting for their own candidate remain attached to the kingship, though they may attack the reigning king. As Evans-Pritchard has put it, the interest in the kingship of a successfully rebellious section may be expressed "at the expense of the king's person" [30]—a nice euphemism for regicide. In this view dynastic struggles are not only competitions for power between princes but are also the culmination of tendencies arising in the technology, the economy, and the distribution of power throughout the state. I have analyzed at length elsewhere[31] the political arrangements that keep these civil wars within

28. On the importance of this point see Andrezejewski, *Military Organization and Society* (1953), following Max Weber.

29. See Schapera, *Government and Politics in Tribal Societies* (1956).

30. *The Divine Kingship of the Shilluk* (1948), p. 38.

31. See references in n. 25, and also my *Custom and Conflict in Africa* (1954). For an excellent similar analysis see the final chapter in Maquet, *The Premiss of Inequality in Ruanda* (1961).

bounds around the kingship. They consist largely—as we shall see for
the Barotse—in establishing a series of allegiances for all men so that
each man is linked to the kingship by a diverse set of loyalties to
varied officials. Hence diverse interests associate him with different
groups of his fellows. These ties thus cut across one another, and
enmesh each man within the whole system. Here I must ask you to
accept that there is evidence to validate this analysis, so that we can
examine the kinds of law of succession and law of treason which are
found in this situation.

A marked characteristic of the law of succession is that often the
successor to the throne is selected from among the princes born to the
many wives of the king in a patrilineal society, or to his several sisters
in a matrilineal society. Alternatively, the law of succession contains
propositions that are inconsistent with one another in that they produce several contestants who can advance equally valid claims on the
basis of different rules. Even where the law of succession gives an
apparently clear and unambiguous principle, its application to the
facts is uncertain. For example, among the Zulu and Swazi the heir is
the eldest son of the great wife of the king; but the great wife should
have several different attributes which may be variously distributed
among several wives, and hence it might be uncertain who was the
great wife.[32] Thus in almost all [33] African tribes at any time, and not
only at the death of a king, there were sometimes more than one
claimant to the throne. The competition was institutionalized only in
some great West African states, which possessed large cities with
guilds of craftsmen, cavalry with cottonwool armor, plantations
worked by slave labor, and large-scale trade with the outer world. But
this institutionalization involved recognition of, and restriction on,
dynastic struggles: the kingship circulated through three dynasties of
the royal family, in an attempt to limit revolts.[34]

This uncertainty about who is to succeed a dead king was found in
so many kingdoms that obviously it must be related to the structure
of the political system as a whole. The same uncertainty existed in the

32. Kuper, *An African Aristocracy* (1947), pp. 88 f.
33. The Bechuana, who name as heir the eldest son of the great wife, who is selected by
the council, are one of the exceptions (Schapera, *Handbook of Tswana Law and Custom*,
1938, p. 55). I suggest that, since they live concentrated in single settlements, the processes
of territorial segmentation did not operate. Attempts on the chieftainship by princes, and
tribal splits, were recurrent in their history.
34. Nadel, *A Black Byzantium* (1942); Smith, *Government in Zazzau* (1961).

states of Asia and Europe during their early history. Kern stressed "the lack . . . of a strict claim to the throne for any individual member of the ruling line in the early Middle Ages," especially in Germany.[35] Maitland [36] reported similarly that a new king was elected by the Witan in Saxon England, usually from among near kinsmen of the dead king, by what he called "usage hardening into law." He went on to argue that the notion of hereditary right—dare I add "narrow" hereditary right?—makes its appearance late in the day. Primogeniture, he thought, spread "from office to property," from the rule defining succession to the king into private law. Rufus, Henry I, and Stephen asserted their titles by election. Maitland thought that the succession of Henry III "did much towards fixing the notion of hereditary rights," a situation continuing for nearly two centuries.

In this period Edward II was deposed. Maitland considered that this presented no difficulty to a constitutional lawyer: Parliament thought it had full power to depose a worthless king. As we might put it, princes and people are under duty to defend the kingship against the worthless king. Maitland further considered Richard II, on the other hand, to be deposed by what might be called a revolution against absolutism, a revolution constitutionally formalized by Richard's abdication. It is important, stated Maitland, that Henry IV asserted a hereditary right, "though in vague terms," even stooping to encourage the story "trumped up that his ancestor, Edmund of Lancaster, was the firstborn son of Henry III—older therefore than Edward I." In this way Lancastrians and Yorkists both asserted valid titles to the throne. I stop here, partly because I think I have oversimplified enough, and partly because I am entering the arena of my bias. In the County of Lancashire we are privileged to toast our Sovereign as "The Queen, Duke of Lancaster" because—since my stock-in-trade is myths—it is said by some that when on the night before the Battle of Bosworth, Henry Richmond's men told him: "Tomorrow when we have made you King of England you will forget your men of Lancaster," he replied: "To you I will always be Duke of Lancaster." The more knowledgeable assert that the privilege was in fact granted by either Victoria or George V.

The complexities of succession and politics in European history are most entangled. I have summarized Maitland's summary of the situa-

35. *Kingship and Law in the Middle Ages* (1939), pp. 35 f. (orig. German, 1914).
36. *The Constitutional History of England* (1908), pp. 59–60, 97–100, 190–95.

tion in England in order to venture the suggestion that this uncertainty over succession, and the possibility that other claimants and pretenders can cloak their rebellions under at least fictitiously valid titles, are not necessarily symptoms of a weak kingship. Maitland stated "that to the end of the [Saxon] period the kingship is not strictly hereditary, but elective . . . that a power also of deposing a king had been exercised as late as the days of Ethelred the Unready, is really rather a mark of constitutional weakness, of a dangerous feudalism, than of popular liberty:—the crown itself may become the prize of the rebellious vassal." [37] With all respect, I submit this is not the case, for the rebellious vassals seem always to have put forward someone with royal title to the kingship. Many complications of different kinds entered into each civil war. Thus, Lady Shenton ascribes to the period of the Wars of the Roses inevitable civil war with the administration "discredited in popular opinion. Magnates with retinues swollen by men who had seen service in the French wars, were rebellious and nervous, likely to make trouble at any moment. They were bound together in great family alliances which might easily convert a personal quarrel into a major civil war." Magnates changed sides rapidly, as Stanley did at the last moment at Bosworth.[38] *Yet* these shifts of noblemen seem on the whole to have been mobilized always behind a contender from the royal line. In his great study, *Feudal Society*, Bloch asserted that "after the recovery which marked the reign of Henry II, the aim of the magnates in their rebellions was henceforth much less to tear it asunder than to dominate it." [39]

Uncertainty over succession to the kingship is logically accompanied by persistent or at least repeated rebellions.[40] Perhaps it is also logical that in this situation commoners who fought behind a prince claiming the throne, or who supported their own chief essaying at power, were not considered to be guilty of treason in its modern sense. Among the tribes I know—Zulu and Barotse—even though commoners fighting behind their rebellious leader might be slain in battle, they could not afterwards be tried for treachery. Zulu were under duty to support their immediate prince as, in feudal times (according to Bloch and Jolliffe) a vassal had to fight for his lord even against the

37. Ibid., pp. 59–60.
38. "English History" in *Chambers Encyclopaedia, 4* (1959), 255–57.
39. *Feudal Society* (1961), p. 431.
40. Cf.: Bloch says of Germany that "no reign in fact was free from rebellions" (ibid., p. 427).

king. Bloch reports that when Hugh Capet retook Melun in 991, the viscount who defended the castle, together with his wife, was hanged. Bloch suggests this was because the viscount's superior lord was in the royal camp, and he had thus broken fealty, rather than that he had rebelled against the king. But the king's own followers insisted that he should pardon the knights who had defended the castle for, as vassals of the viscount, in supporting his revolt they had displayed their "virtue." [41] Pollock and Maitland [42] make a general statement on this point and give as an example: "Henry II, for example, spared the rebels of 1173, though he had thoroughly subdued them and had been within an ace of losing his kingdom. Never was there anything that we could call a proscription of defeated partizans."

The legal basis of the right of a feudatory to revolt in these feudal times was seen as reaction to a lord's denial of justice, even if the lord were the king. Such a revolt was not a rejection of the kingship for, says Jolliffe, "No English magnate of the feudal age ever formed the ambition of breaking loose from the community of English law, and turning his fee into an independent state." It was the reigning king's claim to obedience that was nullified if he failed to fulfill his trust to guard national custom:

> The maxim that the power of a king who acts as a tyrant is illegitimate, which almost exhausts contemporary theorizing about monarchy, and to us seems to be an ineffectual truism, was thus in the twelfth and thirteenth centuries the cornerstone of legal security. . . . when refused legal redress, the aggrieved party is entirely within his rights in declaring his obligation of vassalage at an end, making war upon his lord, and coercing him by every means in his power to do him right. [43]

Dowling similarly stresses that before Magna Carta the royal power was checked only "by the extraordinary feudal remedy of diffidation, which permitted a vassal to fight his lord to protect himself from injustices in breach of the feudal (lord–man) contract." The king was also bound as supreme lord. The right of armed redress was reaffirmed by King John in Chapter 61 of Magna Carta. He empowered the Barons to elect twenty-five of their number:

41. Ibid., pp. 233–34. See also Jolliffe, *Constitutional History of Mediaeval England* (1937), pp. 155–65.
42. Pollock and Maitland, *History of English Law* (1923, 2d ed.), p. 406.
43. Jolliffe, *Constitutional History of Mediaeval England* (1937), pp. 157 f., 446–47.

who shall with their whole power, observe, keep, and cause to be observed, the peace and liberties which we have granted them, and have confirmed by this our present charter, in this manner; that is to say, if we, or our Justiciary, or our bailiffs or any of our officers, shall have injured anyone in anything, or shall have violated any article of the peace or security and the injury shall have been shown to four of the aforesaid twenty-five Barons, the said four Barons shall come to us, or to our Justiciary if we be out of the kingdom, and making known to us the excess committed, petition that we cause that excess to be redressed without delay. And if we shall not have redressed the excess, or if we have been out of the kingdom, our Justiciary shall not have redressed it within the term of forty days, . . . the aforesaid four Barons shall lay that cause before the residue of twenty-five Barons; and they, the twenty-five Barons, with the community of the whole land, shall distress and harass us by all the ways in which they are able; that is to say, by the taking of our castles, lands and possessions, and by any other means in their power, until the excess shall have been redressed, according to their verdict, saving harmless our persons and the persons of our Queen and children, and when it hath been redressed they shall behave to us as they have done before. And whoever of our land pleaseth may swear that he will obey the commands of the aforesaid twenty-five Barons in accomplishing all the things aforesaid, and that with them he will harass us to the utmost of his power; and we publicly and freely give leave to everyone to swear who is willing to swear; and we will never forbid anyone to swear. But all those of our land, who, of themselves, and of their own accord, are unwilling to swear to the twenty-five Barons, to distress and harass us together with them, we will compel them by our command to swear as aforesaid.

Dowling comments that:

Chapter 61, omitted from reissues owing to its largely revolutionary character, was crucial. It tackled the problem of enforcing the contract between king and people in a situation where former kings had hardly scrupled to break their engagements and where the present king's faithlessness was common knowledge. Here, for the first time, a device was advanced which went beyond the sanctions of morality, religion, or even feudal contract. The provision of a standing committee of baronial watchdogs to report and seek redress was perhaps impractical but it was the first real achievement in a long effort to attain the central feature of the English constitution: a method of making government responsive to the will of the governed without civil war. Like most of the great steps to limited government, Magna Carta was the product of a revolutionary situation, the stand of certain classes, here barons and clergy, against deprivation of property, life or important rights. Considering this, the moderation and reasonableness seem amazing. Despite the revolutionary situation, the king was left his dignity and power, and the whole emphasis, as in the Charters of Liberties, and indeed almost all later English constitutional documents, was on specific, concrete details to be mended rather than on pious generalizations about justice and right. There was no wild anarchical doctrine, no vengefulness.[44]

Dowling's comment seems to me, with all respect, to be anachronistic. This was not a revolutionary situation, but a conservative entrenchment of existing doctrine, as defined by Jolliffe and other authorities. The limitation on vengefulness appears to be the explicit provision that after the barons had redressed wrong, with the support of all men commanded thereto by the king himself, they agree to restore John to the throne and by implication not to enthrone another member of the royal family in his place. Civil war was still to be resorted to, with royal approval, but it was to be civil war with limited objectives. The right not only of the barons but also of other approved men to levy war on the king is more than protected; it is almost turned into a duty in the final provision of Chapter 61. The failure to quote this chapter in later reissues of the Charter was not that it was too revolutionary but, I understand, because the next king, shortly succeeding, was a boy aged nine. The right to revolt remained since, in Jolliffe's words, after the defeat of Richard III it was still clear that "a bad or incapable reign broke the bond between the king and the lieges, and that the throne could be claimed and filled with their [the magnates'] assent, was immemorial custom, hardly a departure from constitutional precedent, and certainly not the creation of a new monarchy." Yet each revolution had to be legitimated by legal

44. Dowling, *Cases on Constitutional Law* (1954, 5th ed.), pp. 25, 27 f.

process, in "the permanence and publicity of parliamentary act." [45]

Hence, provided war was properly declared, armed insurrection against the king was hardly an offense.[46] As among the Barotse, this was not a "treason" which could be prosecuted at law and, says Holdsworth, "acts of attainder were . . . a more congenial weapon." [47] My own contention is that this procedure of redress by insurrection against the king has to be related to more than resentment of injustice: it can be connected with the total political process.

Barotse and Zulu carry this doctrine even farther: revolt of a prince is legitimate even if he is not wronged because it is part of the legitimate role of princeship to desire to be king, although a rebellious prince usually made a case against the king for tyranny or usurpation to justify his revolt. In the Barotse's own theory, again, despite the evidence to the contrary, the state is always on the verge of revolt: princes aspire to the throne; the new king constantly antagonizes councillors, for those who were powerful in his predecessor's reign then treated him as a prince, and may find it difficult to accept his new status; and above all those councillors who made him king will not respect him adequately—he must turn on these while he must conciliate his enemies. Barotse always warn: "Never expect gratitude from a king."

I am making an ill-armed incursion into medieval constitutional law to point out that it is not enough to cite the undoubted political weaknesses that arose from uncertainty in the laws of succession to kingship and from granting to rivals the privilege to wage legitimate war against the king. We have to answer the query: Why did no English, or Zulu, or Barotse magnate ever try to turn his fee into an independent state? The wide distribution in time and place of these kinds of laws within polities, which persisted in some equilibrium despite severe civil wars, suggests that the laws might be related to a specific set of social conditions.

It would be presumptuous for me to try to show this for medieval England, but I have consulted authoritative studies of the period, and none of them seems to connect the following facts. Edward III's statute of 1352, which for the first time made it treason to levy war

45. Jolliffe, *Constitutional History of Mediaeval England* (1937), pp. 446–47.

46. Holdsworth, *A History of English Law* (1923, 3d ed.), book 3, p. 288, citing also Pollock and Maitland, *History of English Law*, 2 (1923, 2d ed.), 505.

47. Holdsworth, ibid., p. 292.

against the king, was enacted the year after the Statute of Labourers. This was a more or less abortive attempt to cope with the better bargaining power of serfs and town artisans after the Black Death had so reduced their numbers that men became again much more valuable than land. According to Trevelyan, there was now a quarrel between two classes of peasants—the small farmer and the landless laborer— with the small farmers, formerly serfs, becoming yeomen. The great landlords, now reduced to a few families with very substantial land-holdings, backed the yeomen because high wages endangered the payment of rents by their tenants. There was a "gradual change from a society based on local customs of personal service to a money-economy that was nation wide." Meanwhile "the journeyman in the shop felt the same movement of aspiration and unrest as the labourer in the field. He too struck for higher wages when the Black Death made labour scarce." Trade was expanding and "the harmony of the mediaeval City Guilds was being disturbed by social and economic cleavage between master and man." The Statute was abortive because masters and farmers themselves broke its regulations to get labor.[48]

All this disturbance followed on struggles between landed magnates and city burghers. Sporadic unrest culminated in the great Peasants' Revolt of 1381, and immediately by a new statute "it was made treason to begin a riot." In the same reign it was enacted that it should be treason "not only to compass the king's death, but also his deposition or the rendering up by anyone of his liege homage; and that anyone who procured or counselled the repeal of the statutes passed in that Parliament should be guilty of treason." Henry IV had to have this statute repealed.[49] There is at least a possibility here that the anxieties of the king and of the magnates, who agreed to the new treason law, were provoked by the threat of lower-class uprising into introducing a new conception into the categories of treasonable offenses, while the king himself tried to operate the law against his rivals and the magnates. In practice, the history of the Wars of Roses shows that the new law was not consistently invoked against rebellious nobles and certainly not against their followers. After the Battle of Shrewsbury in 1403 it was not possible "to go to extremes with the rebels," and the lords considered that Edward III's Statute of Treason

48. Trevelyan, *English Social History* (1942), pp. 9–11, 38, and passim. For further complications see Appendix at end of Chap. 2 of this book.

49. Holdsworth, *A History of English Law*, 2 (1923, 3d ed.), p. 450.

did not apply to Northumberland, who was arrested while marching to fight the king. He was found guilty of trespass only, and not of treason.[50] The new system of relations and the old sets of feudal ties continued to coexist, and absolute definiteness in the law of succession denoting a single true heir was not yet established. This comes only with the creation of two further kinds of treason by statutes of Queen Anne: it became treason to hinder the succession to the Crown of the person entitled thereto under the Act of Settlement, or to maintain in writing the invalidity of the line of succession to the Crown established by the Act of Settlement.[51]

I hope that some historian will find this lead worth pursuing. Pollock and Maitland contrasted the 1352 edict that levying war was a treason with the Dictum of Kenilworth, which in 1266 was issued as "an essentially temporary provision relating to the punishment of insurgents," [52] though Jolliffe called it "the sentence upon the baronial regime," opening as it did with "the reassertion of the personal authority of the monarch." [53] But Pollock and Maitland conclude that:

> [This Dictum] shines out in startling contrast to the attainders of the fifteenth century. In part we may account for this by saying, if this be true, that men became more cruel as time went on; but also we ought to see that there had been a real progress, the development of a new political idea. Treason has been becoming a crime against the state; the supreme crime against the state is the levying of war against it. A right, or duty, of rising against the king and compelling him to do justice can no longer be preached in the name of law; and this is well.[54]

With all respect it does not seem enough merely to ascribe these critical changes to the development of a new political idea. Whence came the new idea? Can it be explained by the earlier awkward situation of kings of England who were lieges in other capacities of the king of France, and whose wars in France might have been called treasonable if they named as treasonable their own rebellious lords? Could the English kings then have distinguished their roles sharply?

50. Jolliffe, *Constitutional History of Mediaeval England* (1937), p. 425.
51. Kenny, *Outlines of Criminal Law* (1929, 13th ed.), p. 272.
52. Pollock and Maitland, *History of English Law*, 1 (1923, 2d ed.), 180.
53. Jolliffe, *Constitutional History of Mediaeval England* (1937), pp. 300–01.
54. Pollock and Maitland, *History of English Law*, 2 (1923, 2d ed.), 506.

Was England in the latter half of the fourteenth century undergoing a change, as Trevelyan's summary account suggests, to the kind of "organic interdependence" (Durkheim) in which the division into territorial segments would be countered by the integrating effects of a more differentiated economic system? That is, has some kind of horizontal stratification in terms of economic interests and cleavages begun to emerge, though it was only fully to develop centuries later? Our task as sociologists is to relate new ideas to changing social conditions.

I have thus far confined myself to the recognition of armed insurrection as a treason. "Treasons" were of course in English law a whole class of offenses, distinguished from felonies and misdemeanors, and an important distinction was that if a man were convicted of high treason his land was forfeit to the king. To plot against the king's life was treason, but not to wage open war on him. In addition, other early treasons were offenses against the dignity of the king's person and the kingship: adultery with his wife, violation of his eldest daughter, clipping his money, and usurpation of royal privileges. This is most marked in Africa. Dr. Southwold tells me that in Buganda the king pardoned a page who attempted his life, but a man who lifted his eyes from the ground when a queen was passing would be slain instantly. Among the Barotse to use the eland tail or leopard skin, to wear ivory bangles, to decorate one's fence with royal lashing or one's implements with royal markings, to use a royal name for one's dog or dugout, to commit adultery with a queen, or to speak ill of the king were all more heinous and less forgivable offenses than to rise in armed revolt against him. Among the statutes passed by the Barotse king under the British was one in 1929 protecting these privileges.[55]

The very deficiency in the internal integration of the state's components seems here to heighten the kingship's symbolic and ritual value, as unifying its disparate sections. Hence trespasses on the symbolic and ritual insignia and exclusive privileges of the king and his kingship are grave offenses. The nearer the king's style of life to that of his subjects, the more important are conventions, modes of etiquette, and apparently insignificant material appurtenances in distinguishing king and kingship from the commonalty. I shall have more to say about the influence of this role of convention on the general Barotse theory of power.

One facet of the early medieval law of treason was the offense of

55. See my *Essays on Lozi Land and Royal Property* (1943), pp. 100 f.

"imagining" the death of the king—i.e. to devise, plot, plan, or compass the death of the king, as in 1491 in Act 7, Henry VII, c. 23,
Richard White was charged that he "traitorously imagined and com-
passed the death and destruction of our said Sovereign Lord." As an
anthropologist, I would have been pleased to find that "imagine" here
meant making images, for purposes of witchcraft or sorcery, but alas!
there is no evidence to support this idea. It seems to contrast secret
conspiracy with properly levied and declared insurrection.[56]

We now have the background in which we can interpret the basis
of the Barotse's sumptuary theory of power. In many African states
like the Zulu, the great councillors of the king were rulers of counties
and were princes who had bodies of followers attached to them; immediately and directly they had armies to support them. The king's
own private advisers and stewards, who ran the capital, and the commanders of regiments composed of men of the same age who were
recruited from the whole nation, supported him against these potentially hostile leaders with their independent powers.

The Barotse were at approximately the same stage of technological
and economic development as the Zulu, but the organization of their
council was very different. They had no great men with independent
armies; their nation was not divided for administrative purposes into
territorial divisions; all the men of the nation were attached for jurisdiction, organization for war, and some state labor works to different
great councillors-of-the-right. The men thus attached to a councillor,
particularly in the floodplain itself, were not necessarily neighbors.
Neighbors, and sometimes even members of the same village, might be
attached to different councillors. The members of an administrative
unit attached to a senior councillor were thus widely dispersed in the
nation. I call such a unit a political sector. Several groups of foreign
immigrants in the plain and areas of the outer conquered provinces
belonged to the same sectors, but they rarely entered into state politics
except after a revolt. In result, then, a councillor or a prince did not
have a solid localized block of men, who could develop strong loyalty
to him. As councillors were promoted fairly regularly to higher titles
or moved to other tasks or deposed, there was less chance that loyalty
would develop.[57] In addition, all the men thus attached to councillors-

56. See e.g. *A New English Dictionary on Historical Principles*, ed. J. H. Murray, 5
(1901), part 2, 45–55, under "imagine," section 3.

57. It is impossible to measure rates of promotion and deposition in the past. I have tried to
do so from about 1880 to 1942 in my *Administrative Organization of the Barotse Native
Authorities* (1943).

of-the-right were also attached to stewards and to royals, but in such a way that not all the men who shared attachment to a leader on the right were associated in attachment to a steward or to a prince. These three major sets of attachments thus cut the nation into diverse sets of allegiances, in which men were not constantly associated. Their loyalties to their lords in the capital, which they took very seriously, were divided.

When I studied the Barotse they were working with a territorial system of administration created for, and to some extent by, the British Administration. I was able to work out, but only in outline, the structure of their old system from earlier writings on the Barotse and from what they themselves told me. It is difficult to assess precisely how the system worked, although it still operated within the new system. Jurisdiction for disputes was established by allegiance to councillors-of-the-right. If a dispute could not be settled locally in consultation with important persons, two litigants of the same sector went to the capital where their case was heard at the courtyard in the capital of their senior councillor, supported by other councillors of that sector. If men of different sectors disputed, the case was tried by a combined court of councillors of both sectors, sitting in the courtyard of the senior—i.e. the one who sat nearer to the king. Appeal lay in the full council which heard the case anew. The Ngambela was also owner of a sector but, since he was head of the full council, cases involving members of his sector were heard under the presidency of his own deputy, the Ngambela to the Ngambela; otherwise the Ngambela himself would have had to listen on appeal to a case he had already judged as head of a court, and then it would not have been an appeal. "How can the same man judge an appeal against himself?" ask the Barotse. This applied only to the Ngambela, as titular head of the council; other councillors who had heard the case at lower levels still sat as judges in full council.

These sectors were also the units in which men assembled for war or for state labor. But to work for the king and his queens the nation was mobilized through the stewards, and other stewards mobilized workers on behalf of the prince or princess to whom they were attached.

This division of duties among these three sets of allegiances was constitutional doctrine. In practice an aggrieved person who felt that he might secure justice that way could take his complaints through his stewards to a royal or a queen, to plead on his behalf. I have recorded one case of a man who felt violently aggrieved by his immediate lords; he was prevented by his wife from committing suicide in protest and brought his plaint directly to the king by going through a steward other than his regular one.

I hope I have been able to make clear the outlines of the system. If one wonders whether this is typically African, I can say that there are reports of similarly complex systems. Even among the Zulu, although commoner chiefs ruled territorial areas, the men of these counties (and hence their princely sons) were attached to the king's queens in a system by which adjacent areas held allegiance to different princes, so that in royal revolts the country did not side behind a particular prince in a solid block that might secede from the nation.[58]

In an analysis of a Northern Nigerian kingdom,[59] Dr. M. G. Smith has distinguished administrative action from political action. Political action occurs in systems of relations of power which involve competition, coalition, compromise, and so forth. It is designed to secure control over the means of managing the public affairs of the group and its component sections. One of these means is the system of administrative action through which the business of government is carried on; this system is hierarchical and authoritative, dealing with problems of order and with the associated protection of rights and enforcement of obligations. The distinction between administrative and political action is analytic, because in all polities the administrative apparatus acquires power, and political action has to use that apparatus. The Barotse do not distinguish them, and describe them with one word. Through European history the two systems of relations seem to have become more segregated.

In African states competitive struggles for power tend to occur between the very persons who occupy a series of organized positions in relation to one another in the hierarchy of administration. As stated, the chief of a Zulu county was an officer of the king, ruling his county for the king, and a contender for power backed by the army of his county.[60] In Barotseland, except for a short period, the councillors organized for administration in the hierarchy were also the main contenders for power around the king and, save for small groups of their

58. E.g. Maquet, in *The Premiss of Inequality in Ruanda* (1961), brings out brilliantly how this cross-cutting of allegiances in Ruanda gave stability to their system.

59. *Government in Zazzau* (1961), pp. 15 f. I follow Smith, but amend his analysis somewhat, and for lack of space I necessarily simplify it substantially.

60. Above, this page.

own followers, did not have private armies. When the men assembled in their armies for military or state-labor service, they did so in public, to serve the king.

As allegiance and authority were concentrated in the administrative system at the capital, where the powerful councillors spent most of their time, so struggles for power were concentrated there. Because of the relatively undeveloped economy, and the other factors I have listed, the political system still contained strong tendencies to segmentation, appearing on the surface in dynastic rivalry and rebellion, actual or potential—potential in the sense that the threat of a rebellion hung constantly over the king, and the threat of deposition over a councillor (as an election theoretically hangs over the British Prime Minister). The various kinds of councillors and shifting alliances of councillors did not represent groups differentiated from one another by varied roles in a complex economic system or bound to one another in that mutual interdependence which Durkheim called organic solidarity.[61] In the end, each councillor or steward in the capital represented neither the interests of a territorial group nor a functional group, but only himself. Hence, I suggest, relations among the councillors were marked by incessant personal intrigues, independently of extrinsic factors.

Groups of councillors still move about, whispering to one another about important and unimportant affairs and passing information around in limited circuits, in a way I never observed among the Zulu. The Barotse call this whispering *kusebela,* a verb whose root also describes slandering and calumniating, and other councillors always fear that vital information is being kept from them and that the whispers they do not hear must be to their disadvantage. Everyone tries to get into the series of inner circles which they believe to exist. The administration of justice is palpably carried on in public, and so is the administration of affairs. The head of a court periodically stops a trial to announce some matter and seek the opinion of his fellows or to tell them what has been decided. But there is a feeling that intrigues go on behind the scenes and that circles of information are being closed. And these intrigues focus through factions of councillors on selected princes, since each prince is a potential king. At any one time there are only two or three factions, and these factions seem to have been organized in terms of the administrative linkages.

In Barotseland, contentions for power were in fact rarely marked

61. *De la Division du travail social* (1893).

by the direct threat of the spear. They were pursued in secret negotiations. I suggest that this is one of the main sources of the highly elaborated Barotse theory of power. King and Ngambela, the Ngambela and his deputy, the councillors-of-the-right and the stewards and the princes—all of these are involved in constant intrigues for power and they come to represent and stand against the different categories of persons who comprise the nation. Thus these intrigues for power are absorbed into their discharge of administrative duties for the state and the manner in which they represent the interests of dependents in the administrative hierarchy. Hence each administrative position, which is also a position of power, is seen as posed in ceremonial opposition to a series of other positions, and the interests of the subordinates of each position have to be represented against it. The result is an elaborate network of offices and councils to which the people of the nation are linked in a number of sets of crosscutting ties of allegiance and opposition. Out of this situation there does in practice seem to emerge considerable stability for the state as a whole.

The dominant position of the capital in Barotse polity appears to have an ecological basis and therefore some economic support. The products of the great floodplain differ markedly from the products of all the surrounding woodland regions.[62] Trade lies between the plain and the woodland regions as a whole, and not between those woodland regions. The tribes from the woodlands gained as much as the Lozi themselves from the circulation of goods through the tribute that accumulated in the king's storehouses and was distributed among those who brought tribute. The river routes also center in the plain. It seems safe to say that whoever held the plain was likely to dominate the region by controlling what differentiation there was in the general economy.

Within the plain itself, the effect of the flood on peoples' lives probably accounts for the concentration of power, as well as administration, in the capital. As people move between their dry-season and flood-season villages they do not all move simply from one village to another. Some do, and many plain villages have their marginal counterparts. But the inhabitants of neighboring villages may go to widely separated places on the margins. Some people remain permanently in the plain through the flood, despite its discomforts; others may move

62. I have summarized these differences in my "The Lozi of Barotseland in North-Western Rhodesia" (1951), from a fuller account of *The Economy of the Central Barotse Plain* (1941).

within the plain to temporary camps on uninhabited patches of higher land, or go in various years to temporary camps at different points on the margins. A village in midplain may move to a village nearer the margin, whose inhabitants have moved to the margin itself. The inhabitants of other villages disperse in the flood season, going to different villages along the margin where they seek homes with various relatives or friends. Some members of a village may go to the western margin, while others go to the eastern margin. Young men may take the cattle to graze in small plains in the woodlands, either camping or staying with relatives or with bloodbrothers or friends. In the course of a year the same people are not associated in territorial units. I believe that this set of facts accounts for the absence of a highly organized territorial administrative system among the Lozi of the plain, even though small territorial areas are named and have allegiance to some prominent royal in the neighborhood. In the absence of a territorial administrative system we have the intricate system of sectors leading to the council in the capital, which therefore dominates political life.[63] The outer provinces were not tightly administered from the capital. Their people were attached to councillors in the capitals, but the capital sent representatives to live among them only in order to oversee the forwarding of tribute.

Given that the powerful administrators, who were also rulers of the nation, did not have their own followers concentrated in the capital, there is another general tendency which was likely to produce a highly conventional marking of status within that personnel. I have explained that in states like that of the Zulu the court was filled with great magnates who attended in their own right of power because they ruled counties. They came by their own names as authorities with private armies. In the Barotse capital councillors entered into an established hierarchy of titles. It is a general rule that the fewer the real bases of differentiation between the roles of persons in a society, the more social conventions will exist to mark slight differences of roles. I have developed this argument to explain why tribal societies have more elaborate ceremonies to mark changes of status than modern industrial societies have.[64]

63. Many tribes have similar sector systems on top of a territorial system (e.g. Zulu, Ruanda).

64. For the full exposition of, and the supporting evidence for, this thesis see my "Les Rites de passage" in Gluckman, ed., *Essays on the Ritual of Social Relations* (1962).

In kinship groups which act to achieve a multiplicity of purposes the entry of persons into each role directed to a different purpose tends to be marked by that multitude of conventions and taboos that is characteristic of tribal society. These indicate what role a person is playing at a particular moment. Roles, so to speak, are segregated by customs and conventions and by elaborate mystical theories. Similarly, since there is relatively little actual difference between officials in the Barotse council, conventions and taboos and beliefs and an elaborate theory of power attach to the titles within the council and segregate them from one another. I have already suggested that the less the king is separated from his people by material circumstances, the more elaborate will be his insignia and special conventions, and the more heinous is a trespass on his privileges. The tendency in this direction within the Barotse council is strengthened because in this type of society the palace and the political and administrative council, are the aim of most ambitious men.

In the palace household there is, as seemingly in all royal households in relatively undifferentiated states, a multiplicity of offices and officials and of servants, each with his special duties, secular and ritual. There are royal priests, fishermen and hunters, royal attendants in the bedchambers, caretakers for dugouts and dogs, praise singers and jesters. In the council many more titles exist than are necessary for actual administration, to provide for all the ambitious. There are no barriers to upward mobility, and the brave and able, and even the fruitful, secure appointments of some kind, while marriage to a princess is a shortcut to appointment. The conventions of the titles include ideas of their being linked to one another in terms of their association with Barotse history, for various titles represent ancestral kings, princes and princesses, and great councillors. In this legendary hallowing of titles a dual measure of authority is involved: those near to the reigning and recent kings are in practice most powerful, those representing the early kings are most sanctified. Besides the general idea of power and control of power which the conventional separation of titles embodies, the fact that different councillors represent the history of power in the nation by opposed scales seems to me to account further for the elaborate, and seemingly unusual, theory I am attempting to explain.

I have now, after my long excursion through the laws of rebellion, treason, and succession, offered my answer to the problem posed: How is the elaborate Barotse theory of power, and the manner in which power corrupts, related to other elements of their system? I am not in a position to assert, as a general rule, that the less the material bases which underlie struggles for power within a system where personnel of administration and of political struggle coincide, the more elaborate is likely to be the doctrine of power. I know of no similar treatment of the theory of power in tribal states; my colleagues who have studied African states were not interested in these problems and but few state who sided where in rebellions or by what rules treasons were punished. Schapera (*Government and Politics*, 1956, pp. 157 f.) shows that in S. Africa men tended to support their own leaders, save where tyranny was gross. In Barotseland chance determined what side a commoner took.

The answer to these problems may be found if African states are arranged in a morphological series,[65] ranging from the symbolic ritual kingship of the Shilluk, which lacked administrative powers but represented the unity of the nation, to the great states of West Africa, with their large capitals and slave plantations—states well characterized by Nadel's description of Nupe as *A Black Byzantium* (1942). A step beyond the Shilluk are the small chiefdoms of South Africa, which were subject to constant segmentation. Then come states like the Zulu and Bemba, where princes and chiefs administer for the king territorial counties but mobilize armies of their followers in support of their attempts at power. Next I would place the Barotse-type system, dominated by what I call "politics of the capital." Buganda may fall into this category. In these systems the council of the king does not consist of landed magnates but of a number of titleholders appointed to their positions by the king in council. They are not specialized bureaucrats, since the kingdoms still have the limited technology and economy which I take as a master explanatory principle. The king moves people between offices, to which are attached estates and followers, and no great man establishes permanent ties with a loyal body of followers. Social mobility of the brave and able is still possible. The next type may be the "caste" states, like Ruanda, of the cattle-keeping conquerors of peasants. Here there are caste-like categories specializing in different subsistence activities, and there is a radical restriction of the rights of the peasants to positions of high power. Significantly, we find here, in addition to dynastic struggle and rebel-

65. I have attempted such an analysis in Chap. 4 of my *Politics, Law and Ritual in Tribal Society* (1965).

lion, reports of a religious revolutionary movement of protest among the peasants, such as is not reported from the other states, and which offers parallels with the millenarian movements of the early Middle Ages.[66]

The West African states like Dahomey, Nupe, and Zazzau have a more differentiated economy, with slave labor and external trade on a largish scale. There are great landed magnates, with town and country houses, and factions of aristocrats who, according to one bare statement, seek the support of a city mob in a capital of 50,000 people. Mercenaries and mercenary generals enter the arena of politics. Dynastic struggles still exist but, again, one account reports a large-scale peasants' revolt. I hope the thesis I have advanced will stimulate inquiry in these varied states into the possible interrelations of revolts and how people adhered to rebellious leaders, into the law of treason and the law of succession, and into the indigenous theory of power. Such an inquiry might perhaps illuminate dark periods in our own constitutional history.

With the facts I have now set out we can return to the revolts which beset Barotseland after the Basuto invaders were defeated and mostly killed. They were expelled in a sudden coup by a Barotse prince whom the Basuto chief had reared. He married a daughter of the Basuto conqueror and ruled by Basuto customs: his great men attended his court supported by their armed followers. Councillors who wished to re-establish the old Barotse system plotted to summon a prince from a Barotse kingdom established in the north after the Basuto invasion; they were detected and executed. But while the king was liked for his generosity (notice this theme), the people resented the way he moved around the country, particularly to the distant former capital of the Basuto in a faraway province, and they disliked his habit of taking from his subjects those of their wives he desired. Councillors organized a revolt and he was killed, and another prince was crowned. This prince came from the south, and within a few years councillors from the north drove him out and installed another prince as king. The new king decided to re-establish the ancient Barotse system of administration, which would have deprived the great councillors of their personal armies of supporters. In addition, he proposed to allow people to reclaim land which had belonged to their ancestors before the Basuto invasion, and this threatened these council-

66. Cohn, *The Pursuit of the Millennium* (1957).

lors' holdings. Some of them, moved also by other fears, attempted a coup d'etat, but the king escaped. A prince from the exiled kingdom was brought to Barotseland and installed, but within a year his predecessor had raised an army in the south and regained his throne. The hostile councillors then fled north to raise another army and find another prince. When the one they selected said he had no quarrel with his cousin, they mocked his cowardice and dressed him in woman's clothes. He denied the charge of cowardice and said he would go with them, but refused himself to fight. He and they were killed and their army defeated.

I have listed these facts to show what troubled times followed the Barotse liberation of their homeland. The return of emigrés, the problem of where the capital should be built and which system of rule be followed, and the readjustments of rights to land created internal disturbance. Apparently for the first time in centuries the Barotse were threatened by powerful African states to the southeast. White traders and missionaries were entering the country, and its leaders were divided in their opinion of how they should treat these Whites.

I stress the disturbed conditions because the first missionary to settle with the Barotse, Coillard, has left a record [67] of a savage monarch with murderous councillors, and this is the first full contemporary record of Barotse rule we have. But Coillard's book, written many years later, exaggerates the picture when it is compared with his own unpublished diaries and letters.[68] In addition, these records show two biases. First, like many other missionaries, Coillard understandably exaggerated the horrors of life in the region to which he and his fellows, with great hardship and suffering, were bringing the Gospel and civilization. Second, Coillard and his first Barotse adherents were undoubtedly subjected to capricious support and harassment by the king. My own evidence from old Barotse describes the king as undecided in what he should do about the mission and subject to the pressure of shifting factions of councillors who favored or opposed the

67. Coillard, *On the Threshold of Central Africa* (1904). There are earlier descriptions both of Basuto and Barotse: I cited Coillard's because it was full and reported long experience.

68. The unpublished documents are largely in faded and nearly illegible French and are made more difficult by Coillard's use of private abbreviations. My wife's expert ability in French enabled her to decipher and translate the documents for me. We are deeply grateful to M. Etienne Kruger and Mme. S. Houplain of the Paris Evangelical Mission Archives in Paris for their hospitality and assistance.

mission. Moreover, Coillard had got off on the wrong foot with the king, who was driven out for a year, recovered his throne, and then ruled for thirty years. Coillard had approached him during his first short reign, and after he was driven out Coillard continued negotiations with the new king, against the advice of an English trader who knew the Barotse well.[69] The restored king took a long time to regain his trust in Coillard after what he felt was double dealing.

Nevertheless, the Barotse themselves regard these years after the restoration as times of war; and "in war," they say, "the law sleeps": *inter arma, leges silent*. By the time Major St. Hill Gibbons visited Barotseland in 1898, he found a well-ordered kingdom. The period of relative anarchy may have given birth to the many sanctuaries. I believe they have a long traditional existence, from before the Basuto invasion, and that their multiplicity arises from the highly conventional theory of the separation and opposition of powers which dominates Barotse ideas about their constitution.

A Further Note on the English Law of Treason

It is risky to have summarized so complex a period as the fourteenth century in England so briefly in the course of a chapter devoted mainly to the Barotse. I could not even stress in the text some of the actual complications, or the differing views of various historians, without disturbing the development of my analysis of the Barotse constitution. I set some out briefly here. I state again that I am trying to emphasize only the importance of looking at changes in the law of treason in terms of systematic interconnections, and this summary statement is intended to illuminate that point.

According to Manning in the *Cambridge Mediaeval History*, important changes in the relationships of king and Parliament, and king and baronage also occurred in the fourteenth century. In 1340 Parliament began to show "a disposition to make conditions first," before giving the king money for the war against France. Thus they de-

---

69. Unpublished typescript of Westbeech's diary (in my possession); published since this chapter was written, under the editorship of Tabler (1963), at p. 28. Westbeech (loc. cit., pp. 46 f.) describes the slaughter in these battles and the killings of men, women, and children in the troubled times when he was there. Mataa, the councillor who led the revolt and who is still remembered in Barotse for his cruelty, set a fashion of out-of-hand executions which for a short time provoked King Lewanika to take revenge. My own evidence and some contemporary records, like Westbeech's, show that there were no trials. Lewanika later received all commoners who had fought against him.

manded audit of accounts and the right to nominate his chief ministers. The king came to rely more and more on the hereditary counsel-
ors of the Crown, who seem to have been forming "a definite body,
the peerage." The baronage, lay and clerical, triumphed over the policy of the household. They had embodied in a statute the view that
none of their number could be tried save by his peers in full Parliament. Englishmen were released from the king's claims as king of
France. Edward III did not relish these conditions and later secured
the repeal of some. But though neither baronage nor Parliament gave
Edward "much trouble," his reign "did not permanently strengthen
the monarchy as an institution in relation to its old rival the baronage.
On the contrary, the baronage had made the beginnings of a working
alliance with the social classes that had been lately called to the Great
Council of the nation and that were increasing in political as they
increased in economic importance." [70]

Left-wing historians describe much more intensive and deep-seated
changes and civil strife. Dobb draws attention to the urban disaffec-
tion which entered into the Peasants' Revolt of 1381 and traces it
back among the burgesses to early in the century, especially among
the merchants who were not also landholders.[71] Fagan and Hilton
write: "It is interesting to note that the aldermen who let in the Kent
and Essex rebels [in 1381] were fishmongers—and were not punished
after the suppression of the revolt." [72]

Fagan and Hilton argue that the central state apparatus had developed sufficiently to make possible the implementation of the Statute of
Labourers, which in 1349 followed on the Black Death, whenever and
wherever local powers proved insufficient. Hence, they say, the rebels
of 1381 almost always chose official representatives of the central state
power as object lessons [models] in the administration of popular
justice. They state that the Statute of Labourers was enforced as effectively as any medieval statute could be: "It has been calculated that
between 1349 and 1377" the county quarter sessions, and the central
courts of Common Pleas and King's Bench, "must have considered
something like 9,000 cases and, in almost every case for which there is
evidence, the jury's verdict or the court's judgment was in favour of
the employer and against the employee." The resistance of laborers

70. *Cambridge Mediaeval History*, 7 (1949), 438–41.
71. Dobb, *Studies in the Development of Capitalism* (1946), p. 81.
72. *The English Rising of 1381* (1950), p. 40.

was shown "in the growing tide of revolt revealed by the number of armed attacks which were organised on the justices empowered to operate the Statutes. The peasantry was beginning to extend its political horizons as it broadened its resentment from the well-known local oppressor, the manorial lord, or his bailiff, to the representatives of repression as an organised system, the state system." Opposition, they say, also arose against the Statutes among the richer peasants who might, "at first thoughts, have been thought to favour their provisions." The richer peasants were penalized, since they could not enforce the Statutes and had to pay higher wages; hence, Fagan and Hilton suggest, probably many of the richer peasants were leaders in the revolt of 1381. But they also trace growing peasant opposition to the system under which peasants lived back to early in the thirteenth century.[73]

They then stress that "the nobility during the greater part of the reign of Edward III was very little divided against itself." The later dissension which arose among them was therefore all the fiercer.

> These developments were partly the direct consequences of the war mobilisation, partly the result of the inevitable tendencies in feudal society; the most important of them was the diminution of the great nobility as a class. The wealth of society—in this age, of course, mainly the amount of land owned—became concentrated in ever fewer hands. By the end of Edward III's reign the greater number of the old earldoms and baronies were in the hands of a narrow group of less than ten great magnates, most of them members of the royal family or closely related by blood and marriage. This was the result of a process which had begun under Edward I. An important result of the close family ties between the crown and the great nobility was that dynastic claims to the throne added justification to the claims of each faction to control the state machinery.

They argue that it is historically false to suggest that in feudal society the king stood apart from his barons, and that an examination of the conflicts of the period shows that they arose from divisions inside the ranks of nobility, between a faction "in" with the king, and others.[74]

73. Ibid., pp. 25–28.
74. Ibid., p. 45.

These contrasting analyses seem to me to endorse my suggestion that making it a treason to levy war against the king was not directed against feudal rebels or landed magnates. I have already cited the acquittal of Northumberland after the battle of Shrewsbury in strong support of this suggestion.

Powers were being taken against other classes, and these powers were continually reinforced. The Statute of Treason of 1352 defined treason as compassing the death, or violating the persons, of certain members of the royal house; counterfeiting the Great Seal or the king's money; slaying certain ministers when officially engaged; levying war against the king within the realm or adhering to his enemies.[75] The last two are the new treasons. In 1361 the government took preventive powers "to restrain the evil doers, rioters and all other barrators and to pursue, arrest, take and chastise them according to their trespass or misprision, and to cause them to be imprisoned and duly punished . . . and also to inform themselves and inquire touching all those who . . . go wandering and will not work as they were wont to do before this time." [76] As cited, after the 1381 rising, "it was made treason to begin a riot."

75. *Cambridge Mediaeval History*, 7 (1949), 444. I have altered the order in which the offenses are cited, putting counterfeiting second from near the end of the list, since it was an ancient treason.

76. Fagan and Hilton, *The English Rising of 1381* (1950), p. 99.

Chapter 3

Status and Rights in Land

WHEN I READ books on the early history of land tenure in Europe, I feel that much that appears obscure and ambiguous stems from the multireferential word "ownership." I shall show later that the Barotse apply a word which we can reasonably translate as ownership to describe almost every kind of right or privilege that a person can claim in respect of another person or material goods. I shall argue that the technical vocabulary of Barotse law elaborates distinctions between different kinds of status and different lands or property, and that clarifying the application of these terms determines what issues a court is called on to decide. In this situation the judges are able to work with an apparently unified concept of ownership to cover quite different kinds of rights over other persons and property. But before I can make that analysis, I must examine Barotse landholding—and African landholding in general—in order to clarify the relation between the rights that are held by different persons over the same parcel of land.

Recent jurisprudential analysis has insisted that all legal relations are between persons and therefore, as Corbin puts it, "there can be no such thing as a legal relation between a person and a thing." [1] Even before Hohfeld began to emphasize in 1917 that legal relations exist only between persons, it was at least commonplace, for the sake of clarity, to speak of a person as owning not an object itself but a right to do certain things with or in regard to that object.[2] Despite this commonly accepted mode of clarifying legal situations, even eminent jurists seemed to be so involved in the general concept of "communal ownership" that they continued to apply it to early and tribal land tenure. As late as 1920, many years after jurists had emphatically stated that persons own rights, not objects, Vinogradoff, for example, was speaking of communal ownership; and though he wrote that "when treating of communal organization, one is actually led to ask in what ways the communal principle asserted itself in the actual

1. Cited and discussed in Hoebel, *The Law of Primitive Man* (1954), pp. 54 f.
2. E.g. clearly stated in Salmond's *Jurisprudence* (1st ed., 1902), pp. 268 f.

occupation and cultivation of land," [3] he did not extricate himself from the difficulties inherent in the concept "communal." Even Noyes in 1936, in his learned *The Institutions of Property*, says that in early law there was no individual property in land (p. 92), though later he describes coexisting interests in one piece of land (p. 256), while Vinogradoff described elsewhere layers of rights in one piece of land.[4]

It is therefore not to be wondered at that confusion on this point should influence the manner in which administrators and jurists dealt with African land rights from the 1800s onward into the twentieth century. They were misled by two associated ideas. Since the people themselves in African states spoke of the chief as owner of the tribal land, they tended to think that his subjects had no firm and secure rights in it, but cultivated it only by the chief's permission and to some extent at his capricious will. They were also in consequence misled by the idea of some kind of communal tenure into questioning whether a tribesman had any specific secure rights of ownership over particular parcels of land.

The Judicial Committee of the Privy Council in considering the question whether the conquering British South Africa Company, acting on behalf of the Crown, could claim Ndebele land or whether the subjects of the Ndebele king had private rights in the land, spoke of "indigenous peoples . . . whose legal conceptions, though differently developed, are hardly less precise than our own. When once they have been studied and understood they are no less enforceable than rights arising under English law." Having stated this principle, the judges then held as a fact that Ndebele subjects did not have in the land private rights which could be protected against the conquering power to which the king's rights had accrued.[5] It is the validity of that decision of the Ndebele facts that I examine here. The decision was strange, since, for example, in Nigeria local British judges and the Privy Council had realized how strong were the rights of subordinates and how restricted the rights of chiefs. Ultimately in one important Nigerian case, where land was required for public purposes, the Privy Council held emphatically that the individual African holders were

3. *Outlines of Historical Jurisprudence*, 1 (1920), 325 f.

4. "Transfer of Land in Old English Law," in *Collected Papers*, 1 (1923), 149 f.

5. Hailey, *An African Survey* (1938), p. 734 and Elias, *The Nature of African Customary Law* (1956), p. 35, referring to *Re Southern Rhodesia* (1919, Appeal Cases, pp. 233–34).

entitled to the main compensation and the chiefs only to compensation for what were called their "reversionary rights." [6]

The late Professor Robert H. Lowie, one of the greatest of American anthropologists, pointed out as far back as 1921 that the phrase communal ownership is used often in apparent contradistinction to individual ownership, and he insisted that this contradistinction was false.[7] The validity of his point of view has now been demonstrated by many anthropological and legal investigations of tribes throughout the world,[8] which show that several groups or persons may hold different kinds of rights in the same piece of land while it is devoted to a particular kind of use. It is essential therefore to set out clearly the rights of these various persons over the land as it is exploited for different purposes. Blanketing terms such as "communal holding," "ownership," "possession," "beneficial occupation," and "usufruct" obscure the real pattern of rights over the land. Wilson thus emphasized for the Nyakyusa of Tanganyika that

> Land is not owned in any absolute sense either by the man and his household who live on and cultivate it, or by the village group, or by the chief, but by all of them together. Land tenure among the Nyakyusa is a coherent system of rights in which the chief as overlord, the age-village [a village of coevals] under the leadership of its great commoner, the individual male holder, his wives and children, all participate. . . . Everywhere, whether in civilized or in primitive society, the holding of land is "communal" in the sense that the individual's rights are dependent upon his social relationships, upon his membership of some group with a definite cultural idiom and social organization of its own; everywhere the holding of land is "individual" in the sense that particular people have, at any one moment, definite rights to participate in the use and to share the produce of particular pieces of ground.[9]

6. *Sakariyawo Oshodi vs. Moraimo Dakola and Others* (1930, Appeal Cases, p. 667). Discussed in Elias, *Nigerian Land Law and Custom* (1951), pp. 126–27.

7. *Primitive Society* (1921), pp. 201 f.

8. E.g. among many, Firth, *We, the Tikopia* (1936); G. Wilson, *The Land Rights of Individuals among the Nyakyusa* (1938); Schapera, *Native Land Tenure in the Bechuanaland Protectorate* (1943); Goodenough, *Property, Kin and Community on Truk* (1951); Sheddick, *Land Tenure in Basutoland* (1954).

9. *Land Rights of Individuals among the Nyakyusa* (1938), p. 39

The importance of defining rights in relation to the use made of land is shown by Schapera's record that, though Tswana [Bechuana] say that no one may own grazing land, in a country where water is a major problem the chief gives men rights to graze their cattle in particular places near water, especially if they have dug a well to procure this water. The chief will protect these rights against trespassers. Travelers may cross the land and use it for grazing; and during a drought the rights are abrogated.[10] Among the Zulu also no man may claim rights in pasturage; but if a man takes his cattle to graze where others are accustomed to pasture their herds, and a fight results, the trespasser may be punished for conduct provoking a breach of the peace but not for theft, as he would be if he pre-empted another's garden land. Rights of individuals to graze their cattle in particular places are thus indirectly protected, but again these rights are abrogated for travelers and during drought.[11] In Barotseland the king's cattle are grazed on the new pastures when the floods come; then laws similar to those of the Zulu apply.

The main principles of Barotse landholding,[12] which I am now going to describe and analyze, are to be found in most tribal societies. These principles state that rights to land are an incident of political and social status. By virtue of membership in the nation or tribe, every citizen is entitled to claim some land, whether it be from the king or chief, or from such political unit as exists in the absence of chiefly authority. In practice, among long-settled tribes the tribal land is already allocated to and divided among first-level subordinate political units who, either by joint decision or through their leaders, administer what I shall call "a primary estate of administration"—administration here covering powers to allocate the land further within the group, to dispose of it, to control and regulate its use, and to defend it against trespassers. Within such a primary estate of administration there may be allocation of secondary and even tertiary estates of administration to the series of nesting subordinate groups of decreasing size. Each such estate is controlled by similar powers vested in its administering authority. This terminology enables us to handle the

10. *Native Land Tenure in the Bechuanaland Protectorate* (1943).

11. My own field information.

12. I have given a fuller account of Barotse landholding in my *Essays on Lozi Land and Royal Property* (1943), but the terminology for analysis I proposed there obscures important facts. I follow now the clarifying distinctions made by Sheddick in *Land Tenure in Basutoland* (1954); see below.

direct correspondence of tenure of land and gradations of social status. Rights to land within a particular group are determined by status inside it and by meeting obligations inherent in that status, as well as by the terms of its allocation. Where rights against persons outside a particular group are concerned, the court has principally to determine the facts of allocation.

For simplicity I shall speak of authorities and their subjects as owning rights over land in virtue of their status within the social hierarchy; but clearly they in fact hold rights against one another, and owe obligations to one another, within this hierarchy. In practice in these systems persons can maintain rights of tenure only if they fulfill their obligations both to superiors and to subordinates. Tenure of land therefore arises from, and is maintained by, fulfillment of obligations to other persons and not from title to the land itself. In Chapter 1 I emphasized this fact by reference to the issues which judges consider in many land disputes. Here, although for brevity I speak of rights over land, in the reality of Barotse life these rights reside in obligations between persons in permanent status relationships.

Further, and again for brevity, I shall generally use the single word "right" without continually specifying whether it covers, in Hohfeld's terminology, a demand-right, a privilege-right, a power, and /or an immunity. Similarly, I shall not specify obligations and duties into Hohfeld's four categories.

I stated earlier that the title of the Barotse king, Litunga, means "the land" (Earth), and the king is described as *mung'a,* which we might translate as "owner" of all the land in the kingdom. His ownership embraces certain specific rights: (1) he can claim allegiance from anyone settling on or using his land; (2) he is held to be immediate holder of all land in his territory not yet taken up by his subjects; (3) this gives rise to a power to request that land allocated to subjects but not yet used by them be returned to him; (4) he inherits [13] any land for which no heir of the dead holder can be found, and takes over land abandoned by a family or left by a banished family; (5) his ownership is held to be the basis of his right to demand a portion of the produce as tribute; (6) he can control the settlement of people on the surface of the land; and (7) he has power to legislate about the holding and use of the land. He is supposed to

---

13. I consider "inherit" is the correct word here, as the Barotse see the situation. This is the word they use.

exercise this last right in the interests of his people, and indeed all the examples of land laws promulgated by the Barotse kings-in-council which I have collected might be held to meet this requirement. He is also believed to have ritual powers and duties in connection with the land.

The king not only has rights in the land but also obligations in his use of it. His weightiest obligation is to provide at least a residential site and some arable land for all his subjects. If he accepts a man as a new subject, he should provide him with enough land for these purposes. Should he expropriate people in the public interest, he is obligated to provide them with other suitable land. In addition, he should allow all his subjects to use commonage for pasturing their herds, for collecting wild products, for hunting, and for fishing. He should also protect them against anyone who attempts to prevent their exercising their rights to do these things. In the case of arable and building land, he should protect anyone who has once been granted a right in land from any encroachment on it, even by himself. But as he acts only through his councillors, anyone whose land is trespassed on in the king's name can always summon the councillor who carried out the king's instructions to appear before the court. I recorded several cases of this kind in Barotseland. The councillor cannot defend himself by citing the king's orders; to do so would "work [spoil] the king's name."

This then is the principal aspect of African land tenure that can be called communal: the right of every subject to a minimal use of the tribal land. In my opinion, it is irrelevant whether the land can be described as commonage, as with pastures, or is held and worked individually, as with gardens. The essence of common pasturage is that every member of the tribe, or of a particular group or neighborhood, has the right to expect the king to allow him to find grazing for all his cattle. These rights may be in practice exercisable only in specific pastures. In cultivating, a man is entitled to make a garden in land available to him, and his rights are in that specific garden. Similarly, every subject is entitled to go anywhere to take bark for string and nets, iron ore for smelting, clay for potmaking, and so forth.

Among the Tonga of Mazabuka District in Northern Rhodesia, who lack chiefs, anyone may take wild fruits from trees, even in cultivated gardens.[14] If a Barotse makes a garden in the bush he is

14. See Allan et al., *Land-holding and Land Usage among the Plateau Tonga* (1948); and Colson, *Marriage and the Family among the Plateau Tonga* (1958) and *Social Organization of the Gwembe Tonga* (1960).

forbidden to fell wild fruit trees, by a law of King Lewanika (d. 1916), and these trees come temporarily under his ownership, for no one may pick wild fruit from trees in gardens. As soon as the garden reverts to fallow, anyone may again take fruit from the trees within it, though no one can make gardens in the fallow.

Again, among the Tonga there are shallow pans of water which are stabbed for fish by battues of men in the dry season. Anyone in a defined locality about each pan may participate and take his full catch. Similar pans in the Barotse plain are held by the king and other royals, by councillors' titles, or by families through their appointed heads. Their holdings in these pans entail two rights only: (1) they may set traps at suitable points on the pan's margin; (2) they may appoint a day when anyone who wishes may come to stab in the pan, subject to paying a recognized proportion of his catch to the pan holder. After the first day there is no taxing, and if the holder stabs in the pan before this set day he loses his right to claim a part of the initial catch. Thus, as against the two rights of the holder described above, every member of the tribe is entitled to fish with nets in the pan, to stab for fish on the appointed day subject to rendering a share to the holder, and thereafter to stab as he pleases. The pans are neither privately owned nor communally owned, but certain rights to fish them in various ways are held by different people.

In all these examples we see that the rights form a definite pattern, with one dominant right present in the so-called communal ownership: that every member of a certain social group can claim the right to be given a garden to work privately and to make certain use of public lands or waters. Once he takes over products from these, they are his. And these rights vest in different persons for different kinds of land in terms of membership of different groups. Rights to land thus inhere in what is mainly political status and arise from obligations of this status. Richards says of the Bemba, a Northern Rhodesian people who continually open up new gardens and abandon exhausted ones:

> Rights to the use of land are part of a reciprocal series of obligations between subject and chief. The former accepts the political status of subject and membership of a village group, gives respect, labour and tribute to his chief, and in return he is able to cultivate as much land as he pleases and to occupy it for as long as he needs. The latter [the chief] prays to the tribal spirits in

order to make the land productive, initiates economic effort, feeds the hungry, and maintains his court and tribal councillors —all that the Bemba mean by saying that he is "working" his land.[15]

I have referred to the situation in other tribes in order to emphasize the general existence in South and Central Africa of a claim held by every citizen to some land, a claim that is valid even in the emirates of West Africa. If the king accepts allegiance he must either have the man accepted by some subordinate or find place for him on his own land or on land not yet allocated.

The manner in which land is held in Barotseland itself, and particularly in the floodplain, is as follows. The king's own holdings of land vested in the kingship itself are very large, particularly in the plain and the provinces. Many villages, gardens, fishing sites, pans, and reed beds are specifically his. As I traveled through the plain over several years this was more and more impressed on me. Village after village was pointed out to me as belonging to the king, though it might be held by a queen, by a prince or princess, by a councillor's title, or by an ordinary commoner. Everywhere are *namakao*, the king's gardens, which may not be protected by magic against thieves as commoners' gardens may be, for every traveler and hungry person has a right to help himself from the king's food. The plain contains many royal fenced-off shallow fishing sites (*litindi*) where in the dry season communal battues are held. The king gets a share of the fish caught by the spears thrown into the mud. Most reed beds belong to the king, and he is entitled to one-eleventh of all reeds cut, and to a share of the nestling birds caught in the reed beds and in clumps of trees, but he should not prevent any subject from appropriating reeds or nestlings. (Foreigners traveling down the river have been absolved if they failed to render these dues.) All over the plain are the king's fishing sites for nonreturn traps, though they are worked for him by commoners who take the catch on alternate days. He has pans where turtles are bred and villages where royal cattle are grazed.

The Barotse who work these gardens and other resources do not feel themselves exploited by the king's rights; they look on the king as a father who generously gives them the means of sustenance. Nor indeed does the king exercise his rights rigorously, for he foregoes them when the catch or crop is small. Also, he distributes to others the fish

15. *Land, Labour and Diet in Northern Rhodesia* (1940), Chap. 13.

and other produce which come in to him, although nowadays he can do less than in the past, for supplies have fallen. For the rest, the Barotse seem happy to contribute to the upkeep of the capital.

Thus besides the king's ritual guardianship of the whole land, his secular ownership is always manifest to the Barotse in his own villages and sites. One important sign of this ownership is the canals that score the plain, dug at the orders of successive kings. Each king should dig such a canal, to facilitate the travels of his people, as his distinguishing mark (*sisupo*) on the land itself.

The king's ownership also appears constantly in the Barotse's own holding of land. Whenever they discuss land the king's name is introduced. He enters into the history of every garden: he asked for it, he borrowed it for someone else, he exchanged it for another garden, and ultimately he or a predecessor gave it. Title to land is defined: "My ancestor gave the royal salute for it to King so-and-so," perhaps centuries ago. Whenever the holder dies, the heir is installed both at home and in the capital, and his title is referred to the royal salute he gave when he was presented to the king and his council.

Once the king has given land to a subject the latter has in it rights which are protected against all comers including the king himself. Should the king desire the land he must ask for it, he cannot just take it: "The king is also a beggar," say the Barotse. Barotse have security in their holdings within a well-established and well-defined system of law, administered by an organized judiciary and executive who are alert to protect this security and its premises.

The king may give a piece of land to an individual, but at the present time most land has long been allocated and has been held for long periods by villages in the names of their village headmen. If an individual is now given land by the king, his right to it accrues usually to his position in a village. The pattern of landholding in the floodplain is the attachment of numerous small, dispersed, and intermingled gardens and fishing sites to specific villages, either of titles or of families. The Barotse strongly emphasize laws that prevent a man from "taking land from one village to another." If a man leaves a village he loses his rights in all land he worked as a member of that village, and though a man may work land at his mother's home while living with his father, or vice versa, he cannot move the right to the land to his village of residence. He works the land by grace of the headman to whom it is attached.

The primary allotment of land from the king to his people is therefore to villages, and this allocation is clearly in a political relationship. This is so even if the headman is a prince or princess who occupies that position because of kinship with the king.

The land of a village has been mostly distributed by past headmen among the villagers, and each heir to a headmanship inherits the obligations of his predecessor. Once a member of a family homestead by right of blood or adoption (that is, excluding wives or strangers) has been granted land, he retains the right to use that land and to transmit it to his own heirs, and the courts will protect his rights against the headman. But the holder cannot give the land to anyone but his own dependents, and if he leaves the village the land reverts to the headman. Sometimes land falls vacant and may be redistributed by the headman. Every member of a village by virtue of residence in it has a right to some land from the headman. If a headman has no land, he should not accept a new villager.

Lozi family villages are inhabited by groups of cognates related to the headman and to each other in a variable pattern. Almost all inhabitants of such a village are kindred, with their wives and, in the past, serfs who were adopted as kinsmen, though with lesser rights. The Lozi have a bias to father-right, but in practice a man can claim the right to settle in the village of any of his ancestors. The courts protect the rights of people in the villages and land of their maternal kindred, though Lozi say: "Why do you claim land at your mother's? Claim at your father's."

The heir to a headman is selected from any of a man's kindred for his ability to hold the village together. Preference is given to his brothers and sons, but a son of a junior wife or the younger son of a particular wife may be chosen and often a uterine nephew or grandson is selected. Lozi villages are strong corporate groups which, since they can be built only on mounds in the plain, have long histories. Through a village there has flowed a stream of kinsmen, related at any moment in a variable pattern, but always bound by ties of blood. In landholding, a villager here has rights because he is attached in a political sense to the headman, and because he is kin to the headman.

Many villages are also attached to the king, a queen, a prince or princess, or the title of a councillor. I refer to these as villages-of-titles. Some villages-of-titles are inhabited by groupings of families who are kin to one another, one member being headman on behalf of the titleholder. The inhabitants of many other of these villages have been assembled together by some king or have joined the village with his or the titleholder's permission. Many of them are Lozi or foreign *maketo* (persons chosen by the king), *mahapiwa* (persons seized in raids in the outer provinces) and *batanga* (prisoners-of-war from foreign tribes). In a village of this kind there are many families or expanded families of different stocks and tribal origins who have often intermarried and become interrelated. They are bound together primarily by allegiance to the queen or royal or holder of title to the village. The Lozi consider the titleholder to be parent to all the villagers, and the patterns of behavior in such a village tend to be assimilated to those in family villages. When the royal village is old, many inhabitants tend through intermarriage to be kin to each other; in new royal villages they are "strangers." The inhabitants of such a village have the same rights in their land as those of a family village have in their land. Nevertheless the village-of-a-title is dominantly a group that is held together by political ties, although these ties are stated in kinship terms, and the actual kinship ties are initially of secondary importance.

Thus if we examine the chains of relations in which Lozi hold land from the king, the links between king and village headman, and the links between that headman and his followers differ greatly. A further change occurs within the partition of land inside the village. The heads of the households that constitute the village hold land from the headman in a relationship which is partly political and in a family village is also one of kinship. Allocation of land within each household's share is usually purely within a kin relationship. Nevertheless as the Lozi see the allocation of land, it is in a chain of distribution from the king to the village headman, to household head, to subordinates in the household; and therefore landholding is formulated in a straightforward series of allocations.

Lawyers, administrators, and anthropologists have used various terms to describe these rights in land. Many have called the individual's right to land "usufruct," to cover use of the fruits. But clearly it is more than the Roman law "right of using and taking the fruits of property belonging to another," *salva rerum substantia,* i.e. without the right of destroying or changing the character of the thing, and lasting only so long as the character remains unchanged, which is usually for the life of the person entitled and cannot be for a longer period, and thus corresponds most closely to what we call a "life interest," as Jolowicz summarizes usufruct.[16] For among the Barotse there is no one with a greater right to use the land than its present cultivator, and he has more than a right to take the fruits. He transmits his rights to his heirs. I stress these obligations strongly, with the support of Elias in his *Nigerian Land Law and Custom* (1951, p. 142) and *The Nature of African Customary Law* (1956, p. 165), because contributors to the recent symposium on *African Agrarian Systems* (edited by Biebuyck, 1963) continually speak of usufruct. Others, including the Privy Council and a British judge in Africa, have called this right "use," but clearly, for the same reasons, it is more than a right, in the technical definition, "to the use of a thing, not including the taking of fruits." [17] Indeed the transactions involving usufruct and use appear to have developed in Rome to meet contingencies unknown to Southern and Central Africa,[18] though in some tribal systems there are transactions akin to usufruct and use in this technical sense. But it would muddle issues if they were applied to holdings by virtue of status. Possession again is too weak a term. "Ownership" is clearly not specific enough (see Chapter 5).

Rights to land are clearly attributes of political status [19] in the first place, and then of kinship or marital status. Various kinds of status give privileges to demand varying access to land. In this respect the Lozi system, and even more the system of a tribe whose king has granted counties to chiefs who have granted districts to subchiefs who have granted areas to village headmen, is akin to the system of feudalism where in many respects allegiance in a hierarchy to a series of lords gave vassals rights to land.

The feudal system, with its variations by era and region, is too complicated for me to summarize here, even were I competent to do so. But it shares in common with the system I have been outlining the correspondence between political power plus obligation, usually to provide land, in return for political liability plus tenure of land. Polit-

16. *Historical Introduction to the Study of Roman Law* (1939), p. 282.
17. Ibid.
18. Ibid.
19. Lord Hailey (*An African Survey*, 1938, p. 183) recognized this clearly in stating that "rights to land have the character of a privilege based on membership of a community," but he weakens the right when he adds, "entitling every member to beneficial use of the community lands . . ." since "use" is an inadequate term. He is quite incorrect when he concludes his sentence: "rather than a specific right over specific areas identified with the holder."

ical powers of feudal lords, in a hierarchy with the king at the apex, involved demand-rights to military and other services from vassals and also privileges of jurisdiction, in return for acceptance of obligations to provide maintenance (usually in the form of land) and protection.[20] This hierarchy of lords and vassals might be deep. Pollock and Maitland cite one of eight steps, and add:

> A feudal ladder with so many rungs as this, is uncommon; but theoretically there is no limit to the possible number of rungs, and practically . . . men have enjoyed a large power, not merely of adding new rungs at the bottom of the scale, but of inserting new rungs in the middle of it. At the bottom of this ladder, whether it be long or short, stands the person who has a general right of doing what he pleases with it [and who] is said to hold the land in demesne.[21]

Here cultivation was carried on by villagers and villeins, who might be taken as equivalent to Barotse villagers, since they held and worked their strips of land under custom in some kind of community.[22]

Although tenure of land and the hierarchy of political organization corresponded in many respects with the outline of the African system, and may have given rise to similar political processes, the differences between the two systems are substantial. Marc Bloch summarized the main aspects of the European feudal system as:

> a subject peasantry; widespread use of the service tenement (i.e. the fief) instead of a salary which was out of the question [because of shortage of money]; the supremacy of a class of specialized warriors; ties of obedience and protection which bind man to man and, within the warrior class, assume the distinctive form called vassalage; fragmentation of authority leading inevitably to disorder; and in the midst of all this the survival of other forms of association, family and State.[23]

The class of armored knights, dwelling in manors and later in castles, with finer furniture and materials, supported by a subject peasantry and totaling in England only a few thousands, is not found in

---

20. See Fifoot, *English Law and its Background* (1932), pp. 32 f.
21. Pollock and Maitland, *The History of English Law*, 1 (1923, 2d ed.), 233.
22. Homans, *English Villagers in the Thirteenth Century* (1941).
23. *Feudal Society* (1961), p. 446 (orig. French, 1939/40).

the African societies with which I am concerned. Nor are the cities with their merchants trading far afield, such as are found also in West Africa. The relation of feudal lord and vassal, even after it became hereditary, was theoretically based on a form of contract between individuals and terminable theoretically at the will of either. Status followed on this contract. In the African systems considered here, the relation of superior and subordinate arises from membership in a series of groups which nest within each other, like children's hollow blocks. Status gives rise to obligations, and tenure accrues in virtue of these obligations. The arrangement is terminable at the will of the subordinate, but the superior can expel the subordinate only for gross breach of duties. The rights and duties lying between superior and subordinate are also not narrowly specified, as was the case in feudalism, but are general and diffuse: mutual care and maintenance and respect by all persons of whatever status. The subordinate was in a much stronger position than under the feudal regime. The superior could be expelled by the king from his position for breach of duty to subordinates, while the superior could not introduce intermediate vassals into the hierarchy, of his own will, to stand as lords to subordinates.[24] Lords worked in the fields or fished alongside their subordinates. Often a junior in the hierarchy was heir to a senior, which rarely occurred in a feudal system.

It is therefore inappropriate to apply the forms of feudal tenure to these African systems, and to speak of fiefs and benefices, or of seisin. Nor do they have variations in mutual obligations and claims, covered by such feudal tenures as the unfree and the free, of frankalmoin, military service, serjeanty, and free socage.[25] These complications in themselves exclude treating the two types of systems as similar in respect of the relationship between tenure and status. "Folkright" and "folkland" might be adopted from early Anglo-Saxon law, or "udalsrecht" from other systems, but their specification against "buchland" is uncertain.[26] Besides, they are not illuminating concepts. They do not bring out the layers of rights and related obligations which lie on each parcel of land. Hence it seems wisest to invent a special terminology which will state clearly what the situation is. This

24. Chilver discusses whether "feudalism" was an appropriate term to apply to the kingdoms around Lake Victoria Nyanza and concludes that it is not: "'Feudalism' in the Interlacustrine Kingdoms" in Richards, ed., *East African Chiefs* (1960).

25. Pollock and Maitland, *The History of English Law* (1923, 2d ed.), pp. 240 f.

26. Ibid., pp. 60 f., and Vinogradoff, "Folkland" in his *Collected Papers*, 1 (1920), 91 f.

has been recognized by the Dutch students of Indonesian law, who sought for new terms and described group rights as "the communal right of disposal" and the individual's right to his own parcels of land, his demesne, as the "native right of possession." [27] They spoke too of rights of utilization. The use of these terms led the Dutch into posing a struggle between these rights, with the individual's right encroaching on the community's right, and vice versa. In fact all these rights can exist at the same time over the same piece of land without conflict, since their legal adjustment is determined mainly by how the holders fulfill their obligations in other respects. A British judge was more specific in stating that each community in Nigeria has "rights of distribution" among its members who have "rights of users" over the land allocated to them.[28] We have seen that "user" is too weak a description. These terminologies begin to outline the situation clearly, but the terms are not specific enough and do not emphasize the connection of tenure with status.

Sheddick, [29] working from the suggestions of various writers, appears to me to have made the most clarifying proposals in analyzing Basuto land tenure. He distinguishes two completely different kinds of rights in land in these systems. The first set involved political rights— rights to administer the land—what the Dutch called "communal rights of disposal." These rights of administration involve action as trustees on behalf of subordinates by seniors, the power and obligation to apportion land among subordinates, and to some extent powers to regulate the use of the land. I must emphasize again that these rights carry the heavy obligation of meeting the claims of subordinates, which cannot be denied, so that, as in common usage, administration embraces duties as well as powers. When the superior administers the land, he may do so by granting (delegating) some of his rights to administer to some subordinates, who may grant further rights of this kind before the land is reduced to parcels which people actually use. I describe this hierarchy in terms of "grants," but obviously the grants are not being made all the time. Most land has already been granted, but the people see it as a continuous process. "Grant" has this continuity in legal use.

We also require a terminology which will bring out both the close

27. Ter Haar, *Adat Law in Indonesia* (1948), Chap. 2 (orig. Dutch, 1939).
28. Brooke, "Some Legal Aspects of Land Tenure in Nigeria" (1946).
29. *Land Tenure in Basutoland* (1954), pp. 1 f. I recast his central formulation.

connection of landholding with status, and also that rights of administration are organized within a hierarchy of status. "Estate" seems to
me to be the natural reflection of "status," and to indicate the firmness
of the rights involved.[30] It is sufficiently a word in general and appropriate use to evade any of the implications of its technical meaning in
Western law. By using the adjectives in *primary* estate, *secondary*
estate, *tertiary* estate, we can emphasize the manner in which these
estates of administration overlap on the same parcels of land employed
for some purpose. But among the Barotse and similarly organized
tribes the king or superior chief is in a unique position. I propose
therefore to call him the owner of the land in the sense that the
monarch in Britain is thought of as the owner of all land, who grants
freeholds or fees simple to others, although these latter are commonly
spoken of as owners. The Barotse king's ownership might be described
as a wardenship, for it involves trusteeship.

Rights to use various parcels of land are rights to cultivate, to
pasture stock, to fish, to hunt, or to collect wild products. It is necessary to specify these varied uses of the land because, as Sheddick
insists, a parcel of land in use is not a specific area, but an area used for
a certain purpose at a certain time. My descriptions of rights in various tribes to graze cattle, and to tax and control fishing in pans in
Barotseland bring out the importance of thinking of land as production units, to use Sheddick's phrase. As a further example I cite the
fact that in many tribes, after the harvest all gardens are opened to
permit the neighborhood's cattle to graze on the crop stover; thus at
one time the land is reserved for the cultivation of one person, at other
times the land is accessible to neighbors' cattle.

For economical discussion we need a single term to cover these
varied uses of land. Sheddick, unhappily in my opinion, retained usufruct. I therefore propose to speak of "rights of production," to parallel
Sheddick's demonstration that it is essential to think of land as a series

30. Radcliffe-Brown gave his weighty authority to this anthropological use of "estate" in
"Patrilineal and Matrilineal Succession," in *Structure and Function in Primitive Society*
(1952); while Cheshire on the legal side writes that "the word 'estate' was probably adopted
because in early days it was possible to ascertain a man's status by discovering the kind of
tenure by which he held his lands" (*Modern Law of Real Property*, 1962, 9th ed., pp. 27 f.).
I originally, in *Essays on Lozi Land and Royal Property* (1943), suggested "estates of
holding" (cf. tenement) but think Sheddick has pointed out correctly that this does not
adequately differentiate the rights and duties involved.

of units of production, in which the same parcel of land may be differently used, and subject to rights vested in different persons at various times.

The king grants "primary estates of administration" over cultivable land and some fishing sites to a number of heads of villages, including himself. Some of these heads, who are royals, queens, and councillors holding titles, do not reside in their villages but exercise their control through resident headmen. Other village headmen hold their primary estate of administration in their own right from the king. Each of them must provide land for his dependents in the group. He does this by making further grants within his primary estate of administration to heads of smaller groups or to individuals, whom I call "secondary holders of secondary estates of administration." In a long-settled village he accepts grants already made. If the social organization is more complicated, these secondary holders may grant or have granted tertiary estates to tertiary holders, and so forth. Each of these grants may be called by one term, "an estate of administration," because the rights and obligations involved in the granting and receiving of an estate are similar, wherever the holders lie in the numerical series—namely, fulfillment of obligations of status, even if these obligations alter down the series. Thus the primary holder is entitled to have enough land for all his dependents from the king and in turn has to render obedience, support, and tribute to the king and to control his group according to tribal laws. The holder of a secondary estate is required similarly to assist the primary holder who must grant him adequate land for his dependents, and so forth. The series of estates in landholdings is part of the hierarchical organization of a society like that of the Barotse. Each estate of administration includes similar rights and obligations: the right to secure holding of the estate against all trespassers, including the grantor, even if this be the king himself. The number of estates in the series indicates the degree of complexity in the tribal social organization.

The series of estates also indicates that every senior estate holder has specific rights over the subordinate holdings within his own estate. If the holder of a tertiary estate dies without heirs or abandons his land, it reverts neither to the owner, who is the king, nor to the primary holder, but to the secondary holder; and, correspondingly, only if the primary holder and all his group abandon the land may the king claim the whole estate. The holder of a subsidiary estate is frequently the heir to a holder of a senior estate. Here again, as stated, there is a difference from the feudal system.

This reversion of estates through the series emerges clearly in the Barotse law whereby if one man makes a direct grant of part of his land to another, the latter becomes subordinate to him in the series, and he retains his holding in the land. If the grantee departs, the grantor resumes control of the land. But if a man begs land from the king, and the king acquires land for him from another, the grantee may be held to have been given his estate by the king, and is a primary holder. Therefore if he abandons the land the king may claim it, and it does not revert to the former holder, although if it is a single garden it may be held to have accrued to the grantee's position in his village.

In saying that the primary holder retains his holding in the secondary estates granted in his estate, I again emphasize that this is a reversionary or residual right; i.e. he can exercise it only if the secondary holder abandons the estate or is expelled from the group. Any estate, once granted, is held securely against all comers, including the grantor—and I repeat, even if he be the king.

The superior holders will always also own estates of each order in the hierarchy. The king holds primary estates within which he makes grants to secondary holders, and he himself has secondary estates within his primary estates. The headman of a village holds from the king a primary estate of land which is attached to his title; in this land he has a secondary estate which he allots to his own family, and he himself actually cultivates an estate of production. Estates of production therefore lie at the base of the hierarchy, but their position there may be temporary. For an estate of production can become an estate of administration,[31] if the holder grants portions of it to his children or to others within the village, who then become his subordinates. If they leave the village, their portions revert to the grantor, not to the headman.

To bring out this gradation in the series of estates, I have excluded for the moment one vital point. Each holder of an estate owes obligations to every holder senior to him in the series, as well as to the one

31. Contrast Noyes' statement (*The Institution of Property*, 1936, p. 257) that a chattel cannot be carved into estates. In a tribal society this is only partly true; some chattels can be carved thus.

who has granted him his holding. Correspondingly, every senior owes similar obligations to all the holders subordinate to him. That is, every subject owes obligations directly to the king, and the king has a direct obligation to every subject to see that he has land; the head of a village can claim allegiance from every resident in the village, and every villager is regarded as a "child" of the headman.

In addition, the holder of a junior estate of administration must secure the permission of all his seniors to place someone in a subsidiary estate under him, up to the permission of the holder of the most senior estate into which the newcomer is entering. Thus if a man comes to live with his father-in-law from another village, the father-in-law must secure the approval of every superior up to the village headman. He need not ask the king's permission. However, if the newcomer be a foreigner, the king's approval must be obtained because the foreigner is entering the nation.

The legal holding of these estates appears as a straightforward series, but the categories of social relations in which estates are held alter significantly at different stages, and with them the obligations entailed also alter. Holding by the headman of a village from the king is in a purely political relationship; heads of groups in the village (secondary estate holders) hold from the headman usually in a political and kinship relationship; and in family villages tertiary and subordinate estate holders hold from secondary holders usually in a purely kin relationship.[32]

A kinsman or kinswoman who does not reside in the village may be allowed by grace of the headman to work an estate of production in its land, and if there are not sufficient persons in the village to use all its land, the headman ought to grant this grace.[33] As the Barotse see it, this estate of production held by a kinsman or kinswoman residing elsewhere is his or her security also for his or her claim to return to the village. But I have never heard of such a person holding an estate of administration, and he or she would be prevented from allowing anyone else access to this land. In the case of the headman's fish dams discussed in Chapter 1, the sisters' sons worked the dams on behalf of their respective mothers.

32. See Gluckman, Mitchell, and Barnes, "The Village Headman in British Central Africa," in my *Order and Rebellion in Tribal Africa* (1963), Chap. 5, for the sociological importance of these changes.

33. See Chap. 1 above, pp. 14 f.

I am not here concerned with an analysis of the economics of this situation or with the fact that holders of different kinds of estates are pursuing varied interests: the king to get more subjects, the headman to keep his village as populous as his lands allow or to secure from the king more land if more people are born to or join his following, a family head to provide for his dependents, the holder of an estate of production to produce goods. What I am doing is to offer this terminology in the hope that it clarifies the close association between land-holding and political plus kinship status within a hierarchy. I have in previous publications used hierarchy to cover, in the dictionary definition, "any graded arrangement," without the implication of exercise of authority, such as exists in Barotseland. But since there has been misinterpretation on this point where I tried to apply the terminology more generally, I shall speak henceforth of "a series of estates," except when referring only to the Barotse.

Clearly we can apply to this situation Maine's contention that in early law "the Law of Things can scarcely be distinguished from the Law of Persons." We cannot describe landholding except in terms of the Law of Persons, and we cannot discuss the Law of Persons or status without including an account of rights to land. I shall show later that this applies throughout the Law of Property, and much of the Law of Transactions. But it might also be worthwhile to try to classify the various rights to land of the persons involved as reversionary, qualified, concomitant, concurrent, contingent, etc., in order to facilitate comparison with more developed legal systems. I do not myself feel competent to attempt this task. But I want to discuss the classification of rights which Goodenough suggests in his excellent analysis, *Property, Kin and Community on Truk* (1951), since he too suggests a general terminology which some other anthropologists have adopted. Here Goodenough rejects the terms usufruct and lineage fee simple, which he and Murdock had employed in an earlier analysis of Truk landholding.[34] Instead, he classifies titles to land and other property, as full, residual, and provisional. He writes:

> Two basic forms of ownership must be distinguished. One of these will be called *full ownership*, be the owner a person or a corporation. It confers on an owner what will be called a *full title*. The

34. See his p. 41, n. 13 and p. 42, n. 15, referring to Murdock and Goodenough, "Social Organization of Truk" (1947).

other divides a full title asymmetrically between two parties, either or both of whom may be individuals or corporations. This will be called *divided ownership*. It confers on the two owners two distinct titles, respectively, each characterized by different rights and duties. One will be called a *provisional title* and the other a *residual title*.[35]

A residual titleholder grants a provisional titleholder the right to exploit certain property from which or from part of which the provisional titleholder may make a grant to another provisional holder with the residual titleholder's permission. Further grants may be made. Provisional titleholders are usually heirs presumptive [36] to the holders above them in the series. Only where the residual titleholder also holds the only provisional title over the property is the property held under full title.

This series of titles, and the rights and obligations it entails, varies somewhat for land, pigs, chickens, canoes, fish, fruit trees, and fish weirs. Titles to fruit trees may be differently allocated from titles to the land on which they grow. Since the series of rights is complicated, it would be advisable at least to speak of primary, secondary, and tertiary provisional titles. If as many provisional titles as this are granted, then the secondary provisional titleholder is the primary residual titleholder, while the primary provisional titleholder is the secondary residual titleholder, and he whom Goodenough calls the residual titleholder is in fact the tertiary residual titleholder. This is confusing, and it seems simpler and clearer to conceive of a series of estates of administration. The use of "estate" shows that there is a cluster of obligations and rights, tied to status.[37]

---

35. Ibid., pp. 33–34.

36. I add "presumptive."

37. Generally, see Herskovits, *Economic Anthropology* (1952), p. 360, and Allan, *The African Husbandman* (1965); for a specific application see Mitchell, "Land Tenure and Agriculture among the Machinga Yao" (1951). I have not time to demonstrate how this hierarchy in terms of status appears in tribes with and without chieftainship, but the overlying of estates is clear in, e.g., Malinowski, *Coral Gardens and their Magic*, I (1935), especially p. 370; Firth, *We, the Tikopia* (1936), Chap. 11; Fortes, the *Dynamics of Clanship among the Tallensi* (1945), pp. 177 f.; Holleman, *Shona Customary Law* (1952), pp. 6 f., adopting the Dutch terminology for adat law; Bohannan, *Tiv Farm and Settlement* (1954), p. 31 f.; Meggitt, *The Lineage System of the Mae Enga of the New Guinea Highlands* (1965), where Goodenough's terminology is followed. Pospisil, *Kapauku Papuans and Their Law* (1958), stresses individual ownership except for rights of kinship groups over barren uplands and water. But since he states that land is never taken from a defeated enemy (at p.

Goodenough himself states (p. 29) that since "such important aspects of the social organization as matrilineal kin groups and territorial and political groupings are best defined in terms of the property system," he begins his analysis from property rights. His terminology does not bring out this connection, as mine attempts to do. He in fact shows, as regards landholding, a hierarchy of estates of allocating and administrating (pp. 42, 74) or controlling (p. 49) with powers vested in the senior representative of the group concerned. Thus, "a corporation [of kinsmen] holding provisional title may reallocate its property among its own members without consulting the residual title holder, for possession of the property has not passed outside the corporation to another party. Should the corporation wish to give the property to other than one of its members, permission of the residual title holder must be obtained" (pp. 42–43). Here what I call an estate of production has become an estate of administration over several estates of production—a distinction obscured by the general term "provisional title." This distinction is crucial in order to stress that, though a corporation may hold full title—or presumably subsidiary provisional title—to soil or trees, "trees and soil are usually apportioned among them to work as individuals" (p. 42). Security of title in the series depends upon fulfilling the duties of one's status within a district under a chief or within a kinship group under its senior leader; and a man can be expelled only for a breach of such duty (pp. 42, 51, 140–41). We shall see that these incidents apply to the Barotse hierarchy of estates.

The series of estates of administration is seen most clearly in those tribes that have a more or less fixed system of cultivation, and an elaborate hierarchical social organization. Among the Zulu the organization of estates runs from king to county chief, to the councillor who is head of a local district, to the head of a lineage group of neighboring homesteads, to the headman of each homestead, to the heads of the families within the homestead, and to the different wives of each family head.[38]

---

93) and that an owner of a garden cannot give it to an outsider (at p. 98), it seems that residual rights to administer and inherit the individually worked gardens and forests must vest in a series of nesting groups. The framework of a series of incapsulated estates would clarify this study with its unusual stress on absolute individualism of rights over property. The analysis emphasizes that produce is widely distributed in status relations and relations of "perpetual" friendship, clientship, and trade.

38. My own field data.

Among the Lozi the organization is from king to the head of a
village built on one of the mounds in the floodplain, to the family
groups within the village. The estates are less clearly observed among
people like the Bemba who shift their gardens rapidly through large
areas of woodland. Bemba territory is divided into territorial sections,
one under the king, the others under chiefs of the royal family. Anyone who cultivates in a chief's territory must acknowledge the chief's
authority and render tribute and tribute labor to him, but any subject
may in theory cultivate anywhere in the chief's land, provided he is a
member of some village under a recognized headman. In practice,
people cultivate near their village. Since in the areas described by
Richards in her study of the Bemba, land is plentiful, and the burn-
ing of lopped branches to get ash for a seedbed to some extent eliminates soil differences, people can more or less freely cut where they
will, though at the beginning of each season they announce their
choice of site publicly in the village. A young man will give way to an
old man. The series of estates is therefore simple in this land: from
king to district chief to subject, for once a man has cut a garden it
passes to his heirs and no one may trespass on it. There is a mystical
bond between a man and his newly prepared garden: he cannot lend it
in the first year.

In the king's own district the series is simpler. The village headman
enters into the holding only in that his subordinates must have his
permission to build in the village, and a man must be a member of a
village. However, I venture to suggest, since Richards does not discuss
this point, that where the Bemba have more permanent cultivation, as
on fertilized old village sites or on densely populated Cilubi Island in
Lake Bangweulu, [39] the same series will appear. There the chief alloted
part of his old village to his followers, but once it was allotted "he
could never take a garden back while living relatives of the owner
wished to use it," and these gardens passed to a man's heirs. I would
infer that if a man to whom the chief had allotted a garden gave it to
another, the latter had full rights in it against the grantor, but that if
he abandoned the garden it would revert to the grantor, and only if
the latter and his relatives had departed would it revert to the chief.
The same is likely to be true in all the more permanent gardens around
villages of fishermen and hereditary councillors.

The Bemba, though shifting cultivators, have a developed political

39. *Land, Labour and Diet in Northern Rhodesia* (1940), p. 270.

organization. The Plateau Tonga of Northern Rhodesia have not. Men of prestige in the indigenous system probably had no say in land allocation, and the headmen of villages very little. People cultivated where they could, going in rare cases of dispute to the headman. Once a man cultivated a garden it was his, even when the land reverted to bush, and his permission had to be sought to cultivate there. If he gave that permission, and the new holder went away, the land would revert under the grantor's control.[40] But the series of estates emerges somewhat more clearly among the related Gwembe Tonga who cultivate permanent gardens in the Zambezi River valley.[41]

I believe that this framework of a series of estates of administration is likely to cover most systems of African land tenure and of other tribal peoples. It will be least clear and of least importance in systems of shifting cultivation, while land is plentiful. Its importance will grow as land becomes scarcer, or where in special circumstances cultivation becomes permanent. In hierarchically organized tribes, like the Barotse, Zulu, and Bemba, the gradation of estates will be woven into the social organization; in more undifferentiated organizations, such as the Tonga, the gradation will not always carry with it such stringent social obligations. In tribes with permanent cultivation, such as the Lozi, the series of estates of administration will be part of the social hierarchy, so that ownership of the landholding of a superior estate will give power over all inferior estate holders. The terminology emphasizes that rights over, and obligations in respect of, land inhere in political status at higher levels, and in other kinds of status at lower levels.

In Barotseland, security of title includes the right to give the land to others, subject to consultation with holders of superior estates in the land. Further, security of title includes the right to transmit an estate to one's heirs. It does not include the rights to lease an estate of any type for reward, to sell it, or to pledge or mortgage it. There is also no sharecropping of arable land, though there is of certain types of sites for fishing. Arable land and fishing sites are loaned without rent, though it is appropriate for the borrower to make seasonal gifts from his harvest or catches to the holder. A lender can reclaim his land at

40. Even among the Tonga, who lack chiefly authorities, if a man of one village gets permission from another village to cultivate in its old lands, he requires approval of the granting village to place a third person in this garden (Allan et al., *Land-holding and Land Usage among the Plateau Tonga*, 1948).

41. Colson, *Social Organization of the Gwembe Tonga* (1960).

will but he must give reasonable notice of his intention to do so before
the next productive season begins, to enable the borrower to seek for
other resources. He is also barred from reclaiming his land until the
borrower has exhausted the rewards of his improvements—whether
this be the clearing of bushland for garden, the manuring of other
gardens, or the building of a fish dam. The period of bar of action is
determined by the judges' decision on how long it will be before the
cleared garden should be allowed to revert to fallow, or how long the
amount of manuring of the soil will increase yields (usually three
years). The judges work here from their own experience as cultivators.

It is general in South and Central Africa that there was no traditional pledging of land, and that powers to pledge land did not develop in the rural areas and were resisted by tribal authorities where
these existed. Some pledging seems to have occurred sub rosa. But in
Chapter 22 of his *Land Law and Custom in the Colonies* (1949)
Meek summarizes accounts of pledging of land in both West and East
Africa which show that it has been customary for very many years. I
cannot here enter into a full analysis of the situation, but it is essential
to note that when a man in need wishes to pledge land, in most tribes
he should consult others involved in the series of estates of which the
land is part, and he might be required to give them preferential
claims. Theoretically also, the rights of holders in the series of estates
to redeem the land never lapsed. Interest was not payable on the
money given against the land. Outright sale was achieved by circum-
venting the law, the pledgee giving the pledgor far more than the
land was worth. Mortgaging land was not a traditional procedure.

Nevertheless, these developments have not yet obscured the original
system, even though West Africa has been influenced by trade across
the Sahara and by sea with the northern hemisphere, and by the slave
trade, for more centuries than have the regions of Africa on which I
have concentrated. Of recent decades cash cropping has been an important part of the Africans' economy, and land has not been only a
reserve from which men migrated to earn money as laborers. Yet
Elias' authoritative analysis, *Nigerian Land Law and Custom* (1951),
showed how the persistence of a series of rights held by different
groups over parcels of land has been recognized not only by indigenous courts but also by the British courts in Nigeria and by the Privy
Council on appeals from these courts. Elias has worked through re-

ports of indigenous tenure and reported judicial decisions. He sums up
the situation by saying that when a chief has allotted land to a family,
"the head of the family is, like the chief, a trustee beneficiary of the
family lands." The rights of these leaders are reversionary only. And
when the head allocates land to a member of the family he cannot
eject that person provided he fulfills his obligations (see pp. 137–38).
As cited above, Elias insists (p. 142) that the cultivation rights are
more than usufructuary rights or rights of use. But he is still, in my
respectful opinion, hampered in clarifying the whole situation by accepting the restrictions imposed by the terms drawn from English law
which the judges have used. I venture to suggest that the conception
of a series of primary, secondary, etc. estates of administration, leading
to estates of production, would clarify the analysis of these Nigerian
systems of landholding. I note that Elias sees a parallel between those
systems organized under the authority of paramount chiefs and subchiefs, and systems where the rights of groups are expressed through a
single elder or councils of elders. He excludes from the pattern only
the Benin kingdom in a period of autocracy, and in the Northern
Nigerian emirates those lands worked by slaves for the nobility, but
not those worked by villagers who yielded large tributes to their lords
from the harvest. He shows that even slaves developed on the land they
worked estates which were protected at law.

I make the same comments on Lloyd's recent excellent study in
Nigeria of *Yoruba Land Law* (1962). Here too the analysis of four
Yoruba kingdoms, introduced by a general discussion (Chapter 4),
emphasizes the close connection of landholding with status and fulfillment of obligations of status. Newcomers can be accepted onto an
estate generally only with the permission of what I call holders of
superior estates of administration (p. 128). But this discussion of
superiors' rights in terms only of trusteeship and possession of reversionary rights seems to me not to be sufficiently clarifying, and the
use of "usufructuary" to describe the rights of cultivators, hunters,
and collectors is, as shown, misleading, since these rights are strong,
transmissible to heirs, and capable of transfer to others.

There are many restrictions in the public interest on how an African
may use his estate of production. Among the Bemba he may not fire
the piled brushwood he has lopped from the trees before the chief
gives the signal, lest he start a fire which destroys others' brushwood
before it has been piled. I have recorded a case among the Tonga

where a man who had dug a well in his garden had to replace a cow which fell into it while grazing on his maize stalks, since everyone may put his cattle to eat anyone's maize stover. Among the Barotse, tribal laws fine a man who fells fruit trees and, latterly, parent bush trees, and a man who neglects to dig the channels in his drained land and thus spoils the gardens of his neighbors may be fined and ultimately expropriated.

The working of the land and the appropriation of its products within this system of land tenure are highly individualistic. In the use of public land and waters, immediately a man kills game or fish, or collects fruits or wild vegetables or medicines, or gathers thatching grass, clay, iron ore, bark for rope, etc., these fruits belong to him, though he use them in certain customary ways which often entail sharing. Cattle that graze on commonage are owned by individuals or small groups. Only certain people have rights to the crops grown in gardens. In order to understand landholding fully, it is necessary to analyze ownership of the produce.

Generally it may be said that produce of a garden belongs to the holder of the right of production. The king may have the right to claim some as tribute, as our state demands a portion of our income in taxes. Otherwise, except under specific agreements of metayage, partnership, etc., we say that in our system the products of the land belong to the owner of the lease, fee simple, or share in the land. In Africa, ownership of the crops is more complicated. Among the Lozi, a man and his wife ultimately have a right to a half each of the produce grown by her on a garden given by him, since they divide the crops on divorce or on the death of one spouse. They are in a sense joint owners of the crops. Often the Lozi speak of the man as the owner, but his rights to touch the crops are very limited. He is entitled, with his relatives, to be fed from the granary of his wife, and his wife should consult him before selling from it; if he divorces his wife or she dies he can claim half the crops in it. But, woe betide him if he go to her granary himself to take food. An old man was foolish enough, in his wife's absence, to sell a basket of her maize. He gave her the shilling. He also took food from the granary to feed her visiting relatives. The wife sued and obtained divorce. The court accepted the man's defense that he had not stolen the food, indeed had sold it to help his wife, but he had no right to touch her crops, grown in his land allotted to her. He ruefully commented, "Of course, she would not have claimed a divorce if she had not long been looking for an excuse to leave me. She would just have scolded me."

Sometimes a Lozi settles in his wife's village. Then she is cultivating her own land and he has no claim on any crops she grows. The crops he grows on land allocated him are his own.

The husband, in addition to giving each of his wives a garden (and each wife has a right to claim one), usually keeps one garden at least for himself. If asked to state the law, the Lozi will say that no wife has any ownership in the produce of this garden, even though every wife helps to work it. However, every wife has a right to demand food for herself and her children from it, and a reasonable amount of European goods bought from the proceeds of its crops. Further, every wife has a right to demand that her husband treat her as well as his other wives, both in distribution of food and of goods purchased from it. If he favors one the others can claim divorce. Thus though the man is the owner of the granary in which the food is stored, and will be so described by the Lozi, his wives have certain rights to control his use of it.

In Loziland, there are certain sites for fish traps that belong to individuals. No one else may trap there. A man must feed all his wives from his traps, equally. But while he is bound to give each wife a garden, and she may claim divorce if he does not, he would be foolish to give each wife a trap site in his fish dam. For fish are uncertain things, and if one wife had plenty of fish from her trap while the others had none, a witchcraft charge would soon flare out. The wise man keeps his fish in common and shares them out among his wives.

The above analysis applies to the products of almost every type of land. Among the Barotse, game and fish in public waters and wild fruits belong to the tribe, through the king. That is, grazing land, stretches of water and rivers, trees, grasses, and mineral deposits are not granted to any individual, but anyone can exploit them. The king holds the estate of administration; every subject has a right of production. We have seen that when a man leaves wild fruit trees in his garden he acquires a right to all their fruit while he is still using the garden. In a communal hunting battue, the man who first hits a buck gets the major portion of the beast, but a second man who finally kills it is entitled to a foreleg. If the king has summoned the hunting party he is entitled to half of all kills, but he has to give some of this to unsuccessful beaters and to people who have remained at the capital to

watch over the country. Some parts of certain game are royal property
—the ground tusk of an elephant, lion skins, leopard skins, parts of a
hippo, and eland switches and sinews and some meat—and these have
to be rendered to the king while the hunter keeps the rest. The king
must reward the hunter for producing a lion skin or leopard skin, and
everyone present in the capital has a right to eat of hippo meat.[42]

Thus an outstanding feature of rights over produce is that though
the producer has a dominant power over his goods, he owes duties to
distribute some of these to specific persons within a complicated pattern established by status relationships. He has to yield part of his
produce to the demands of his superior holders of estates of administration lest he lose his rights in his estate of production: the series of
consumption rights runs in the opposite direction from that of estates.
Some obligations he owes to persons outside that hierarchy. There is
thus a complex clustering of rights over all material goods, and these
rights inhere in membership of differing groups or social relationships.
Once we recognize this, we can define the rights and their corresponding obligations precisely. This appears clearly in Richards' account of
the Bemba.[43]

While there is a certain sharing in consumption, I emphasized, as
Richards does, that the basis of this system of sharing is individual
appropriation. The sharing of one individual's produce with others is
an expression of the relationships between them in a social organization based on highly personal contacts. The more a man can give, the
more important his status; the good hunter acquires prestige by killing meat to give away. Production is individualistic. This individual
basis remains untouched even in what are commonly called the "collective aspects of African agriculture"—working parties to hoe or
plant or weed or harvest, attracted by beer, tobacco, salt, or food.
Every person who helps can claim a share in the feast, and others do
too; but the crop belongs to the landholder. Where the people collect
to work for the chief, the crop is his, though each helper may claim a
basket from the harvest.

The Barotse can recite to an inquirer a series of what, following
Ehrlich, we might call "legal propositions" which their courts state
and follow in judging disputes. "If you leave my village you lose your
rights in its land," and its converse, "If you enter my village you are

---

42. These so-called "kingly goods" differ from tribute (see below, Chap. 5, pp. 152 f.).
43. *Land, Labour and Diet in Northern Rhodesia* (1940), passim.

entitled to a share in its land," are examples of such propositions. I have cited a number of others. It is rare for any dispute in court to be simply a question of who, in this case, has what right to a particular piece of land. Since land is held by virtue of position in a series of groups or a complex of relationships, disputes over land frequently hinge on whether individuals have fulfilled the multifarious duties of their stations.

The situation is as described by Goodenough for Truk: many of these duties are not legally enforced, in that specific performance will be ordered or damages levied for breach. They are observances of moral obligations or customary and conventional modes of behavior —not legal demands. But the court may hold that a litigant has so flagrantly broken these obligations or conventions, which are not themselves directly enforceable at law, that he must forfeit his status and with this his rights to land. Thus they are indirectly enforced. And in determining who has rights to a particular piece of land, the court may allot it to a particular estate but advise that it be granted to another, in terms of more diffuse customary obligations of status. Thus in a state like that of Barotse, there is a body of legal rules which courts can define on cases stated. In settling cases the courts introduce many norms, customs, and ideas of justice within the standards of what is reasonable fulfillment of duties, in a specific situation, by a person holding a particular status. Custom, convention, and current standards of reasonable fulfillment are sources of law on which judges draw to lay down legal rulings on rights and obligations in disputes between holders of estates of administration and estates of production. Rights to land arise from obligations of status; status does not arise from transactions involving land. The situation is in fact the reverse of the feudal situation.

The background of this system of landholding was an economy without the luxuries that would enable rich men to raise their standard of living markedly above their poorer fellows. It did not pay the king or the primary owner of a big estate of administration to retain land for his own use far above his subsistence needs, for he could not gain profit from it or a raised standard of living. Instead, he acquired social power by granting holdings within his estate to dependents who became subordinate to him in the social hierarchy. The induction of Africa into the modern world economy potentially changed the value of land, since goods were now available to enable individuals to raise their standards of living. Nevertheless, the chiefs and holders of superior estates have not increased their own workings by enclosures of the land to the detriment of their dependents.

In 1943 I surveyed [44] what had happened in all the South and Central African tribes under British control where landholding developments had evolved in this situation without the White governments' interference. I found that generally the tendency had been to emphasize the right of every member of the tribe to some arable land, and that within groups smaller than the tribe there had been a similar emphasis in respect of their own members, which could be explained by the facts that many tribal areas were too distant from markets to develop the sale of crops and that most tribes therefore looked for their money income to meet new wants to their able-bodied men who went out of the tribal area to work for White enterprises. These migrant laborers had a great interest in retaining their rights in tribal land against the insecurities of industrial employment,[45] and rights in land were involved in the whole complex of tribal social relationships. In effect, the chiefs and superior holders of estates in tribal land looked for gifts of money and goods from their subordinates, who migrated to labor in White enterprises, and in return the superiors granted or held for these subordinates estates of land. As pressure on the land increased with increase of population, following often on restriction of tribal territory as land had been taken for White settlers, chiefs tended to take over unused land already allotted in order to fulfill their obligations to the landless, and even to take over fallows after a short period of rest. At this stage land was becoming short under the prevailing system of cultivation. The ultimate end of the process was found in Basutoland where each married man was entitled to only three small fields. Most of these developments were reported from South Africa and the British Protectorates, but I detected the germ of similar developments in a few scanty reports in Northern Rhodesia.

Reports from this South-Central African region which are now coming in, twenty years later, indicate that wherever possible the major development is in the same direction, though there are additional complications. In an article on "Effects on the Xhosa [of South

44. In my *Essays on Lozi Land and Royal Property* (1943).
45. See my *"Anthropological Problems Arising from African Industrial Revolution"* (1961) and works cited therein.

Africa] and Nyakyusa [of Tanganyika] of Scarcity of Land"
(1963), Professor Monica Wilson concludes that in both these tribes
"the attitude . . . is still that the use of land for cultivation and
grazing is a right to which every man is entitled and in practice they
criticize any individual who lays field to field and leaves his brother
landless." In the Xhosa tribal reserves, the area of land for each man is
officially restricted by village headman and White Native-Commis-
sioner. Where some families have been settled many years ago on freehold and quitrent farms, they or their descendants have tended to
accommodate landless relatives; but lending and leasing of land, and
particularly sharecropping, are widely practiced. The Xhosa's main
source of income is labor migration.[46]

The Nyakyusa have developed cash-cropping on richer land in ancient craters, but even this land is not yet leased or sold, though
Wilson believes these transactions will soon become common. Wilson
says that the effect of land shortage has been to stop the redistribution
of land periodically as new villages of coevals were established, and to
make all land inheritable in the agnatic line, as the rich crater land
always was. Men are more tied to old villages, there is less movement
and, whereas formerly villages tried to attract new members, they no
longer do so. Land is not so freely lent.[47] Quarrels can no longer be
settled by sections of villages or individuals moving away. But generally the stress is still on the rights of all men, and presumably women,
to land for their support, though not necessarily to land which will
carry the cash crops. Migration of men to labor centers keeps the system going.

In Xhosaland in South Africa many married men cannot obtain
fields and are left landless. Mr. Basil Sansom has recently studied a
similar situation in one Pedi chieftaincy in the Northern Transvaal.
He has not yet published his analysis, but he has allowed me to summarize here his findings of a type of social development not reported
from any other tribe. The chief has endeavored to maintain the principle that each married woman is entitled to a tract of land to produce
food for her household. But the chief has not been able to ensure that
a second category of land, in which title is held by men, is equitably

46. There is a fuller analysis of the situation among the Xhosa in Mills and Wilson,
Keiskammahoek Rural Survey, Vol. 4: *Land Tenure* (1952).

47. In his *Lineage System of the Mae Enga of the Central New Guinea Highlands*
(1965), Meggitt suggests as a general rule that as land becomes scarce, the dominant principle of affiliation and inheritance will be increasingly enforced.

distributed. Technically, title to land cannot be gained or relinquished without the chief's approval. However, wealthy men "borrow" and work the land of poorer tribesmen. A poor man in debt to a wealthy man may virtually surrender his land to his creditor. In this way some men in the chiefdom are able to build up large holdings in "men's land" to the detriment of the holdings of others; they emerge as a set of "land brokers," manipulating debts and land as much for social power and prestige as for monetary gain, since the main source of Pedi income is labor migration. No traditional authorities have entered into these pursuits, and the chief apparently turns a blind eye toward them.

Only one study, by Jaspan,[48] of a small tribal reserve in southern Natal in the Republic of South Africa, carried out in the mid-1940s, suggests that a chief in this region of South and Central Africa has tried to gain land at the expense of his subjects. Jaspan states that the chief began to compete with his subjects for land from early on. The chief possesses more livestock than any of his subjects. Eventually some brought a suit against him: they claimed that he had used his official position unlawfully to monopolize the grazing rights in a Government-trust farm where grazing was restricted by proclamation. "Part of the reaction of the Chief to this unprecedented act of opposing him at a supra-tribal level was to accuse the leaders of the 'opposition' and their sympathizers of attempting to destroy him by sorcery and witchcraft. The Chief has for many years steered clear of the district in which the 'opposition' is centred; he neither eats nor drinks, nor attends any ceremonies or meetings there." Jaspan's implicit contention seems to be land shortage in this reserve has reached a point where the whole traditional system must break down. The chief cannot even begin to meet his obligations to his subjects. The reserve is so severely denuded of fertility that in many respects it is a reserve residence for men working in White towns, with most of the men absent at any one time. The chief, facing the competition of better-educated men for prestige, maintains his wealth at the expense of his subjects. It is the only report I know of a chief acting thus.

Nowhere in South Africa or in the British Protectorates or the Rhodesias or Nyasaland had there been a spontaneous development to a Western type of tenure in which lease and sale of land are allowed,

48. "A Sociological Case Study: Communal Hostility to Imposed Social Change in South Africa" (1953), especially at pp. 105–08.

presumably because few areas here gained their main income from cash cropping, which was important in territories not dominated by White settlers. There, in East and West Africa, and in the regions around the Congo, pledging, leasing, and even sale of land have emerged in many areas. These transactions have to some extent been accommodated within the old series of estates,[49] but they strike hard at the traditional social organization.[50]

Although, in the regions on which I have concentrated, the right of all tribal members to be given some land has been emphasized, all developments also stress the individual basis of landholding. The example set by immigrant White settlers was not likely to lead to more collective working of land by Africans, though cooperatives for marketing have emerged. In addition, the bias of indigenous use of estates of production was also individualistic. A producer used his fruits to fulfill his obligations and by generous distribution to acquire prestige —in short, to meet the demands of his status as citizen, villager, and kinsman. But in certain areas, as among the Northern Rhodesian Tonga where cash crops are grown, it has been possible for individuals markedly to increase their holdings under tribal law, and to raise their standard of living above that of their fellows.

In no tribe has there been a general evolution to collective working. The Barolong chief in Bechuanaland divided his territory into farms, held mostly by his relatives, but as what I call "estates of administration." During the 1939–45 war Tswana tribes cultivated "war-lands" collectively, the produce being held for the tribe. This is in a sense a development from the communal working of the chief's lands, for though the produce from these went to the chief, he used it to feed his court, to help the needy, and so on. This was true too, for example, of the Bemba, but the abolition of tribute labor has reduced the Bemba chief's power to maintain his gardens. By special proclamation, the Barotse king also abandoned his rights to tribute labor, but some of his gardens are still worked by communal labor, freely rendered. He and other members of the royal family now keep the produce for their own needs but usually reward the workers with a basket of crops.

49. For good accounts see Lloyd, *Yoruba Land Law* (1962), and Obi, *The Ibo Law of Property* (1963). There are many others, referred to in Biebuyck, ed., *African Agrarian Systems* (1963).

50. See ibid. for a convenient collection of several studies dealing with this situation.

Since this type of analysis applies to the Ndebele (Matabele), with all respect it seems that the Judicial Committee of the Privy Council was incorrect in holding that Ndebele tribesmen's rights did not fall into the category of rights in private property which the Crown should recognize, and which the committee itself had recognized in Nigeria and elsewhere. When Sir Harry Johnston negotiated a protectorate treaty with the Baganda and granted freehold estates to Baganda chiefs, he overlooked, in Low and Pratt's words, that

> The importance of land to the Baganda chiefs was essentially political. A chief needed control over land so as to settle followers upon it. To the British, missionaries and administrators alike, this was not clearly apparent. To them there was a plain distinction between the connexion which linked ownership and land on the one hand, and that which linked administrative area with chiefly jurisdiction on the other. Land-ownership and chiefly authority were to them, that is, separate issues. But to the Baganda the essential connexion very largely cut across the British distinction. It lay in the connexion between land and chiefly jurisdiction. No one "owned" land in Buganda. A peasant occupied land which his wives cultivated. A chief exercised authority over peasants who occupied land within his jurisdiction, or over lesser chiefs to whom he delegated portions of the land and peasantry over which he himself had been given jurisdiction. In both systems there was control over the land. But control to the British implied ownership; to the Baganda control implied jurisdiction. During the negotiations these differing conceptions were never adequately distinguished.[51]

The path of clarity in these respects was emphasized by Pollock and Maitland, as far back as 1895:

> At the present time there is perhaps some danger that a little too much stress will be laid on the communal traits of mediaeval history. The apparent communalism of old law covers an individualism which has deep and ancient roots. Every right, every duty, however communal its character, spontaneously becomes the right, the duty, of an individual by attaching itself to the land that he

51. Low and Pratt, *Buganda and British Overrule* (1960), p. 49 and passim.

holds. Because he holds a certain messuage he may turn out two oxen on "the common of the vill"; because he holds a certain messuage he is a doomsman of the county court.

As I have put it, rights and duties are individually held in terms of political status. And political status is involved in a hierarchy for, say Pollock and Maitland, "the community is a community not because it is a self-sufficient organism, but because it is a subordinate member of a great community, of a nation. The nation is not a system of federated communities, the king is above all and has a direct hold on every individual." Pollock and Maitland thus far might be describing Barotseland. The change comes when they go on to add that "the communities are far more often the bearers of duties than of rights; they appear before the courts chiefly as punishable units; the proudest city will lose its liberties if it exceeds or abuses those powers that are given to it from above. But above the king himself—thus even a royal justice (Bracton) may think—is the greatest of all communities, 'the university of the realm.' " [52] For in Barotseland rights and duties are reciprocal. I propose my terminology in the hope that it may clarify these relations. But in Barotseland the law also emphasizes duty—in disputes it insists on fulfillment of the obligations of status, from which rights arise.

As I complete this manuscript for publication, my original proposal (made in 1943) of the above terminology, has been considered in a newly published symposium on *African Agrarian Systems* (1963). Rather than confuse the development of my argument by inserting the comments of the editor, Professor D. Biebuyck, on my proposals, I am dealing with them here. I cite in translation the relevant passage from Biebuyck's Introduction:

> Usually a certain number of social persons and groups could avail themselves of rights over the same patch of ground, without necessarily being in conflict or without there being present a phenomenon which M. Gluckman calls a "hierarchy of estates of holdings." This plurality of rights exercised by different persons and encumbering the same plot must not indeed necessarily be conceived in terms of a sort of hierarchy of tenures, which would presuppose, as C. M. White has underlined [in an essay in

52. Pollock and Maitland, *The History of English Law* (1923, 2d ed.), pp. 687–88.

the symposium], a successive series of attributions of land carried
out by a specific land authority to holders of domains and plots,
socially and/or politically situated below it. M. Gluckman has
moreover admitted that this hierarchy is more clearly found
among peoples who have a more or less fixed agricultural system,
and a well-elaborated hierarchic social organization, and that its
importance is growing where there is some measure of land shortage. Thus what is important is the consideration of this network
of rights, exercised by persons and groups on each of the different
types of land employed to specific purposes. Moreover, what characterized these traditional systems was above all the rarity of
litigation and serious internal conflicts over land. [Pp. 15–16.]

Clearly Biebuyck is here conceiving that use of the word "hierarchy" necessarily implies the existence of an organized system of
authorities, holding estates and continuously dealing with land distribution. I do not consider that the phrase "a hierarchy of estates" does
imply this; it merely states that the holding of estates of administration retreats or advances in a graded arrangement. I therefore consider
it applicable to situations where groups, without authoritative leaders,
devolve estates on their component segments, down to the individual
cultivator. Nevertheless, to avoid this misunderstanding, I have now
substituted "series" for "hierarchy" to cover situations where the estates are not held by authorities whose rights are supported by legitimate force, as among the Barotse. Given this clarification, I believe my
proposals accord with Biebuyck's analysis, and particularly with his
exposition of his own findings among the Nyanga of the Lake Kivu
region (his Introduction, at pp. 4–9). He does not discuss my later
distinction between estates of administration and of production, in
which I followed Sheddick.

I agree that the series of estates is less well developed where land is
plentiful, but I have dealt with this point in the text of this chapter. I
have also considered how the analysis can be fitted to the different uses
of different kinds of land, at various times and for varying periods.
Biebuyck's analysis emphasizes the connection between landholding
and social organization, but gives no means for handling this relation.

Since Biebuyck quotes White with approval, and White has written
an essay on "Factors Determining the Content of African Land-
Tenure Systems in Northern Rhodesia," citing tribes I have myself

considered (Bemba and Tonga), I am compelled to say that I consider White has misinterpreted studies of those tribes. This comment does not bear upon his own analysis of field data which he collected in various tribes. These indicate a growing neglect of the rights of what I have called estates of administration within which estates of production exist—which White says are held now in "a highly individualistic manner." He argues that "commercialization of land and pressure of population upon it appear to play a part [in the full emergence of rights of individuals which can be discerned], and in particular seem to affect the degree to which land sales appear." These land sales are mostly concealed under an apparent sale of improvements to the land itself.

Chapter 4

IMMOVABLE PROPERTY AND CHATTELS
IN SOCIAL CONTINUITY

BOTH DEVELOPED AND UNDEVELOPED legal systems distinguish sharply between immovable and movable property. Basically the distinction is between rights and duties of persons in relation to land, and rights and duties in relation to others with respect to goods, animals, and people. The English speak of real property and chattels or personalty; the Romans divided *res mancipi* from *res nec mancipi*; and the Barotse distinguish *litaba zamubu* (cases over soil) from other cases. I shall later cite similar distinctions from other tribal legal systems. As Maine pointed out,[1] the difference between the two types of property is not absolutely between land and chattels—between immovables and movables. The Roman *res mancipi* included slaves, horses, and oxen besides land. Maine cites Scottish law as ranking a certain class of securities with land, and Hindu law as grouping slaves with land. And he then says English law separates "leases of land for years from other interests in the soil, and joins them to personalty under the name of 'chattels real.' " In terms of my own data on Barotse law I examine here some problems arising from this dichotomy in the law of property and will consider briefly the examples raised by Maine and try to show why other kinds of property are classed with land.

There must be many reasons to explain the existence of this fundamental and, I believe, universal legal distinction. No important phenomenon can be analyzed in terms of one set of relations alone. Land is everywhere a basic means of production and hence highly valued. This is perhaps especially marked among a people like the Barotse, who (as cultivators, herdsmen, and fishers) live almost entirely off the land and its waters. We would therefore expect their land law to be highly important. But land will produce food only through seed, cattle, and the tools of production whose ownership is sometimes protected, and their transfer effected, under a different set of laws. Deal-

1. *Ancient Law* (1861), p. 283 f. (1909 ed.).

ings in land are more complicated, often ceremonial. Why should there be this difference? Indeed, why should this distinction have persisted so tenaciously into modern times in England? The trucks of a transport company are more important to production than is the garage in which they are housed, but the trucks can be sold by ordinary contract, whereas the sale of the garage involves a prolonged process. Similarly, the few acres of ground on which a factory stands are not in themselves so productive as the complex machinery, yet the machinery is easily transferred and the acres are not. Hence I do not believe that the importance of land as a productive resource is sufficient to explain the dichotomy of property law or its persistence into periods far removed in every way from an agricultural economy.

This problem is well put by Cheshire, and he suggests that answers lie in the former value of land in an agricultural community, and in the high possibility that land can be encumbered with numerous contingent rights, whereas chattels are usually not so encumbered. For the benefit of anthropologists who may not know these complications, I quote from Cheshire at length:

> Between 1837 and 1922 the [British] legislature became more and more active in the sphere of real property law, but most of the enactments were directed towards the simplification of conveyancing and the extension of the landowners' powers of enjoyment. No comprehensive effort was made to smooth the path by abolishing the substantive defects which had settled on the main body of the law like barnacles on the hull of a ship. Then came the war of 1914, and with it a general desire to set the social life of the nation in order. One of the results of this desire was to give an impetus to land legislation, and it will be as well to state at the outset the main idea which lay at the back of the legislation that resulted. It was nothing more than a desire to render the sale of land as rapid and simple a matter as is the sale of goods or of shares. A layman knows that if he desires to transfer to another the ownership of a chattel, such as a motor car or a picture, the only requirement is the making of a contract which names the parties, records their intention, describes the article to be sold and states the price to be paid. The moment that such a contract is concluded, the ownership of the article, in the absence of a contrary intention, passes to the buyer. At first sight it is

difficult to appreciate why the same simple expedient cannot be adopted in the case of land, and not unnaturally a layman grows impatient of the long and expensive investigation attendant upon the conveyance of a piece of land worth perhaps one half of the car which can be effectively sold in a quarter of an hour.

But the difference is inevitable, and the explanation is that in the great majority of cases the possessor of personal goods is their absolute owner, and therefore able to pass a title which will confer upon their deliveree an equally full and unencumbered ownership. If *A* is in possession of a piano, it is probable that he is its owner, and in most cases a buyer is safe in paying its value and taking delivery of possession. No doubt the maxim of the law is *nemo dat quod non habet,* and if it should happen that *A,* instead of being the owner, is merely holding the piano under a hire-purchase agreement, then a buyer from him will not acquire ownership. But the fact remains that despite the risk a buyer is generally justified in assuming that the possessor of goods is also the owner, and as a rule there is no need to go to trouble and expense in order to ascertain whether some person other than the possessor has any interest in them. It is a legitimate risk to take. But for a purchaser of land to be content with the word of the vendor and with the appearance of ownership which flows from his possession would be an act of sheer folly.

Land and goods are and must ever be on a different plane. Land is fixed, permanent and vital to the needs of society, and a subject matter in which rights may be granted to persons other than the ostensible owner. *A* is in possession of an estate and is obviously exercising all the powers of enjoyment which amount to the popular idea of ownership, but none the less it is by no means certain that he is in fact entitled to dispose of the interest that he may have agreed to sell. He may be merely in possession under the lease for any period from one to 999 years or more, or he may be a mere life tenant holding under a family settlement; and even though he holds the fee simple—the largest interest known to the law and one that approximates to the absolute ownership of goods—it is likely that he or his predecessors have granted to third parties rights, such as mortgages, restrictive covenants and rights of way, which continue to be enforceable against the land regardless of any transfer to which it may have been subjected.

So long as third parties can in this way have legally enforceable rights against land which outwardly appears to belong absolutely to the possessor, it is difficult, in the absence of compulsory registration of title, to devise a system under which conveyances of land can be conducted with the facility of sales of goods, and it will always be incumbent on a purchaser to make careful searches and inquiries in order to see that the land is unburdened.

We may start, then, with the assumption that no effort of legislative genius can, from the point of view of simplicity and rapidity, put conveyances of land on an equal footing with sales of goods. But when the question of reforming the law came before Parliament in 1922, the result of 600 years of development from a feudal origin was that the law of real property contained so many antiquated rules and useless technicalities that additional and unnecessary impediments had come into being to hinder the facile transfer of land. The real property law as it existed in 1922 might justly be described as an archaic feudalistic system which, though originally evolved to satisfy the needs of society based and centred on the land, had by considerable ingenuity been twisted and distorted into a shape more or less suitable to a commercial society dominated by money. The movement of progressive societies has been from land to money, or rather to trade, and a legal system which acquired its main features at a time when land constituted the main part of a country's wealth can scarcely be described as suitable to an industrial community.[2]

I propose to suggest that in tribal society at least there is an additional important difference between land and most chattels, and that this difference contributes to the distinctions made in classifying these types of goods. My hypothesis is that immovable property and chattels have different functions in the maintenance, through time, of a social system as an organized pattern of relations. Immovable property provides fixed positions which endure through the passing of generations, through quarrels, and even through invasions and revolutions, and many social relationships are stabilized about these positions. Movables establish links between individuals occupying different immovable properties, and tribal practice artificially accelerates movement of these goods. The two kinds of property therefore acquire different symbolic

2. *The Modern Law of Real Property* (9th ed., 1962), pp. 5–6.

values in the law and ritual of tribal society. This difference in social function is based on the obvious fact that all social systems, including those of nomads, are settled on land which changes but slowly, while the living personnel of the system and their interrelations change comparatively rapidly. These attributes may help to account for the fact that the distinction is so sharp in tribal society, although their ownership of chattels, unlike ours, was not generally free or unencumbered by demand-rights held by others than the producer or possessor. In Barotseland, as in other African societies, any chattel may be subject to a number of rights held by different persons.[3]

This point may help explain why in some societies slaves, stock, and titles are associated with land, whereas in English law leases of land for years are chattels real— a significant paradox. I concede that the hypothesis in itself is patent enough, but it gains in interest as we trace the elaboration of its implications through other institutions in different types of social system. I begin with the working out of the principle among the Barotse, but I shall also make some comparisons with other cultures.

I have described how the floodplain Barotse have to dwell in villages built on mounds raised by themselves or by termites. Only in these places can habitations survive the floods, even though in many years the huts are badly damaged. Therefore, the most ancient island mounds have been centers of settlement throughout Barotse history. They have names, with praise songs attached to each, which go back deep into legendary history. The villages on these named islands have been enduring cores of settlement through a long period. For nearly thirty years, from 1836 to 1864, the Barotse were ruled by Basuto invaders; the identity of these villages survived this conquest and the later Barotse liberation of their homeland. A mound newly built by the king fits into the scheme with a new title. Abandoned old mounds retain their former status.

A Barotse village consists of more than the mound on which it is built. To each village are attached scattered gardens, since cultivation is possible only on pockets of fertile soil dotted between the sands and thick mats of grass on the plain's surface. The percentage of cultivable

3. See e.g. Colson, "The Role of Cattle among the Plateau Tonga" (1951); Evans-Pritchard, The Nuer (1940), pp. 79–80; Gluckman, Essays on Lozi Land and Royal Property (1943), pp. 65 f.; Schapera, Handbook of Tswana Law and Custom (1938), pp. 214–30.

land is low, and what can be cultivated is very valuable. Sites suitable for fishing by nonreturn traps, fence traps, communal battues, and certain other methods are also scattered and scarce and are attached to villages, though net fishing in the waters of the river and in its gulfs and pans is free to the public.

Most of the valuable land of the nation is distributed among existing villages, and the main outlines of this distribution have persisted for many generations. The Barotse see this distribution as an important core of their history, since many villages are attached to titles of royal persons and national councillors, and others are the cenotaphs of dead kings. Their history is marked on the land through the titles of villages. Each village has a headman whose title devolves on his successor, so that its history is also told in the persistence of headmen's titles. The land of a village vests in the title of a headman; he holds it from the king, and he must distribute it fairly for cultivation and fishing among his villagers. He cannot disturb their existing rights, and neither can his successor, so long as they respect the position of headmanship.

In one important respect, therefore, Barotse society consists of a large number of villages, enduring through the centuries and through radical social changes. Through each of these villages there has flowed a stream of people, related to one another by varying ties of kinship or brought together by royal command, but united in allegiance to their headman. All citizens live in one or another village, for citizenship in Barotse society is not only immediate by allegiance to the king but also mediated through membership in a village. Every man must live in a village, so he must have a headman. The nation is thus organized as a system of villages. But the organization of people into villages also involves organization of its land, which is so essential a part of it that if a man leave the village, he loses his rights in its land. Moreover, if he wrongs the headman so as to justify expulsion from the village, he loses his land rights there.

These rights he gets, first, as a subject of the king. Second, since every subject must live in a village, he derives these rights from the king through his headman. In short, the organization of the nation into villages of people and into land units largely coincides, and the headman occupies a critical position under the king in both these systems of relationships.

Chattels (cattle, spears, axes, hoes, clothes, grain, fish, etc.) do not enter *directly* into these systems. Huts which are fixed to the soil did, however, and could not be sold until legislation, influenced by new economic values, allowed this in 1940. Land was thus separated in Barotse law from chattels: rights of any permanency in land were derived from status as a citizen and status as a villager. Transfers of land were handled publicly and ceremonially; they were reported at the capital if important, at local councils if unimportant. To transfer land one had to go to law to have the transfer legitimated. Allocations of land received from the king were acknowledged with the royal salute, as was installation in a headmanship.

In many cases I have heard the judges insist on protecting this structure of landholding centered on the headman, and remind litigants that if they wronged the headman or left his village they lost their land. But is was in a case in which the judges tried to avoid applying the letter of this law, in favor of a headman who was in the wrong, that I came clearly to see the significance of this land law. This is the case, summarized in the first chapter,[4] in which a new headman demanded that his sisters and their sons rejoin his village or return his fishing dams to him. He was upheld by a district court. His kin appealed to the court in the capital. The judges all felt that the headman was behaving immorally, but the senior judge sitting held: "We cannot change the law against Mahalihali [the headman's title] . . . Our law comes from long ago . . . Mahalihali is the owner of the dams . . . He gave the royal salute when he was installed as heir." The head of the court was absent, but when the situation was explained to him, and he found the headman still insisting on his claim, he applied a new sanction. The dams undoubtedly belonged to the title Mahalihali, but if the present incumbent was ungenerous in exercising his rights the court would discharge him from the title and appoint a more generous successor.

The brilliance of the solution was that it left untouched the basic premise of Barotse land tenure: the dams remained vested in the title Mahalihali, but the judge evolved a sanction by which he could force generosity on any incumbent of the title. He distinguished incumbent from title and thereby left untouched the structure of Barotse law, in so far as it protected headmen's titles and their rights to administer a village's land. In this case the structure of the land-tenure system, and

4. Cited on pp. 14 f. above, and analyzed fully for its application of equity in my *Judicial Process among the Barotse* (1955), pp. 178–87.

its involvement in the system of village settlement, was made manifest in another passage. In an earlier quarrel between the headman's father, Mahalihali I, and the latter's brother Sabangwa, the court had allowed Sabangwa as a temporary measure to build a small separate hamlet away from his quarrelsome senior, but within the village estate where he continued to cultivate and fish. In the present case Sabangwa appeared as a witness for his nephew, the new headman Mahalihali II. One of the senior judges noticed this, and asked why Mahalihali was not demanding Sabangwa's return to the village: he was dwelling apart, yet was using village land. The judge upbraided Sabangwa for not telling Mahalihali that it was wrong to bring suit against the sisters, and ordered him to return to the village. The other senior judges took up this point and confirmed the order. The words of one bring out clearly how the Barotse nation endures as a system of villages under the king. He said: "Let the title of Sabangwa on the bank of the canal die, that the title of Mahalihali be made great."

Like all people, Barotse pursue many ends, both as individuals and as members of various relationships and groups. They marry and beget and raise children. They work in various ways for their living. They strive for prestige. They serve many other interests. In the course of their activities they quarrel, and patch up their quarrels or part irremediably. Or they deliberately seek new alignments of friends, of in-laws, of political allegiance. Their ties are constantly altering. Outside events may also influence these ties: the king may move some people to new villages. For thirty years their homeland was under the sway of alien invaders who drove many of them into exile and moved others. Nowadays the Barotse go out to work at distant European centers. Yet through all these changes in relationships Barotse social structure has in large measure endured as an ordered arrangement of relationships of various types between social positions. One of the most important, the state organization, I shall shortly consider again from another point of view. We are concerned for the moment with the nation as an organization of villages, each with its land, each under its headman, all owing allegiance to the king. Through these villages the nation has flowed, and at every moment the varying sets of ties through which people have achieved their purposes have been based on their residential allegiances. This, though the nation consists of people, these people occupy residential positions as king, headman, and villagers.

It is this system of relations, in addition to land itself, that is in-

volved in "cases of the soil" (*litaba zamubu*) and which is particularly protected by the separate rules of land-tenure law. That is, the
law of land tenure has defined and defended the fixed positions on the
land through which successive occupants of the throne, successive incumbents of headmanship, and successive residents on hut sites in the
villages have flowed, as the generations have come and departed, as invasion and rebellion have disturbed political relations, as modern col-
onization has altered the pattern of Barotse life. These positions on the
land are therefore a fixed and enduring part of the social structure,
about which more ephemeral relationships are established. Hence a different sort of law applies to them from the law that applies to chattels,
which can move with people and be transferred to people fairly freely.
Herein, I believe, resides what Radcliffe-Brown called the "dynamic
structural continuity" of society. Among the Barotse through all the
changes, there persist the capital, the villages, and the hut sites. And
their persistence is largely controlled by the ecological situation.

The persistence of this residential structure, based on the land, is
achieved by the public exhibition of changes in landholding, and by
judicial care in protecting the distribution of land. Barotse severely
criticized to me the judges who held that the headman Mahalihali
had lost his control over the dam, since this disturbed these landholding arrangements. But I must note that the judges held in effect that
Mahalihali could not oust his kin from the fish dams unless they had
wronged him or he needed the dams for his own villagers; the same
judges would probably have upheld Mahalihali if he had been object-
ing to his kin's attempt to transfer the dams to persons in other
villages.

According to Barotse legends, this basic arrangement of villages in
relation to the kingship has endured from near the beginning of time,
when the Barotse evolved as a nation whose king was descended from
God. There still exist the village where lived the daughter-wife of God
who bore the first king, the pool where kingship was founded, the place
where God saved the people and where offerings are still made to him,
the sacred point where the king's younger brother entered the ground
and trees sprang up, the capitals and cenotaphs of all past kings, and
the villages of many ancient princes and princesses.[5] Historical rec-

5. Malinowski dealt with this symbolic historical perspective of geography in his *Argonauts
of the Western Pacific* (1922) and *Myth in Primitive Psychology* (1927). A good recent
study is by Cunnison, *History on the Luapula* (1951) and *The Luapula Peoples of Northern
Rhodesia* (1959).

ords vouch for the existence of some such system at least 150 years ago, and probably it has existed for a far longer period. After the Barotse recaptured control of their homeland from the Basuto, one of their kings set about restoring both Barotse state organization and Barotse settlement in villages according to ancestral affiliation. Many of the Lozi had fled to the north; others had remained in the plain under the Basuto, who frequently moved them to other villages and placed villages under prominent men of their own or of the Lozi themselves. The Basuto also brought people of many other tribes to settle in the plain: Yeyi, Mbukushu, Shanjo, Subiya, Totela, etc. King Sipopa reconquered Barotseland in 1864, but he had grown up with the Basuto and had been ruled by their customs. He continued to handle people and land as the Basuto had. King Lewanika (1878–1883, 1884–1916) reconstituted the Lozi political bodies and titles, and to achieve fully the return to the old Lozi regime he passed an edict enabling Lozi to reclaim the villages and lands which their ancestors had held before the Basuto invasion—this was *kuliulula*, to free the land.

The disturbances in power that followed helped provoke a rebellion against him. But after he regained his throne many Lozi successfully established these claims. However, the Lozi had been in exile for a generation, and many old people of the time of the Basuto invasion had died, while middle-aged people had also died or had been killed in battle. Lozi growing up in the north had become woodland cultivators who delayed claims in the plain. Claims of people for ancestral lands therefore continued as they became aware of their rights, or desired to move elsewhere and wanted some land, or coveted particular parcels of land to which they could raise some ancestral title, or decided they wanted to work land in the plain. Under Lozi rules of inheritance, title could be claimed in any line of descent. These claims were being made as late as the 1920s. Under the prodding of the British, King Yeta in 1927 passed a law, known as the law of *muliu*, which barred suit to free land in virtue of ancestral title after midday on 27 April 1928. This law was designed to stabilize the existing allocation of land. It also prohibited claims by the king against occupiers.[6]

The passing of the original law allowing claims to ancestral land, at

6. See my *Judicial Process among the Barotse* (1955), pp. 54, 56 f., 287–88. See also pp. 69–70 above.

a time when the Barotse king was re-establishing the intricate political system of the capital, shows how importantly the residential system was regarded. In result, the major part of this residential organization has endured through the passage of generations, exile from and return to their homeland, conquests of many neighboring tribes and the importation of some to the plain, internecine war, and peaceful absorption by an alien civilization. This structural continuity through radical change shows in the relations of king to village headmen and in turn of headmen to their villagers, and also in the arrangement of positions at the capitals which I shall soon consider.

The continuity is clearly exhibited by a judgment in a land dispute, heard in 1942, between a man called Liwalela Mutome and a prince holding the title Mubukwanu. The seventeenth Barotse king was then reigning. The title Liwalela had originally been the name of a great hippo hunter in the reign of the fourth king. Here is the judgment: "Mutome [defendant], the soil is [the prince] Mubukwanu's, not this Mubukwanu, but the old [prince] Mubukwanu of long ago. Liwalela was given land because of his hunting: and this was in the time of King Ngalama [the fourth king]. . . . The garden falls to [these princes], not to Liwalela's name." [7] The judges spoke of the present incumbent of the princely title Mubukwanu and the commoner title Liwalela as if they were the long-dead founders of the titles, and of the dead founders as if they were the present incumbents. Though we may call these legendary references, they expressed the structure's endurance clearly. [8]

This case, like Mahalihali's case, shows that the Barotse at once identify, and distinguish between, a social position like headmanship and its present incumbent. They speak of the present incumbent as if he were the position, and often as if he were the past holders. But they also say, "There is the title and there is also its holder" (*kunani libizo ni mung'a lona kiusili*), and "The title is greater than the *holder*" (*libizo lifita mung'a lona*). Hence they see clearly what is factually true, that

7. In "The Case of the Prince's Gardens" in my *Judicial Process among the Barotse* (1955), pp. 56–61.
8. Cunnison has the best exposition I know of in describing how the incumbent of a title speaks of himself and of all his predecessors in the present tense as though they were one person (*History on the Luapula*, 1951, and *The Luapula Peoples of Northern Rhodesia*, 1959). He shows how this leads to the maintenance of fixed positions in genealogies at a particular depth. On this point see also Watson, *Tribal Cohesion in a Money Economy* (1958), pp. 145 f.

the title persists through a series of incumbents. It is the persistence of titles that is the enduring part of Barotse structure. This continuity is made possible by a mechanism which is found in many societies and is known best in the Roman form of succession to a *universitas juris*. Maine, whose views still prevail among students of Roman law,[9] held that the chief form of universal succession was the replacement of a dead person by a live one. He wrote:

> A *universitas juris* is a collection of rights and duties united by the single circumstance of their having belonged at one time to some one person. It is, as it were, the legal clothing of some given individual. . . . A universal succession is a succession to a *universitas juris*. It occurs when one man is invested with the legal clothing of another, becoming at the same moment subject to all his liabilities and entitled to all his rights.

When a man died the most important demand was for an heir on whom could be bestowed the universal succession: *haereditas est successio in universum jus quod defunctus habuit* (an inheritance is a succession to the entire legal position of a deceased man).[10]

The mechanism of universal succession is found in many African societies, who describe it as "taking the name" or "the spirit," or "eating the name" (in Barotse, *kuyola libizo* or *kuca libizo*). Richards called it "positional succession" and "positional inheritance" for the Bemba, and Professor Mitchell accepted this term in his analysis of Yao villages.[11] Many other anthropologists have drawn attention to similar types of succession in different societies and have applied various terms to them; in essence, they are all the universal succession of early Roman law.

Dr. Richards' use of the adjective in *positional* succession draws attention to an important limitation of universal succession in most African societies. The heir of a dead man succeeds to his universitas juris in a particular position, and not to his individual legal clothing,

---

9. Jolowicz, *Historical Introduction to the Study of Roman Law* (1939), p. 128.

10. Maine, *Ancient Law* (1861), pp. 191 f. (1909 ed.). See also Radcliffe-Brown, "Patrilineal and Matrilineal Succession" (1952).

11. Richards "Mother-right in Central Africa" (1933); Mitchell, *The Yao Village* (1956). Richards recently wrote an important analysis of this institution in a general consideration of "Social Mechanisms for the Transfer of Political Rights in Some African Tribes," Presidential Address to the Royal Anthropological Institute of Great Britain and Ireland (1960), pp. 179, 181, and passim.

as in Maine's phrasing. Clearly even Maine erred in his choice of words, for he himself pointed out (p. 144) that "the Patria Potestas did not extend to the Jus Publicum"—so that a man dying in public office did not pass to his private heir the rights and duties of his official position. Similarly when the Barotse chief councillor, Ngambela Munalula, died in 1941, a member of his family was universal successor to the universitas juris attached to the name Munalula, and Wina at his installation as Ngambela became universal successor to that office and its property. "Killing from the title," as the Barotse describe dismissal of a councillor, deprived Wina of that universitas juris in 1948, but not of the bundle of rights and duties attached to the name Wina. Universal succession, among the Barotse and probably everywhere, is thus not to a person, but to a position or *persona*. And the positions to which there is universal succession are mainly positions on a specific place on the land.

In some African societies, but not in a developed form among the Barotse, a man may occupy more than one position, each with its own universitas juris, within a kinship system, and each universitas may devolve at his death on a different person. Thus among the Shona of Southern Rhodesia a man inherits an estate from his father and should pass it on whole to his father's other first-generation descendants (his brothers) while succession to his own earned estate is confined to his own descendants (Fig. 2).

Thus when a Shona dies the number of "estates" (estate is the nearest English equivalent of universitas juris and is the term I proffered in the previous chapter), which were united in him as an individual, are dispersed among the different persons who succeed to his various positions in an agnatic lineage structure. This process is clearly related to the maintenance of the lineage structure, though in practice it does not work indefinitely, since other social processes prevent endless proliferation. Holleman examines how in practice conflict arises between the principle of community of estate with its unified control and the preferential claims of different houses within the group, and how this conflict is adjusted at law.[12]

Devolution of estates among the Zulu is somewhat different. Here a rich man with several wives divides his estate into "houses" (*izindlu*) centered on each wife. The wives are grouped into bevies under two or

12. Holleman, *The Pattern of Hera Kinship* (1949) and *Shona Customary Law* (1952), Chap. 8. (Figure 2 on next page.)

three senior wives, with the first-married wife occupying a special position. She gives birth to a son who becomes *uyise wabantwana* (*isizinda* in Natal), "the father of the children" who replaces the father ritually. The father's central position devolves on the *inkosana* (little chief), a son born of the great wife. The *ikohlwa* son is heir to another part of the father's property. Within the bevies of wives

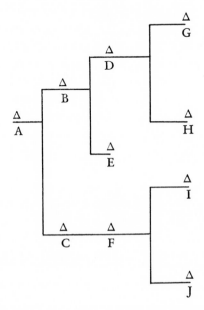

Figure 2. Inheritance of estates among the Shona of Southern Rhodesia.
When A dies, the estate A passes to B who becomes AB. When B dies A passes to C who becomes AC, but estate B passes to D who becomes BD. When C dies, A passes back to D who becomes ABD, while C passes to F who becomes CF. When D dies, A and B pass to E (now ABE), while D passes to G (now DG). When E dies, A passes to F (now ACF) and, since E has no son, B and E both pass to G (now BDEG). On F's death, A returns to the senior line to G (now ABDEG), while C and F remain in their line to I (now CFI), and so on.

attached to the inkosana and ikohlwa each wife has her own estate of land, cattle, and rights to marriage payments for daughters. Thus a rich Zulu's estate consists of several subsidiary estates, literally houses, each of which estates has its own universal heir. Here wives in an agnatic lineage structure become the nuclei of subsidiary estates within a man's major estate, and each wife transmits rights to her own sons as against the husband's sons by other wives.[13] Holleman and Barnes have shown how this system is related to residential alignments.

I have made this comparative excursion to emphasize that universal succession among the Barotse, and elsewhere in Africa, is to a position or *persona* rather than to an individual. This point is basic to the whole analysis, for the result is that certain positions become permanently linked irrespective of who occupies them. In some tribes the headman of a new village is linked to the headman of the village from which he leads out his following as, say, brother, son, sister's son, brother-in-law, or son-in-law. Thereafter the two incumbents of these headmanships will always regard each other as related in this specific way whatever their actual genealogical tie as individuals. They are in what Cunnison called "perpetual kinship." And the incumbents will observe norms of behavior that fit with their perpetual kinship. One of the linkages between villages, and a chief and his headman, is a series of perpetual kinship ties of this sort.[14] It is a permanent structure of relations.

Maine compared the results of the Roman universal succession with the endurance of the English corporation sole, "an individual, being a member of a series of individuals, who is invested by a fiction with the qualities of a Corporation," as the king, or the parson of a parish.

> The capacity or office is here considered apart from the particular person who from time to time may occupy it, and, this capacity being perpetual, the series of individuals who fill it are clothed with the leading attribute of corporations—Perpetuity. Now in the older theory of Roman law the individual bore to the family [i.e. the extended family or lineage] precisely the same relation which in the rationale of English jurisprudence a Corporation sole bears to a Corporation aggregate.[15]

13. See my *"Kinship and Marriage among the Lozi of Northern Rhodesia and the Zulu of Natal"* (1951); Holleman on Zulu: "Die Zulu Isigodi" (1941); Barnes on Ngoni: *Politics in a Changing Society* (1954), *Marriage in a Changing Society* (1951), and "Seven Types of Segmentation" (1955).

14. Good studies of the political importance and legal significance of this institution are Mitchell's *The Yao Village* (1956), Cunnison's *The Luapula Peoples* (1959), and Watson's *Tribal Cohesion in a Money Economy* (1958). See also Richards, "Social Mechanisms for the Transfer of Political Rights" (1960).

15. *Ancient Law* (1861), p. 200 (1909 ed.).

These concepts are almost cast to fit the structure of Barotse society, and I hope I may use them despite the fact that Maitland demonstrated in effect that Maine did not appreciate all the complications involved in the history of the corporation sole in English law.[16] In Maine's terms, each Barotse village is a corporation aggregate, with its rights and duties vested in a headman, who holds a specific title—a corporation sole. The village is in set and permanent relations with the king, also a corporation sole, and with other villages and headmen. But the nation as a whole is a corporation aggregate, organized in an elaborate structure of subsidiary corporations aggregate and corporations sole. I have described some of these in Chapter 2. Besides the king, there is the council. The palace, the council chamber, and other royal edifices are always placed spatially in the same relationship to one another. King's palace and council house face each other in seemingly linked opposition across a large open space, *Namoo*, which must be treated with respect. I was told by one informant, but did not check this adequately, that Namoo means "mother of the nation," and it is defined by Jalla as "open space reserved for the king." [17] No man bearing a burden, and no woman, may cross Namoo. The king's throne in the council faces the palace. The set of councillors who represent the commons sit on the king's right hand, the source of his authoritative power. The stewards who represent this king himself sit on his left hand, the side of his own life, and priests at national shrines also sit there. The stewards are called "wives of the king" and they care for his wives and for stores of food. It is the king's feminine and ritual side.[18] Opposite the king is the place for the royal family.

16. Maitland, "The Corporation Sole," reprinted from *Law Quarterly Review* (1900) in 3, *Collected Papers,* 209–43.

17. Jalla, *Dictionary of the Lozi Language* (1936).

18. My information on these points is not very good. Compare Turner's full account of how, among the Ndembu of Northern Rhodesia, "a bow is feminine, (a) because it is shaped like a container—gourds and calabashes are regarded as womb-symbols in divination, and (b) because it is held in the left hand, while the arrow is held in the right. The arrow is masculine." A chief is a woman before his installation (Turner, "Three Symbols of *Passage* in Ndembu Circumcision Ritual," 1962, p. 133 and passim). Needham has a penetrating discussion in "The Left Hand of the Mugwe" (1960) on the feminine and ritual power of an East African religious dignitary's left hand as against his masculine and secular right hand. This is in commentary on Bernardi, *The Mugwe, A Failing Prophet* (1959). Needham notes that this is uncommon, since the right hand is usually privileged (citing Hertz, *Death and the Right Hand,* 1959, and Wile, *Handedness: Right and Left,* 1934).

This is the spatial distribution of the basic three elements that the Barotse see in their state and its kingship.[19]

Royals have titles of ancient princes and princesses and sit in fixed order, as do stewards who hold the titles of servants of ancient kings. Above all, certain councillors of the right have titles of the private Ngambelas of ancient kings. As each king appoints his private Ngambela to sit below the councillor who is a sanctuary (the Giver-of-Life), the private Ngambelas of preceding kings move farther from the throne. These perpetual titles, with their fixed order, thus place in spatial positions the history of the throne. It seems probable that this is an actual history, for legends fit with the order of seating. When I first studied the seating, the title of the private Ngambela of one "king" seemed out of place. This title was too far from the throne, below the Ngambela of the first king, though the "king" concerned "reigned" after the sixth king. I learned that this man had never reigned as king; according to legend he acted on behalf of his very aged grandfather, but had died before the grandfather. He was so beloved by his own people that when he lay sick to death they covered his hut with very finely woven mats to keep out death. But death entered, and the prince died. In reward for his loving care of the prince, the prince's chief attendant was given a titled place in the council, below the title of the first king. History here again has a spatial dimension: the treasured past is set out in plan on the ground.

The nation is attached to the commoner councillors and the stewards in three series of administrative divisions which lead to king, queens, and members of the royal family. This elaborate structure, which I have described in Chapter 2, endures because the titles are on the whole perpetual, both in themselves and in their positions in relation to one another.

This principle is extended throughout the capital and land. Every council title, like royal and conciliar storehouses, has a special site in the capital. So does each queen and royal. Other state servants and priests have these specific positions also. Within the palace, the house of the king, his drummer's shed, the national altar, his private store-

19. The literature on the symbolic significance of space is voluminous. This significance is marked among many North American tribes, particularly perhaps the Pueblo. In Africa it is a theme on which the late Marcel Griaule and his colleagues have concentrated. See Griaule and Dieterlen, "The Dogon of the French Sudan," and references therein, in *African Worlds*, ed. C. D. Forde (1954), pp. 83–110.

house, each with its own title has its own site. Indeed, every material object involved in the kingship and the council has its special place in an edifice in the capital: national drums in Nateyo storehouse, king's drums in the palace, the king's own dugout in Nayuma storehouse, and so forth. The objects, like the edifices, have titles and praise songs. The royal edifices, goods, and symbols form an enduring part of the structure of the Barotse nation, in a spatial representation. And if one rots or is destroyed ("dies"), it must be replaced, often ceremonially —a process called *yoliswa,* the same word that is applied to the installation of a new incumbent of a title, be it king, queen, councillor, headman, or villager.

Like the village system, this elaborate system at the capital has survived through the vicissitudes of history, and through changes in the personnel of the nation. New subject tribes have been absorbed into it and administrative changes brought about by British occupation. Changes in personnel and changes in functional relations have all been brought into and under a limited number of titled positions, though there has been some change in these. But these changes at the top have been relatively small. We can say therefore that the central structural continuity of Barotse society has been a persisting arrangement of relations between a limited number of corporations aggregate and a limited number of corporations sole, in some of which vest the powers and liabilities of certain corporations aggregate. The corporations sole are maintained in perpetuity in themselves and in relation to one another by the device of universal succession.

Furthermore, all these corporations, sole and aggregate, are based on the land, either in themselves or in symbolic form, and their specific importance comes from their rights over land, whether it be the rights of a headman to control the land of a village or the rights of a councillor to sit in a specific place in the council by virtue of his title. Herein, I suggest, resides a symbolic importance of the law of immovable property in tribal systems. Position in space establishes the enduring elements of social structure. Certain types of movables are attached to this immovable property because they amount to immovables (e.g. fixtures on the soil, long leases for years, slaves bound to the soil, horses and cattle in some circumstances). "Incorporeal property," in the form of titles and other privileges as well as heirlooms, also are so attached. In fact, among the Barotse, as a movable becomes tied to a specific piece of land or immovable property, it becomes hallowed, and often requires to be replaced in perpetuity.

Chattels otherwise are less likely to develop this particular symbolic significance. They are employed mainly in transactions that measure the fulfillment of obligations between the occupants of what I may call "linked landed positions" within the hierarchy, or in transactions between holders of independent positions. This is of course in addition to their utilitarian value. It appears to me, therefore, that their easy transfer is encouraged by the law, as against the transfer of property connected with landed positions.

This emerges vividly in Barton's analysis of Ifugao (a Philippine tribe) classifications. He states that, as he alleges, the Ifugao's

> language, and indeed his thought, is very poor in abstractions, . . . he bases his classification upon the difference in the method of transferring property by sale. The one he calls *ma-ibuy*, "that for whose transfer by sale an *ibuy* ceremony is necessary"; and the other, *adi ma-ibuy*, "that for whose transfer by sale an *ibuy* ceremony is not necessary." . . . Classifying them upon their essential differences in status in Ifugao law and culture, the former [is] family property and the latter personal property.

Family properties consist of rice lands, forest lands, and heirlooms. These have all been handed down from generation to generation and "cannot be the property of any individual. Present holders possess only a transient and fleeting possession, or better, occupation, insignificant in duration in comparison with the decades and perhaps centuries that have usually elapsed since the field or heirlooms came into the possession of the family." A field may be sold to acquire means to provide sacrifice for the ancestors, in order to secure the recovery from dangerous sickness of a member of the family. The heirlooms are gold neck ornaments, gongs, rice-wine jars, beads, and "jewels." "These articles are used fully as much by the owner's kin as by the owner himself: for they wear the beads and ornaments, play the gongs in feasts, and brew rice wines in the jars. . . . The scale of family property is registered by ceremonies in which the nearer kin of both buyer and seller take part. In comparison with the solemnity of these transfers, our [American] real estate transfers are commonplace." [20]

20. Barton, *Ifugao Law* (1919), pp. 39 f.

This difference between the treatment of immovables and chattels is again an aspect of tribal law that has escaped the explicit attention of anthropologists. But several have reported on a phenomenon that may be associated with the symbolic difference between enduring landed positions and the cross-linkages established by chattels. In societies organized on the basis of unilineal descent groups, such as agnatic lineages, it is the mother's brother who frequently gives to his sister's son the property that differentiates him as an individual and draws him out of the tight loyalty of his agnates into relationship with others in "alien" groups. A custom frequently found in systems of this kind is that the sister's son has the privilege of taking chattels, without leave, from his mother's brother.[21]

This privilege is important among the Tallensi of Ghana, where the sister's son "has no property rights in the lineage or clan of his [mother's brothers] but is, in theory, allowed certain liberties with things belonging to them." They do not contract debts to each other, since repayment of loans cannot be demanded. When a lad becomes capable of productive labor, his mother's brothers give him the fowls from which he may with care build up his individual property, independently of his rights to property in his own lineage. At his death, this independent property becomes in its turn lineage property.[22] In Tallensi and Nuer society, on the other hand, blocks of land and their inhabitants are set in relations of perpetual kinship by the agnatic genealogy of the lineage system. And among the Nuer, the mother's brother can curse his sister's son's cattle; this is the obverse of the situation outlined above. He has not those mystical powers over his sister's son's land—those mystical powers which so often in tribal society are vested in the "submerged line," i.e. the line without jural rights.[23] In the situation, for example, of the matrilineal Trobrianders, Uberoi has shown out of Malinowski's own material that a father does not give to his son valuable articles in the great ceremonial circle of exchange only out of father-love, but principally because position in this circle of exchange takes the individual out of the solid corporateness of his lineage and interlinks him with individual trading partners in other lineages.[24] Significantly, as we shall see, among the

21. See Radcliffe-Brown, "The Mother's Brother in South Africa" (1923), reprinted in his *Structure and Function in Primitive Society* (1952).
22. Fortes, *Web of Kinship among the Tallensi* (1945), pp. 305 f.
23. Evans-Pritchard, *Kinship and Marriage among the Nuer* (1949), pp. 164–65.
24. Uberoi, *Politics of the Kula Ring* (1962), pp. 106 f.

Barotse, who had no unilineal descent groups, any kinsman had this right to take of his fellows' movable property. Chattels thus in practice break up the exclusiveness of corporations aggregate by drawing their individual members into other relationships. This means that links denoted by the transfer of chattels are socially as important as, and not less important than, links through immovable property. In some societies the apparently most significant groups have no base on the land, like Anglo-Saxon kindreds which claimed wergild, or the clans of the Plateau Tonga of Northern Rhodesia.[25]

The situation I have summarized all too briefly by these few citations is most sharply developed in double unilineal descent systems— systems in which there exist both patrilineal and matrilineal descent groups. These types of systems have been known to us for many years from South-West Africa, West Africa, the Sudan, and the South Seas. We owe our basic sociological understanding of how they work to Forde's work among the Yakö,[26] but since then substantial research has been carried out on several such systems.[27] In his recent *Death, Property and the Ancestors* (1962) Goody has specifically discussed the concept of property, in general and with specific reference to these systems.[28] In view of this accumulation of knowledge and analysis, it is hazardous for me here to attempt a summary of the complex situation and the variations in these systems. For my purposes I want only to draw attention to the fact that in many of these systems the one type of group formed by unilineal descent holds land and tends to be based on the land, which is inherited in that line, whereas the movables of a deceased member are distributed to relatives in the other line, as well as to other kin.

Goody[29] points out that a distinction in the rules of transmission of

25. See my *Politics, Law and Ritual in Tribal Society* (1965), Chap. 3.

26. Forde first reported on the Yakö in the 1930s, but see for this purpose, "Ward Organisation among the Yakö" (1950); other papers are cited in his most recent paper: "Death and Succession. An Analysis of Yakö Mortuary Ritual" (1962). These papers have recently been published together in book form (*Yakö Studies*, 1964, Oxford University Press for the International African Institute).

27. See Goody, "The Classification of Double Descent Systems" (1961). See also Schneider "Double Descent on Yap" (1962), and Schneider and Gough, *Matrilineal Kinship* (1961), for general and particular discussion there of these systems, passim. There is also a discussion of the political implications of one system in Harris, "The Political Significance of Double Unilineal Descent" (1962).

28. Especially Chap. 14.

29. Ibid., p. 295.

immovable and movable property by inheritance was characteristic of many early European societies. He argues[30] that

> Land is a focus of a multiplicity of interests; contiguity, for example, is everywhere a criterion of eligibility for membership in significant social groups. Furthermore, in settled societies, a hierarchy of interests can be built up more readily in land than in other objects of property that are simple to divide. Property in land is characteristically distributed in a series of aggregates of rights, known as estates of interest, held by different holders or holding groups in the society, and different segments of a lineage may have different interests in the same territory.

Often these rights cannot be sold, and this bar is buttressed by ritual beliefs. Goody compares this situation in tribal society with that in early England, where alienation was barred until it was introduced for purposes of the Church and even then was limited to the most superior kind of right, with restrictions on alienation persisting in other forms of tenure. He divides the rights that inhere in land into two analytic categories: those based on land as locality, being thus the basis of social organization, and those based on land as a productive resource. In both respects land is distinguished from movables, as in early Roman law *familia* (*res mancipi*) covered the land and those persons, instruments, and things essential to its use, while *pecunia*, chiefly herds not required for farming, were *nec mancipi*. Pecunia could be disposed of more freely, by alienation and then by testament. He notes that the property around which the corporation of the family was organized was thus protected, and quotes von Ihering: "The *familia* is fixed, stable, continuous; the *pecunia* is passing, changing, floating." Similarly, he says, in early Germanic law movable property could be dispersed by transmission through both sexes, but land was retained in male hands.

Goody[31] then discusses how among the Lodagaa, movables, starting with food, are exchanged to acquire other commodities (and nowadays money), which in their turn can be used "to acquire rights in persons, most commonly sexual rights," by the transfer of marriage payments. He does not seem to me to press far enough the point involved in his statement that "by throwing large feasts, or by more

30. Ibid., pp. 297 f.
31. Ibid., pp. 299 f.

direct forms of gift, food may be translated into hierarchical position of either a permanent or a temporary kind, that is, into rank or prestige." For it is characteristic of tribal societies that an enforced pattern of gift giving and feasting increases markedly the circulation of movables within the tribe, and perhaps among its neighbors,[32] so that in the absence of differentiated trade, people are in fact exchanging the same types of goods. These feasts and institutionalized gift giving exhibit what Pound might have called "a social interest" in the continual circulation of movables between occupants of landed positions in a particular hierarchy and members of other hierarchies. In the double-descent systems this interest appears in rules by which movables are distributed after death to the line that does not carry rights to inherit land and the social positions attached to it.

I am not of course suggesting that this was done by design; for whatever reasons they developed, these double-descent systems exhibit an efflorescence of a principle which I have exhibited by citations from other societies not thus organized. The situation appears most sharply among the pastoral Herero of South-West Africa, where matrilineal clans hold secular herds and the means of utilizing their products, while patrilineal clans, the cores of local groups, hold sacred herds for sacrifices to the ancestors and various sacred objects.[33] Here we see ritual and symbolic beliefs operating to make distinctions where none exists, and to exaggerate those distinctions that do exist, a process remarked on in my analysis of the Barotse theory of power. Through the social interest in accelerating the circulation of movables in societies which do not have sufficiently differentiated types of goods to link together occupants of landed positions in mutual interdependence, the law favors "artificial exchanges," and compels them in alterations of status relations, as we shall see subsequently. On the other hand, ritual and symbolic beliefs restrict the exchange of landed positions and their accompanying insignia. This refers to positions as "localities," fixed in relation to one another. These beliefs exaggerate the fixity of

32. For a classic study see Malinowski, *Argonauts of the Western Pacific* (1922), and Uberoi's analysis of these Trobriand data in *Politics of the Kula Ring* (1962). Mauss on *Essai sur de don* (1925) is still a leading theoretical analysis, but the most sophisticated treatment recently is Lévi-Strauss, *Les Structures élémentaires de la parenté* (1949). For a general discussion of the point made here in the text see Gluckman, *Politics, Law and Ritual in Tribal Society* (1965), Chap. 2.

33. Goody, *Death, Property and the Ancestors among the Lodagaa* (1962), citing Vedder, *South West Africa in Early Times* (1938) and Gibson, "Double Descent and its Correlates among the Herero of Ngamiland" (1956).

localities. That land as a productive resource is also involved is obvious, but this is not sufficient to account for the forms of law and ceremonial exchange. Both attributes must be looked at, as Goody insists. Hence Ifugao rice lands are ceremonially tranferred for they are linked to the political structure, but sweet potato lands merely change hands, for they are not.[34]

The difference between the two kinds of property, with reference to their contribution to processes of continuity, is well shown in two passages in Firth's account of the island of Tikopia. The first is:

> The device of giving permanent names to house-sites has provided the Tikopia with a most valuable mechanism for the preservation of social continuity. Houses decay, men perish, but the land goes on for ever. Hence whatever may be the vicissitudes of human groups, the dwelling-site name furnishes always a basis for the crystallization of kinship units in residential terms. Though the married pair who reside there may change their name in conformity with the needs of the political and religious organization, personal inclination, or the desire for children, the place is known as before. In European society it is the family name which tends to remain constant, whatever be the changes in the name of their house.[35] In Tikopia, the opposite obtains, a state of affairs apparently to be related with the small society which allows of an intimate personal knowledge of everyone, no matter what name they bear. The permanency of dwelling names, combined with that of orchard names, tends to emphasize that feeling to which every Tikopia gives expression now and again, of the stability of land compared with the human beings who inhabit it. . . . That the system of house-site names provides a useful basis of social continuity is recognized by the custom that such names are borne (with rare exceptions) by married people only, *i.e.* by those who are in a position to provide the offspring who will tend to perpetuate the situation.[36]

Tikopia is a very small island, but it contained then both some 1,300 people (at the time of Firth's first study) and a limited number of house-sites and orchards, water points, etc. Whatever the vagaries

34. Barton, *Ifugao Law* (1919), pp. 39 f.
35. I shall question this statement below, p. 138.
36. *We, the Tikopia* (1936), p. 86.

of demographic chance in the way of fertility and barrenness, of lives and deaths, this population has had to be fitted into the fixed landed positions in terms of an agnatic lineage structure (taking this as given); and Firth's study shows the "laws and customs" that achieve this end and the social continuity to which his Tikopia referred.

The other passage describes the distribution of movables at a death:

> Further light is thrown on the continuity of the family and the nature of the sentiments between its members by the customs of inheritance. On the death of the head of a household, the family property—mats, sinnet cord, bark-cloth, paddles, bowls, fish-hooks, and tobacco—is largely absorbed in the various ritual payments to the mother's family of the deceased and other mourners. Apart from this, goods go to his daughters in other households, since their children are the *tamu tapu* [daughters' and sisters' sons] of his and his sons. Land interests may also be transferred.[37] Some other goods remain with the sons, especially sinnet belts, clubs, spears, and ornaments which have been the property of the family ancestors. These are *tauarofa,* heirlooms, of which the history is known and which are not lightly given away.[38]

These citations from Firth, dealing with other problems, cogently state the contrast I am making. The law of property is here influenced by the same undifferentiated economic situation I have emphasized throughout, to exaggerate the distinction between immovable and movable property beyond the needs of the productive situation. In addition to the value of land as a main resource, social continuity through position on landed property, and above all on landed properties linked to others within the major social system, is protected and stabilized by law and by ritual. In Barotseland, major elements in the concept of the state are symbolized by where people sit in a hut, where huts are placed in a village, where edifices and objects are sited in the capital, and where councillors are seated on mats. Movables are encouraged by ritual and law to circulate as rapidly as possible, to set up cross-links between these positions.

The problem here is the general relation between a social structure,

37. Few plots were transferred in this line, and as population pressure on the land increased, fewer still (Firth, *Social Change in Tikopia,* 1959), pp. 158 f. This point is made by Meggitt, *The Lineage System of the Mae Enga* (1965), and in my "Foreword" to that book I discuss again some of Firth's data.
38. Firth, *We, the Tikopia* (1959), p. 180.

as a set of permanent social positions, and the personnel who flow through these positions and among whom there are ever-changing ties dictated by short-term interests and satisfactions. I believe that it is important to emphasize continually the difference between a house, the position of a householder, and the occupant of a house. Firth, in contrasting the Tikopia with European society (cited above), missed the point that, though we retain our family names, we also move through farms and houses, factories and offices, and schools and universities which do not change their names. In relations with neighbors an individual may be known by the name or number of house or farm. More importantly, it is in virtue of local position as a householder or tenant that a person acquires civic rights and duties—to vote, to serve on juries, to pay taxes, and to be assessed for other costs. Local position is also significant in many aspects of economic life. A vagrant, that social misfit, is a person of "no fixed address."

There is continuity in the position of a householder into modern times. Mr. Justice Oliver W. Holmes, Jr., spoke of the theory of succession to persons deceased as "founded upon a fictitious identification between the deceased and his successor." [39] He pointed out that this fictitious identification applies even *inter vivos,* for a right of way can be established if a succession of holders of property uses it adversely for a combined total of twenty years: "the heir has the advantage of sustaining his ancestor's *persona,* and the right is acquired," [40] even if the ancestor be not a lineal ancestor, but a predecessor in a landed position. For the sociological problem persists. As the Tikopia saw in their own system, in our society houses and factories, schools and offices, farms and railway lines, persist through the passage of generations. A factory is a factory whosoever holds its shares. It may persist through great social changes. The endurance of land and buildings, and how this endurance is related to constant changes of personnel, is a problem for investigation by students of tribal society because high ritualization of succession thrusts itself on them. Ritual to mark all changes of status has steadily died out, and with it ritualization of the transfer of the position of householder. But does the problem disappear for society and for sociological investigation in the industrial era?

At the same time the distinction between the two types of property

39. *The Common Law* (1881), p. 342.
40. Ibid., p. 353.

Plate 1. Barotse court at the king's capital, looking over backs of stewards, across the dais where the king sits when he is present, to the councillors-of-the-right.

Plate 2. A newly installed junior councillor-of-the-right, supported by adherents of his title and by his own relatives, gives the royal salute to the palace.

Plate 3. The late Mshiyeni, descendant of the great Zulu kings, adjudicates a disputed chieftainship (1938).

Plate 4. Matolana, of the Ndwandwe clan in Zululand, listens to evidence in his district court.

Plate 5. View of the Barotse plain in the dry season.

Plate 6. A Barotse plain village in the flood season.

Plate 7. The Barotse king's barge, followed by the barge of one of his queens, on their ceremonial voyage from dry-season to flood-season capital (1947).

Plate 8. The end of the voyage. The king's barge is farthest away; next is a barge carrying goods, then the barge with the national drum, then the dugout that led the voyage with the national spears. Note the varied headdresses of the paddlers.

Plate 9. Ceremonial voyage to Barotse dry-season capital. The ruling king's Ngambela beats one of the great national drums; the state Ngambela, in overcoat, captains the craft.

Plate 10. The king's band plays behind the shelter in which the king sits in his barge.

Plate 11. The Barotse Princess Chief, led by her xylophone and followed by her drums, walks from her palace to sit in court. On the right, her husband goes separately to sit at the head of her councillors-of-the-right.

Plate 12. The paddlers of the king's barge, on returning to the Barotse flood-season capital, break into the royal dance to the sound of the king's drums.

Plate 13. Men draw the great Barotse royal net up a branch of the Zambezi (see Chapter 6).

Plate 14. The royal net, attached to floating reed trays, is drawn through the water. Men in dugouts wait to stun fish which leap onto the trays.

Plate 15. A Barotse communal fishing battue in a privately owned pool. Each fisherman's catch is tagged by the owner (see Chapter 3).

Plate 16. A Barotse pool owner fencing off the waters to prevent the escape of fish.

is being reduced to the necessary minimum described in the long citation from Cheshire at the beginning of this chapter. Here perhaps not only changes in economy, but also possibly concomitant changes in familial structure have been significant. Maitland stated that the two systems of property law were really "two systems of inheritances, or if that phrase be incorrect, one law of descent and another law for the distribution of an intestate's goods and chattels. This is the one central, all-important fact from which the two systems diverge." At that time he pointed out that "the Statutes of Distribution, which, being but two centuries old, we may call modern, may not be perfect; but at least they start from the sound cognatic and 'gradualistic' principle, which is, as a matter of fact, the principle of the modern family." [41] He added too that "centuries have not sufficed to convince the people of England that the word 'heir' is quite inapplicable to personal property; they cannot or will not believe that we have two schemes of succession." [42] These passages on England's past might be applied to double-descent systems, and they exhibit the tenacity of ideas that fit the law of societies based on kinship alone. The power to devolve property by will eventually eliminates the persistence of these two systems of kinship ties, cutting across each other.

41. See Maitland, "The Law of Real Property," published first in the *Westminster Review*, 1879, and later in his *Collected Papers*, I (1911), 162–201.
42. Ibid., quotations from pp. 171, 179–80, 192.

Chapter 5

Ownership and the Technical Vocabulary of Barotse Jurisprudence[1]

IN HIS GREAT *History of English Law* Sir William Holdsworth says that primitive law has no technical vocabulary. This seems correct if we are thinking of a specialized vocabulary to define different kinds of rights and duties arising from the relations between individuals out of property holdings and out of contract and tort. The Barotse, for example, discuss most of their legal situations in terms of three main conceptions: *swanelo,* derived from a verb that can be translated as ought and which covers both right and duty; *mulatu,* which covers both fault or wrongdoing and debt; and *bung'a,* which may be reasonably translated as ownership. But Barotse jurisprudence is highly elaborated in its definition of various kinds of status. In addition there is a complex vocabulary to distinguish different kinds of property in terms of their significance in specific status relationships. Students of early English and feudal laws will immediately be reminded of their similar construction.

I shall examine here how the judges work with the very embracing concept bung'a to discuss disputes involving a variety of rights and obligations standing between persons. I have stated that bung'a can be reasonably translated as ownership, and its personal form, *mung'a,* as owner. I am sure that the reasonableness of this translation will emerge as I proceed, even though bung'a in Barotse law does not confer any absolute title and does not correspond exactly with our everyday conception of ownership. Mitchell,[2] among other anthropologists, has pointed out the difficulties in other Central African languages of

1. An earlier form of this chapter was published in the *American Anthropologist,* and I am grateful to the editor for permission to republish it in amended form. It was then published as a tribute to the memory of Paul Radin and his remarkable analyses of the ideas of tribal society. I gave it also as a Munro Lecture at Edinburgh University.

2. Mitchell, "The Yao of Southern Nyasaland" in Colson and Gluckman, ed., *Seven Tribes of British Central Africa* (1951) and *The Yao Village* (1956); also Mitchell (with Gluckman and Barnes), "The Village Headman in British Central Africa," *Africa,* 19 (1949), 89–106, reprinted in Gluckman, *Order and Rebellion in Tribal Africa* (1963).

translating the corresponding words by ownership and owner, and he himself uses "warden" when it applies to the leader of a group of kin. But this is an awkward word to use in relation to things. "Proprietor" has been suggested to me, but this has no advantages over owner. Both these words also lack, in addition, the great advantage of a verbal form. Owner comes from the Old English *aegen,* and a time when our legal concepts were more like those of Barotse law, and this lends some traditional sanction to using the word here.[3] I ask that difficulties of appropriate translation be borne in mind throughout.

The reason I had to invent a terminology in an earlier chapter to cover various rights in land was that the Barotse handle these with the single term mung'a, or more often with simple, possessive grammatical constructions. Yet we saw that rights in land, and obligations arising from its tenure, vary somewhat, and I showed how in Barotseland, as in most systems of law, rights to land and rights to chattels are handled very differently in the process of law, but both sets of rights are covered by the same term.

The apparent confusion that can arise from this use of a single term is shown in the following extract from the judgment of a court far from the capitals of the country.[4] A teacher at a rural school had quarreled with a number of immigrants from Portuguese Angola, and he had threatened to have them driven out of the country. The head of the court rebuked him: "This affair of driving the people out of the country—soil has no owner! Soil has one owner?—it is soil of the king." In this compressed phrasing the judge expressed astonishment that a man should speak as if there were no ultimate owner of the soil and the land who controls the rights of people to reside in the land; he asked rhetorically if a parcel of land can possibly be thought to belong to one person; and he then stated that all soil and land is the king's, and he stressed in this context that the king alone can drive a man out of the land, just as he alone can give people permission to settle on the land.

The third chapter describes the right of a citizen to be given land

3. Diamond (*Primitive Law,* 1935, at pp. 261 f.), states that "primitive law has no such conception as 'ownership.' It knows no name for the relation between a man and his goods." I cannot accept this. He adds that the word "ownership" was not found in English till 1583 according to the Oxford Dictionary, but that "own" is found as early as 888, though with the meaning "to take." He then considers words in a series of other languages. (See p. 169.)

4. Case reported in detail and analyzed in my *Judicial Process among the Barotse* (1955), pp. 71–76.

by the king, and how land throughout the kingdom is held in grant from the king in a large number of primary estates of administration by village headmen, who make further grants to their dependents. Land is thus in fact parceled out so that a hierarchy of rights exists over all parcels of land, a hierarchy of rights corresponding with the hierarchy of status in the political and social organization. In this series of holdings the Barotse regard the king as ultimate mung'a, owner, of all land. Judges emphasize this in many cases, as in this case of the teacher who threatened the Angolan immigrants. The manner in which the king's ownership is connected with the political system is shown in another rebuke by a judge to the teacher: "Do not talk of wretched Angolans: the Angolans have come here to strengthen our king, perhaps tomorrow they will surpass us in strengthening him." [5]

The king's obligations, arising from his ownership, are among his heaviest duties, to be discharged faithfully by the council. In 1942 the Barotse council worked British civil-service hours for Northern Rhodesia, where offices closed at 4 P.M., even if officers did not stop work then. I have heard the council adjourn a case which awaited only their judgment when the four o'clock drum was sounded, though the litigants came from a considerable distance. The principal occasion on which I observed the councillors continue in session after 4 P.M. was once when a suppliant came to ask them for land near the British settlement, so that he could cultivate vegetables for sale to the European residents. Land in this area is very valuable, since a market is near, and markets are scarce in Barotseland. The council could not find land for him. It offered him land in other places, and a prince volunteered to take him into his village. The suppliant refused; the councillors became angry and told him everyone wanted land near the settlement and that beggars cannot be choosers. But he insisted. They continued discussing the matter until evening, and then adjourned it till they could summon local councillors to ask these if vacant land was available.

In the total hierarchical series of holdings from king through holders of estates of administration to holders of estates of production, the Barotse describe everyone as a mung'a, an owner: king, royal or concilliar village head, village headman, villager, or villager's dependents. In different contexts king, prince, village headman, and villager are described as mung'a of the same garden.[6] This causes little confusion,

5. Ibid., p. 75.
6. Ibid., pp. 56–61.

for disputes are not normally over how the land was obtained but over how far status obligations have been fulfilled.[7] Yet cases do arise in which the title to land is not clear, and then the rights of commoners against the king himself may come under survey. In these circumstances, commoner may be called mung'a, owner, against the king. For example,[8] six men in 1942 complained to the court in the capital that their gardens had been taken from them by the two most senior stewards. Questioned, they said that the stalks of their last year's crops were still in the ground, and their cattle were staked in the gardens to manure the soil. They were told by the two senior stewards to remove their cattle. They said that the gardens had been taken for a prince from the far north who had come to work in a local store. They complained that the gardens were theirs and had been their fathers' and their grandfathers'. The stewards were not in the court, which was recording the complaint, but the head of the court explained that the prince had asked for gardens from the king, who had replied that he had none in the area. The prince pointed to these gardens, and the king replied that they belonged to the title of his senior steward and he could not take them. But the steward agreed to give them to the king, and both the prince and the steward gave the royal salute to the king to mark this transaction.

The second senior councillor in court objected: "The gardens are the steward's gardens-of-the-title (*masimu aluu*); he is not giving his own, we should have been consulted"—with the implication that the council owns rights over gardens-of-a-title. Some judges then said that they could not hear the case when the chief councillor, the Ngambela, "the owner of soil," was away on business in Livingstone. Others maintained that this would apply if people were begging for gardens, which could not be handled in the absence of the "owner of the soil," but this was a complaint by people turned out of their gardens, and there was the problem of whether they could continue to cultivate. It was finally decided that the issue was being prejudged in the absence of the defendants, and a summons was sent to the two stewards to appear in court that afternoon. But the judges continued to discuss the case; they seemed to know that the complainants and their ancestors had cultivated these gardens for many years, and referred with astonishment to the eviction of the "owners" from the gardens. When the complainants explained that they had refused to take out their

7. Ibid., pp. 37–43, 178–87. And see above, pp. 12 f., 103–04, 143.
8. Reported in full, ibid., pp. 102–03.

cattle, a senior councillor approved: "Be strong." The plaintiffs said that they did not quarrel with the prince and stewards because they knew these were lords: "We did not get carried away with anger. Now, a week afterward, we are bringing our complaint to the Malozi" [Barotse]. They were then told to wait till afternoon, but judges continued to discuss the gardens and their history, which some knew, and to cite decisions in similar cases, all to the effect that people could not be turned off the soil of their forefathers.

In the afternoon the senior steward, sitting with the other litigants, said he knew nothing of the gardens. They had been pointed out to him when he was installed as gardens of his title, by certain appointed persons, who should be called as witnesses. He did not know what he was being sued for, since he was not taking the gardens for himself, but only giving them on the king's gift. Fearful of a fine, he insisted that he was not claiming ancestral land. The head of the court said the witnesses should be summoned and taken to a senior councillor, lest the steward corrupt them; upon which the judges commented that a corrupted witness can answer three or four questions, but then surely breaks down. The head of the court instructed the other judges not to discuss the case lest the litigants should feel it had been prejudged. In fact the case never came up again; the plantiffs were confirmed in their holding as owners of the gardens (i.e. as estates of production within the estate of administration of the steward's title).

We see then that in this case where the king was trying to resume rights of administration and disposal over specific gardens of his closest steward's title, he had to beg the steward for them, and the ultimate ownership (bung'a) of the king in all land, as well as his rights in the title's ownership in these gardens, were irrelevant. The council as a whole, and various members, referred to the chief councillor (Ngambela) as owner of the soil because his courts distribute land and protect the rights of the subjects, and one judge by implication referred to the whole council's own rights to control redistribution of gardens of its constituent titles. The senior steward might also, as holder of the title of senior steward, be owner of gardens attached to it; but the holders of the estates of production in the gardens are also owners who have to be protected in their rights.

Similarly, if a prince claims the power to take over a garden in a village attached to his title, when the garden is being held and cultivated by one of the villagers, the villager will be held to be the mung'a unless he has so neglected his duties that he can be expelled from his position in the village and his garden. Then only will the prince be declared the owner.[9] If another village headman claims that the garden belongs to his village, the prince will or will not be held to be owner against him, depending on the facts. In short, application of the term mung'a to a garden depends on the context of dispute; in any particular case the term is applied to the person who has the stronger claim.

A man is compelled to give each of his wives at least one garden of reasonable size or she can claim a divorce, but a wife does not transmit rights in her garden to her heirs—not even to her children by her husband as against his children by other wives, as is the case in South African tribes. When a Barotse man dies, any gardens he has allocated within his own estate to his children remain theirs, and his heir cannot expropriate these gardens. But his heir can take over the gardens allotted to the deceased's wives, and the heir has power to redistribute these gardens as he pleases. All a widow can claim is half the crops she grew on land given her by her husband. Thus a wife's rights differ fundamentally from the rights held by persons in the social hierarchy which I have so far described. A husband remains mung'a of a garden that he allots to his wife, in view of his rights in it. He can dispossess her, and she cannot sue for the garden as can a villager if he or she is dispossessed by the headman. All the wife can do is to assert that her husband, by stripping her of her garden, has ceased to treat her as a wife, and therefore she sues for divorce. Yet in a case of this kind the judges will refer to the wife as mung'a of the garden, even though they will not restore it to her. In speaking thus, they are stating that as a wife she has claims on the garden against her husband, and if he does not recognize his obligations to accept her "ownership" she is entitled to a divorce.[10]

The word mung'a does not cover all rights in land. In Barotseland, arable land cannot be sold, leased for rent, pledged or mortgaged (though there is sharecropping of fishing sites). Arable land can be lent freely, and a borrower of land is described by a separate term. But a borrower of land is the only type of person who, aside from the

9. For such a case, see my *Judicial Process among the Barotse*, p. 152, where the rights of a princess' people to control heirship to titles in her village are also involved.

10. Gluckman, "Kinship and Marriage among the Lozi of Northern Rhodesia and the Zulu of Natal" (1950).

king, does not assert his rights to land in terms of status relationship with a superior mung'a. If he can make this assertion, then he claims to be a mung'a, and I have records of cases of borrowers who claimed that, by virtue of the generous way in which they had treated the lender of the land, they had entered into the equivalent of a kin relationship, so that the lender had lost the power to reclaim his land.[11] In the cases I heard, the claimants were unsuccessful.

To repeat, the Barotse describe the person who has the strongest claim on a piece of land in a particular case as the mung'a; therefore when king or another person is judged mung'a of a piece of land, the judges are not asserting that he has any exclusive power over the land, nor are they denying that other persons have enforceable claims on the land. The successful contestant is only mung'a in relation to another contestant. In the course of adjudicating on a dispute the judges do not have to inquire into the nature of the rights held by the contestants; their main inquiry is into the status relationship between the ligitants and, once they determine this, they know what rights are involved, and they can enter on an inquiry into the titles of the litigants in terms of how the land was granted or inherited. For, as shown in Chapter 3, title to land arises from relationships between persons. The inquiry may then lead to an investigation into how far the parties have respectively fulfilled their obligations to each other. But throughout, the judges are able to work with a single term, mung'a, to cover a series of different rights: the elaboration of their jurisprudence is in the definition of status. For them there is a specific kind of relationship between particular people and a particular type of land, or indeed a particular type of product; and if a dispute arises, determination of the status of the parties immediately clarifies the forensic issues.

Barotse terminology is secondarily elaborated in the naming of special kinds of gardens or other property. Thus if the king gives a garden to a man he has no claim on its products, beyond a general claim to a certain amount of tribute. But the king has also special gardens of his own called *namakao* (royal gardens), which are worked by the people of a neighborhood. The king has the right to take of these crops but he cannot do so inordinately, for those who look after the gardens are also owners of it, and they may take freely, but reasonably, of the crops. Indeed, any traveler who is hungry may take

11. E.g. my *Judicial Process among the Barotse* (1955), pp. 62–64.

sufficient to sustain himself from the edge of the garden, for the nation is also owner of the royal gardens; and the king is not entitled to protect his gardens magically against thieves as ordinary cultivators are. This ban also applies to all members of the royal family and to the most senior councillors.

Similarly, a distinction is made in naming the gardens which a man reserves for himself (though they are worked by his wives) and the gardens which he allots to his wives for them to work for themselves. As we have seen, a widow or divorced woman is entitled to take half the crops of the garden given to her, and if she dies her own kin can claim this half against the husband. This is in the *simu yamusali*, the garden of the wife. But the wife, upon widowhood or divorce, or her kin upon her death, cannot claim the crops of a garden which the husband has reserved for himself under the name *simu yasolume*, the male garden, even if she helped cultivate it. In addition, a husband can use crops of the male garden as he pleases, save for a general imprecise right of each wife to some support from these crops and a more precise right of each wife to equal treatment with other wives in this support. But a husband can use crops from a wife's garden for himself only by her permission; he cannot take of them for other wives, and he must call on the crops of all wives equally for his support.

A man can give a new wife part of his male garden. He cannot give a new or old wife part of a garden he had allotted to another wife, without the latter's permission. The crops from these different gardens go into different granaries, and a wife can claim divorce if her husband so much as looks into her own granary. Yet husband, like wife, may be called mung'a of garden and of crops; and if a husband neglects to support his wife from crops grown by her in his male garden, the court will ask whether she is not also mung'a of this garden and its crops. In all these cases the sanction is that the wife will be granted a divorce.

Though they make these distinctions between types of gardens, the Barotse have not refined the general term, ownership, which describes the various rights that the different parties hold in these gardens and their crops. Thus there is no vocabulary of reversionary, contingent, concurrent, concomitant, qualified, etc. rights. Both husband and wife have bung'a (the abstract form of mung'a) in each other's garden, just as king and headman and villager have bung'a in a single garden. The Barotse thus recognize only one general relation between a person and land—the relation of bung'a—except for the rights of a borrower. This relation of bung'a is not a simple definition of an individual's claim to land; rather, it defines the rights and duties of a person occupying a specific social position of status as part of a complex of rights and duties held in the same land by other persons occupying related social positions. These rights are relative and specific to persons and disputes, but they are all defined by a single term. Thus bung'a defines all stabilized relations between persons and land, from which people cannot be expropriated without altering their social positions. For example, if the husband expropriates his wife, she ceases to be his wife, and a headman can expropriate a villager only if the villager has behaved so badly to him as to deserve expulsion from the village. These stabilized relations to land can all be called by one term, without resultant confusion, for if the rights inhering in them come under review in court, the judges have to investigate the relative social positions of the litigants—king and subject, headman and villager, husband and wife. Cases first are inquiries into social positions and this immediately clarifies the kinds of rights and duties involved, and there is no confusion if all are described by a single term. Within the inquiry into social positions, which sets the context of trial, the court has to establish the facts: whether the garden was allotted, and by whom, and to whom. Here, as between husband and wife, confusion might arise, and there are specific terms to define two different kinds of gardens. Similarly, the rights of a man in a garden derived from his political position are basically the same as his rights in a garden derived from his position in a kinship group. But rights of other persons in these gardens vary, and the gardens of political positions have special names. Nevertheless, here again rights are fixed by speaking of one person as mung'a as against particular contestants.

We are already in a position to see that Holdsworth was wrong if he meant that "primitive" legal systems lack any refined and developed vocabulary, even if their terminology for types of rights and duties be relatively simple. It is true, on the Barotse evidence, that there may be only one major term to define relations between persons and property, but there is a complex vocabulary in the Law of Persons. This follows from Maine's description of the domination of status in early law. We can add that there is a complex vocabulary to define different kinds of property. That is, in the situation of Barotse law there are no terms to differentiate precisely relationships between a person and other persons and things, as Holdsworth emphasized more generally; but the definition of these relationships is implicit in the terms for social positions considered in relation to one another and in the names of things themselves.

The implications of this situation can be pushed farther. The essence of the Barotse legal situation is an interest in the Law of Persons, in how people related to each other in terms of status discharge their obligations to each other. People acquire rights in land in virtue of their status, as citizens, as villagers, and as kinsfolk. They can maintain their rights only if they discharge faithfully their status obligations: the recalcitrant villager who merits expulsion from the village thereby loses rights in land. Hence when we consider property rights, we find that what is critical in Barotse jurisprudence are rights over, and obligations to, other persons in relation to land and chattels. Property is important in status: this emerges clearly when we examine Barotse ownership of titles and other privileges.

I have described the three sets of councillors who constitute the Barotse council: the commoners, save for the royal sanctuary, who represent the nation on the king's right hand; the stewards who represent the king on his left hand; and the royal family in front of him. Commoner councillors and stewards, and to some extent princes and husbands of princesses, do not sit merely as individuals: each of them holds a title that occupies a specific position in the ranked hierarchy of the council. If a councillor or steward dies, or is promoted or discharged, a new incumbent is selected who assumes the title and sits in its traditional position, for the ranking of the titles is fixed by the historical development of the Barotse nation. Titles were created by certain kings, and some titles represent important events in Barotse history. Thus history is deposited, one might say, in the order of seating in the council, like fossils in a series of geological strata.[12]

The present incumbent of any title is most commonly and emphatically described as the mung'a of the title, but other persons and groups, both superior and subordinate, may in certain situations be called mung'a of the title against the incumbent, if he defaults in his duties to them. For every title is a nexus between many different social positions, whose incumbents are bound to render duties to, and

12. See my *Administrative Organization of the Barotse Native Authorities* (1943) and "The Lozi of Barotseland in North-Western Rhodesia" (1951).

may exercise rights against, one another. Any of these positions may
therefore be called mung'a of the title, depending on whose rights or
duties are being emphasized. Thus in a case where the children of a
titled headman had assaulted a villager, and had been supported by
their father, the senior judge said to them: "You live in a village of
the king, it is not your own village . . . The title of your father,
Saywa, is not a title that belongs to your family, and you need not
think that you will inherit it." [13] Here the judge was emphasizing the
right of two owners in the title Saywa as against the incumbent: first,
the ownership of the king, and second, the ownership of the villagers.
For the incumbent of the title Saywa owes duties to the king and to
his villagers; and it is to their right to demand fulfillment of the
incumbent's obligations to them that the Barotse ascribe bung'a—
ownership. Normally the incumbent of such a title is called *mung'a
libizo* (owner of the name), because of his rights to the title itself and
to its property, including its demands on the duties of others. Rights
of ownership in a title may therefore be vested in several positions and
persons.

The number of positions which are held to be owners of a title
depends on its importance. All titles of authority critically have three
owners: the incumbent, the king, and the subordinates of the title.
The ownership of the incumbent is that he may use it as his name and
administer its property; his property includes rights against the king
and claims on its subordinates. The king's ownership is his power to
appoint or discharge incumbents and his claim on the incumbent's
services with those of all subordinates. The subordinates' ownership is
their power to demand that the incumbent fulfill the duties of his
office. Many more social positions have holdings in the kingship itself,
besides the ruling king: the dead kings through their representative
councillors, the royal family, the national council, the nation at large.
For the ruling king has obligations to all of them: hence Barotse say
these "own" the king. And they speak of the king, as he himself
does—and indeed the British of their monarch also—as *mutanga wasi-
caba,* slave (servant) of the nation.

Again, in addition to the incumbent of the title Ngambela—who is
chief councillor of the nation—king, council, nation at large, a large
number of special adherents of the title, and members of a political
unit attached to him, may all be called owners (*beng'i*) of this title.

13. See my *Judicial Process among the Barotse* (1955), pp. 83–90.

Which ownership will be emphasized depends on the situation. Thus where the council was appointing a successor to a junior title, the head of the political unit concerned told me of the selected man: "We were worried about his drinking beer, but the Princess Mbuywana and the people of her district, the owners of the title, want him." But a few minutes later he described himself, and then the council as a whole, and then the king, as owners of the title.

Another interesting use of mung'a which I recorded, occurred when I traveled to the southern capital with a prince, son of a king who had reigned, in my entourage. After the litigants in a case had presented their pleas, the head of the court called on the prince: "Here is a dispute, enter it." The prince replied, "I'm a stranger here," and the court clerk, also a prince, said: "You a stranger!—don't say that. You own the capital." The head of the court capped him: "Yes, no prince is a stranger here." [14]

It may seem that I am merely stating at some length that the Barotse say of anyone who is interested in some office or piece of land, that he has a right in it. But what I am trying to emphasize is that the Barotse work with a single conception of ownership of rights, as entailing corresponding obligations, because all land and all titles are involved in a complex of social relationships—a complex of statuses, to follow Maine's terminology. In a society at this stage of development, where most transactions occur between persons already related by status, the law is interested in property as an incident of a social relationship, in addition to the property's material value. To enable social relationships to endure, the law stresses the obligations to other persons involved by the holding of a piece of property, even beyond its stress on claims to rights over the property. The series of rights of ownership over property constitute an essential part of the status structure of the society; rights in property, and obligations to use property generously thus define the social relationships themselves. Each piece of property, land or title or chattel, may be a link in a complex set of relationships between people who are bound to one another permanently.[15]

14. Ibid., p. 152.
15. Leach (*Pul Eliya*, 1961, p. 305) has recently written: "I want to insist that kinship systems have no 'reality' at all except in land and property. What the social anthropologist calls kinship structure is just a way of talking about property relations which can also be talked about in other ways." This statement is made in apparent contrast with statements he believes summarize the works of other anthropologists. In my opinion, these summaries

I exhibit this point further in considering royal property. The main capitals of the nation, both northern and southern, are laid out on a set plan. There is a palace within a fence, and in the fenced area, in specific positions in relation to one another, are the king's house, the shed of royal drummers, the altar, the hut of the privy council, and the private storehouse of the king. Across a sacred open space in front of the palace stands the council house. The national council is seen by Barotse as opposed to the king. Every royal storehouse, every titled queen's house, every councillor's house, has a fixed site, as have royal granaries, sheds for royal canoes, and so on. Each of these edifices, containing special objects, has its praise song containing historical lore and proverbial wisdom. Wherever the king travels, his camp is set out on this pattern; and when the several rulers of Barotseland assemble, as in 1946 to greet King George VI, they camp in relation to one another in the respective directions of their capitals; within each royal camp edifices are erected as in the home capital. Here, I think, is shown how the rights of specific persons to build in certain places—their rights of ownership—form a complex exhibiting the structure of the political system. Thus it is hardly surprising that I have even heard Barotse speak of a building, a barge, or other material object as the "owner" of a special position, and therefore of the person whose social position is connected therewith.

The significance of bung'a, as defining rights and obligations within a complex of status relationships, emerges also in the distinction which Barotse make between what we may call "tribute" (ng'amba) and "kingly things" (zasilena).[16] This distinction shows the capacity of the Barotse to elaborate legal distinctions and the fact that they do this by giving different names to various types of property. Under their protectorate treaty with the British, the Barotse kings abandoned their rights to demand tribute from their subjects. In 1941 the king claimed that "tribute," the word used in the Treaty, which was writ-

---

do not accurately represent their analyses. The meaning of Leach's assertion is not clear to me; it does not cover how rights to property are acquired through status or transmitted by descent, and distributed at marriage, etc. He seems here to have struck the phenomenon I am trying to analyze; but sweeping criticisms of his colleagues lead him to a one-sided presentation, which I consider obscures the problem instead of clarifying the role of property in kinship relations, as against the use of idioms of property and kinship. Contrast Evans-Pritchard's clear statement of the issue in *The Nuer* (1940), p. 89, cited below, pp. 167–68.

16. For a fuller description see my *Essays on Lozi Land and Royal Property* (1943), pp. 78 f.

ten in English, did not cover his rights to one tusk from all elephants killed in the country and to hides of hippopotami.

I was asked to investigate this, and found that the Barotse made a sharp distinction between the king's power to levy imposts on all subjects for certain annual payments of grain and other products (fish, honey, cattle, canoes, hoes, spears, axes, etc.) and the king's claim on parts of certain wild animals. These were one tusk of an elephant, parts of a hippopotamus, lion skins and lion manes, leopard skins, genet skins, eland tails, lecwe antelope, blue-monkey skins, and a number of other things. They called the regular imposts on all products *ng'amba,* and I feel this is correctly translated as tribute. But they call the specific parts of wild animals, all which have to be rendered to the king, *zasilena*—literally, "things of kingship." (These rights are like the British monarch's rights to wild swans, and to sturgeon and whales caught in coastal waters, in which the monarch has what Halsbury called "a qualified ownership." [17]) The Barotse cited to me eleven different ways in which tribute and kingly things were distinguishable.

1. They are named differently, and everyone knows the difference.

2. Some things are designated as kingly things, and everyone knows which they are.

3. Tribute was rendered compulsorily and failure to bring it was punished; people were not compelled to seek for kingly things, but if they were lucky enough to kill a royal animal they had to bring the designated portions to the capital under threat of severe punishment. That is, production and bringing of tribute was compelled, kingly things were obtained by choice and chance.

4. Tribute was part of what people produced in these goods; everything designated as a kingly thing had to be brought to the king.

5. People could themselves freely use the kinds of things they brought as tribute; they could use only some of the kingly things and then only by special generosity and permission of the king.

6. Tribute goods could be used to pay fines and compensation, but kingly things could not be used thus.

17. Lord Halsbury, *Laws of England,* 7 (1909), pp. 216–17.

7. Rewards for killing fierce kingly animals were given from tribute goods.

8. Tribute was given back to the people in great quantities; on the whole kingly things remained at the capital, mainly with the royal family and very important councillors.

9. Others besides the king shared in tribute before its redistribution: princes and princesses, queens, great councillors. On its way to the king some tribute was stolen by councillors and the king's attendants, and when it was being distributed in council, jesters used to "steal" from it. All kingly goods went to the king and were used on his instructions.

10. It was mainly the subject tribes who brought tribute, for the work of the dominant Lozi themselves for the royal family was not classed thus. But if a Lozi killed a royal animal, he had to render the kingly parts to the king.

11. They stressed particularly that the procedures for handling tribute and kingly things were entirely different.

When tribute was brought to the capital, it was set down outside at a special spot and left for the night. During the night part of the tribute (now given a special name, *bumbuyi*) was taken for the king to his Mushukula storehouse. In the morning, the rest was taken to the council house, and a further portion was taken for the king to his Nateyo storehouse—the only royal storehouse which is also described as in the ownership of the council as a whole as well as in the ownership of the king. First shares went to a special priest who alone makes sacrifice on behalf of the nation to God, then shares to certain councillors in special order, and some perhaps to a prince who had a claim on the tribute bringers involved. Finally, the king distributed the balance among all the people present because, say the Barotse, "the nation is owner of tribute." Here again nation, and the king, senior councillors, priest and prince, are all called owners of the tribute. The king's warrior attendants and court jesters could steal from the tribute, for they were owners of the tribute also, in view of their right of privileged license in the capital.

Kingly things were handled quite differently. The hunter who had killed the animal brought the relevant part to the head of his political sector in the capital, who informed the chief councillor. The hunter then took the goods to the steward of the royal storehouse (there were five royal storehouses) to which he was personally attached. Thence all kingly things went to Mushukula storehouse (where the night tribute goes), save for lion skins which were publicly exhibited in the council house and then went to Nateyo storehouse, and leopard skins which went after exhibition to Kamona storehouse, the only storehouse standing in the Palace itself. But the killer of an elephant came into the capital with a party firing guns and took portions of the elephant straight to the king's hunting shrine, Lioli, in the palace courtyard, where the sacred spears of the nation are kept. After being thus deposited, various kingly goods were used in quite specific ways, which I have no space to detail. I mention only that lion skins and manes were used to dress councillors at certain ceremonies, so that some councillors told me they were not kingly things at all—not *zasilena*, but *zamulonga*, things of government. They were exhibited in Nateyo, the storehouse of the council as well as one of the storehouses of the king— the storehouse in fact that is a sanctuary from the king.

The Barotse thus differentiate kingly goods from tribute, and then further differentiate each type of goods in that category, by the whole concatenation of social relationships and institutions of which each is a part. They look at the path of authority along which it is rendered to the king, the storehouse to which it goes, the way it is disposed of, and so forth, as well as at the king's right to demand it and the subjects' duty to render it. Ownership of these goods is highly specific in its definition, in terms of its significance as a nexus between social positions and institutions. This being so, the single word ownership (bung'a) is used to cover the rights of everyone.

This implication of ownership in Barotse law can be exhibited vividly in the ownership of hippopotami. Living hippo are considered to be the property of the king but, before they were protected in 1942, any subject had the privilege of killing hippo anywhere save in designated reserves. However, immediately a hippo was killed, rights of ownership by the king, the chief councillor, other councillor-titles, and hunter, and nation, vested in different parts of the carcass. First, in the past it was taboo to skin a hippo unless the king ordered this be done to make whips. Now, when hippo hides are valuable, all hippos are skinned. The hippo was cut up, and divided as follows: the king was given the meat from both sides of the chest, the corner of the mouth, the chin and lower lip, between the ribs, the chest and belly, the two hindlegs and one foreleg, and all the fat; the chief councillor (the Ngambela) was given the right ribs, the meat of the right loins, the tripe, and the inner stomach; the private Ngambela of the king (Solami), and the Ngambela of the Ngambela in his own political sector (Imandi), shared the left ribs and loins; and the hunter took one foreleg, the bowels, and the strip of meat from the tail to the nose. Notice that these two councillors are specially linked to king and Ngambela.

The king's share had to be disposed of according to special rules: Half the stomach was cooked in Newa storehouse, and half in Mush-ukula storehouse, and taken to the Palace to be eaten by the king and his wives and children. The inner meat between the ribs and a hindleg were cooked in Nateyo storehouse (the storehouse of the council and hence of the nation) and then taken to the council house where it was eaten by the councillors and all the people present. This meat should not be taken home but should be finished in the council house. One day I heard the senior councillor, before dividing hippo meat in the council, summon all the men in the capital till they filled the house. He said that though there were so many of them, they must each have a piece, even if only to get a taste, for that was the law. I was not given any, and one of my attendants complained bitterly to me that this spoiled the division: therefore he had broken the law and brought a piece home for me.

The Barotse usually describe two persons as owners (beng'i) of the slain hippo: the king and the hunter. The chief councillor and the two other councillors who get special portions are added afterward as own-ers of their specific portions. That is, the king and the hunter stand in a masterful relation to the hippo as a whole, and both derive prestige, though of different kind, from this general ownership. In addition, they and the three councillors have rights to special portions, but the king is obliged to dispose of parts of his portion in special ways.

The Barotse do not normally discuss rights to a hippo in these terms of ownership. What is significant for them is the statement of social positions involved in the division of the hippo: the relations among king, council, special titles, hunter, and nation. Ownership of the specific portions is important and is emphasized as demonstrating these relations. Therefore their descriptions of ownership invariably include an account of the way in which the meat is ceremonially handled—what storehouse each part is cooked in, and where and by whom it is eaten. They are concerned with the meat not as property of which someone is master or owner, but as property that binds social positions and persons in institutionalized links. They have no need to define types of ownership or types of rights, and the single word mung'a indicates all positions with claims in the institutional framework.

Rights and duties involved in titles, in tribute, and in kingly things bring out sharply the dominant interest of Barotse law in status relationships and the elaboration of their jurisprudence about social positions and different kinds of property. Other scholars have made the same point in studying tribal economics. The situation is well summarized by Firth[18] in his study of the economy of Tikopia, a small and isolated Polynesian island:

> From the transactions in labour and goods I have described, it emerges that there are at least three separate series of exchanges, or spheres of exchange, the goods in which are not completely convertible into those of the other series. At the lowest level is the food series. Small objects such as arm-rings, small services such as the loan of a canoe, non-specialist labour of taro planting, paddling, or ordinary timber working are paid for by food. Gifts of food, whether raw or cooked, are returned in kind, though not necessarily in the same state. On the next level is the bark-cloth sinnet series. Payment for timber, for bowls, coco-nut grating stools, or specialist skill in canoe or house-building, damage to valuable tools, the unauthorised use of a canoe, and in some circumstances payment for a ritual presentation, is made in one or other of these items (the sinnet here is of the ordinary light kind). Attached to this series is the pandanus mat which is its highest expression. The third and most important series from the point of view of utility of the goods, though not from the frequency of the transactions, is that including bonito-hooks, turmeric cylinders, and canoes. The objects and services in these three series cannot be completely expressed in terms of one another, since normally they are never brought to the bar of exchange together. [Nor can they be often substituted, save temporarily, for one another.] But generally, it can be said that the social context is different in each case. The services of a burial party at the death of a chief or the son of a chief are of a complicated kind charged with high emotional significance, and though

18. *Primitive Polynesian Economy* (1939), pp. 340 f.

compensated for by economic goods could not be paid for only in
bark-cloth and food, the types of goods by which specialist and
non-specialist skill are rewarded. In other contexts again, obligations which are satisfied by bark-cloth or sinnet cannot be met
simply by an increase in the amount of food handed over. Each
kind of object is appropriate to a particular kind of social situation.

And each social situation is defined by the status relationships
between those who take part in it. Other studies also vouch for this
restriction of types of property to particular sets of relationships, each
of which is hence in some respects defined in terms of the property
appropriate to it.[19]
   Among the Barotse, all these forms of property are discussed in terms
of ownership, and it seems that the position is not dissimilar in other
tribes. Firth was told about the peculiar position of the bonito hook
given by a chief in Tikopia: "If a commoner has a good tree for a
canoe growing on his land . . . and a chief desires it, the man may be
unwilling to part with it. But if the chief presents him with a bonito-
hook his objection vanishes. I was told that he will hold the hook
among his treasures, but he will not term it his; it is held as 'the
property of the chief.'" Nor will he ever hand it to another commoner, but at the death of a chief and the accession of his heir he may
present it to the new ruler. If a commoner has a bonito hook not given
him by a chief, he can use it to exchange for a canoe.[20] Yet here, as in
Barotse, it is the social relationships centering on property which are
of interest to the people, and these social relationships define all legal
and forensic issues. There are no distinctions between general kinds of
rights and duties: indeed the Barotse have but one word in most
common use to cover both right and duty, derived from a verb we
can translate as "ought."[21]
   These principles involved in holding land and titles and in distribut-

   19. The recent study by Goody, *Death, Property and the Ancestors* (1962, pp. 286 f.)
has a good account of what he calls "the circulation of objects in different non-communicating
systems of exchange." He cites other authorities, as does Firth (preceding footnote). An
account by Bohannan describes well the three circles of exchange among the Tiv of Nigeria
("Some Principles of Exchange and Investment among the Tiv," 1955).
   20. *Primitive Polynesian Economy* (1939), pp. 338–39.
   21. Gluckman, *The Judicial Process among the Barotse* (1955), pp. 166 f., and see Chap. 1
above.

ing tribute and kingly things apply also to holding chattels and to rights over and against persons. After land, the most valuable Barotse possession is cattle. Although some cattle are more or less owned outright by one person (I shall explain the meaning of this statement), many cattle are subject to a complex of rights of ownership by groups and individuals. For example, when a man marries a presumed virgin he has to hand her kin two cattle as *sionda* (marriage payment).[22] If he does not, she is not his wife. She is his wife whether he makes the payment to a representative of her father's or her mother's kin. Provided he gets her from, and makes a gift to, an apparently accredited guardian with whom she is living, he meets his legal obligations. As far as he is concerned, her kin are not differentiated. The first beast is payment for the girl as his wife, the second is for her untouched fertility. Should he divorce her and she has not conceived, he is entitled to recover the second beast and its progeny. This is therefore called "the beast of herding" (*komu yabulisana*); i.e. the bride's people merely herd it for the husband until he has impregnated their "daughter." They have the right to hold it and to sue for it, but it is not theirs, it is still the husband's, though he cannot claim it without divorcing his wife. Nor may he slaughter it.

Whichever side of the bride's family receives the two beasts, should give one to the other side. Within each side, if he slaughters the beast, the recipient should divide the meat among his kinsfolk, including the bride who draws from both sides, as do her full brothers and sisters, since they belong to father's kin and to mother's kin. The maternal kin can sue the paternal kin for their share, and vice versa, although I never heard of an action in court on this issue. "It would ruin kinship," say the Barotse; and the only sanction in fact used by an aggrieved group is to refuse to aid the others if troubles arise in the marriage. They say: "We know nothing of this marriage."

Within each group of the bride's kin, the recipient should divide the meat among his kin, if he slaughters the beast. Different kinsmen are entitled to specific portions of the beast; the bride, for example, gets the tongue, "for is she not the owner of the beast since she brought it to the village?" But these claims by other kin against the recipient are not enforceable at law; they are moral claims only.

---

22. Gluckman, "Kinship and Marriage among the Lozi of Northern Rhodesia and the Zulu of Natal" (1950), pp. 193 f.; £2 may be paid instead. For clarity, I discuss only payment in cattle.

Three points about the legal ownership of the "beast of herding" emerge.

1. As far as the husband is concerned, payment to any one of the bride's kin is payment to all and gives him conjugal rights. But on divorce he can sue only the person he paid for return of this beast and its progeny.

2. Once any of the bride's kindred receives the marriage payment, the two groups are differentiated into her father's and her mother's kin, and each has a legal right to half the payment.

3. Within each of these groups there is a further division in which the other group is not concerned, but claims are not legally enforceable.

If the payment is £2 instead of two beasts, the principles of division are similar.

Therefore "ownership" of marriage cattle consists in a complex arrangment of rights. The second beast remains the husband's until his bride is impregnated, but he cannot claim it, and the bride's kin hold it against the world. All her kin have varying claims on the two beasts; all are owners of the beast and so is the bride herself.

If the bride is not a virgin, only one beast is given. If it is killed by the person who received it, he should share the meat with the bride's kin on both sides according to fixed rules. If the beast is kept to breed, say by the father of the bride, he must give the mother's family the first and then all alternate calves. Thus he owns the beast but not all its offspring. The court will enforce these claims against him.

The rules for distribution of the marriage payment, here given in simple form, show how a chattel may be subject to a cluster of rights which define relationships within the kinship system. Again, all rights may be defined as the ownership of any interested party in opposition to others within the context of a particular dispute. Now it would obviously be possible, and also I believe valuable, for a Western lawyer to classify the different rights which various persons have in the marriage payment beasts under terms from our own law. Thus I suppose we might say that the husband remains owner of the beast of herding, whereas the bride's kin and the bride hold it in trust, perhaps as a gage, until the fruitfulness of the marriage is established, when ownership vests in them. The rights of the rest of the bride's kin and the bride may be a form of joint ownership, or each may have a contingent lien on specific parts of the meat, if the animal is killed, or on its progeny if it is not. As stated above, rights might be classified as concomitant, concurrent, reversionary, qualified, etc.

Obviously this sort of classification would read doctrines into Barotse law that do not exist there, though it would clarify the structure of that law and enable us to make comparative analyses. What I want to bring out here, however, is how the structure of the Barotse social system, with its emphasis on status, is related to the ideas of Barotse jurisprudence. In considering the ownership of marriage cattle, Barotse lawyers cannot think only of the relation between an individual and a beast or a part of its carcass; they are concerned with the whole concatenation of interdependent status relationships which are focused on the transaction setting up the marriage, and thereafter on the marriage itself. Hence two kinds of rights are sufficient to clarify the issues: bung'a, ownership, and bulisana, herding. And the bride's kin, till she becomes pregnant, are only herdsmen as against the husband, who is owner; against the rest of the world, the bride's kin are owners.

A similar concatenation of rights is revealed in the herding of royal cattle, which have a specific name, *zambuwa*. The king used to allot his herds to various herdsmen, again with a special name, *boimutongo*. The king was obviously mung'a of these herds. But the king could not take cattle from any one of these herds without the herdsman's permission. The herdsman could refuse this permission if he felt *his* herd —as Barotse speak of it—was being depleted. Nor could the king take the herd from a man unless the man had wronged him. For the herdsman was also mung'a. The herdsman could use the meat of cattle which died, and he could even kill a beast if he wished and use beasts from the herd for marriage cattle.[23] This form of royal herding is different from a contract by which a man put out cattle to be herded by another, under agistment, where the herdsman (*mulisana*) could not kill a beast, eat the meat of a dead beast, or use the cattle for marriage payments. These cattle were not zambuwa, but *mafisa*. And the king, like any commoner, could put out cattle to herd in this way. But these types of quite different rights in the cattle are all covered, as are marriage cattle, by the terms ownership and herding. The elaboration of Barotse jurisprudence is in giving different names to the herders and to the different types of cattle, as well as to the transactions, but

23. Schapera, *Handbook of Tswana Law and Custom* (1938), pp. 67 f., 248 f., reports a similar institution.

not to the rights created by these. As with land and titles, so with cattle: the main interest of Barotse law resides in the complex of relationships between persons, which is built around property, rather than in the rights of individuals over property.

Of course not all chattels are subject to the same complex ownership as marriage cattle. The vast mass of chattels appears to be held in the private ownership of individuals: crops, hoes, spears, axes, utensils, clothes, mats, canoes, fishing traps and nets, and many cattle. One person can usually assert a dominant claim to these against others, and he is called the mung'a. But even chattels are subject to the claims of other persons, related in specific ways to the owner, to use or take or consume. These claims appear in the institution of *kufunda,* which the Lozi Dictionary calls a privileged theft. A man was allowed to take anything belonging to a blood kinsman: he could kill a beast, take crops, spears, anything. And the person whose property was taken could not reclaim the thing taken. But if a man was unreasonably extravagant in taking the goods of his kin in all lines, they could sue to have him expelled from kinship—i.e. his kin sued to have his status altered, so that he lost the privilege of taking anything from them. Barotse grumble and do not always cheerfully yield these rights to their kin, but if they have to choose between a breach of kinship and loss of possession, they prefer to abandon possession. Thus ultimately no individual has absolute rights over anything, even when he is called mung'a, for all his kin are beng'i, owners, and can take his property. People with whom a man enters into bloodbrotherhood acquire similar rights over his own, but not his kin's, property.

In the past almost every chattel was held by an individual subject to a complex of claims by others, arising from the social relationships around the owner and the role of the property within those social relationships. Through a man's chattels run his relationships to a variety of other social positions. In Barotse life disputes spring up over the handling of apparently trifling amounts of property, because the way people deal with their property exhibits whether they feel the sentiments of love and affection appropriate to a particular status relationship. In Barotse, I have known cases to be fought over sixpennyworth of beer. The significant aspect of ownership for the Barotse is thus the part it plays in a nexus of highly specific relationships. Ownership itself is a very vaguely defined right without specific terminological qualifications. It states that X stands in a masterful relation to the object, privilege, or person in terms of certain social relationships. Rights to property define and are attributes of social position. For example, the chief councillor, the Ngambela, is defined as follows: "Even if it is only a tortoise which comes to the capital, the chief councillor gets one leg." He is nearly as powerful as the king and stands against the king; he shares in everything given to the king.

In summary, Barotse property law defines not so much the rights of persons over things as the duties between persons in respect of things. Indeed, the critical property rights are demands on other persons in virtue of control over land and chattels—not any set of persons, but persons related in specific ways. Or if new relationships are created, this is done through transfers of property, as at marriage, or in making allegiance. Hence ownership, bung'a, is constantly used also in defining social relationships themselves, even where land or things are not immediately involved. This may have given rise to the idea in early writings, and in modern political statements about the position of African women, that persons are chattels in tribal society. In conclusion, therefore, I briefly illustrate this final use of the concept of ownership.[24]

Any position in any social relationship may be described as ownership, depending on whose rights to demand the fulfillment of obligations are being emphasized. Dominantly, the senior in the relationship is called owner, even when his rights are not being emphasized or called in question, because he has greater obligations as well as stronger claims. The king, political authorities, and senior kinsmen are all politely addressed as "my owner." The king would never address a subject thus, though in discussion or dispute over constitutional issues the Barotse state that the nation is owner of the king, as it is of councillors. But councillors address one another, even seniors their juniors, as "my owner"; and a very senior councillor may speak thus to an ordinary commoner whether he is exhibiting his courtesy and willingness to help or his inability to oblige. Most strikingly, councillors thus address litigants or accused whom they are severely reprimanding. They do this in order to emphasize that they are discharging an obligation to the wrongdoer by pointing out to him the error of his ways: for they speak not in anger but because the law requires them to do so. Their duty is to uphold the law, and they have this duty even to those

24. Cf. Kroeber's statement that Yurok made no distinction between rights in things and in persons, "Yurok Law" (1928), p. 20.

punished by the law. Similarly, adults frequently call a child "my owner" as an affectionate endearment, especially if it is fretful or hungry, to emphasize readiness to serve the child. But the adult also uses this address when he is reprimanding the child; thus he states that he reprimands the child as a duty, for he owes it the obligation of bringing it up to be a good citizen. Wives commonly call husbands "my owner," and a husband speaks thus to a wife to mark his respect for her, to thank her, and above all to placate her if she is angry.

These forms of address exhibit the constant emphasis of Barotse law on obligation to others which is involved in their concept of ownership. The background of this situation is the complex network of rights and obligations lying between a person and others occupying related social positions in a society dominated by status. And a court will ascribe ownership to any of these social positions, as against another, depending on who is failing to fulfill obligations. Thus most commonly a husband is called "owner" of his wife. We must remember that in Barotseland a woman cannot sue her husband for having sexual relations with another woman, i.e. for adultery, unless she is pregnant, when sexual relations with anyone except another wife threaten the health of her unborn child. But if a husband neglects his wife to fornicate with other women, the court calls the wife "owner of the husband" and "owner of the marriage," in insisting that the husband must sleep with her a reasonable number of nights. Or the wife may be called "owner of the marriage" if she sues for divorce on grounds of neglect, or failure on her husband's part to treat her as a wife, which he does if he entrusts to a kinswoman duties which are his wife's rights, such as receiving visitors or caring for his property.

The ownership of the husband over his wife, in terms of rights, is emphasized especially against adulterers. In a divorce suit by a wife (husbands divorce their wives at will), the court will refuse a divorce by stating that the husband is "owner of the woman." If divorce is granted the court states that the father or other guardian is "owner of the woman," thus stressing the control over her, and obligations to her, held by her kin as against her husband. But obviously father's and husband's rights over a woman, and their obligations to her, differ markedly.

When they thus speak of a wife as in a man's ownership, the court is thinking of a complex of rights and duties lying between her and her husband and her kin. She is not in the status of a serf, for a woman or man who is a serf is related to the owner by quite different rights and can claim different obligations from the owner.

A man who has been injured by his child may even sue the child's maternal kin for redress, referring to them as "owners of the child." Or the reverse may happen. The aggrieved kinsman or woman thus thrusts responsibility and obligation onto the relatives of the opposite side. I omitted to enquire into the problem of incest adequately, since I was told that a person committing incest would be killed. But it is worth noting here that Barton records of a Philippines tribe without chiefs, that if an Ifugao father commits incest with his daughter, his own family cannot take action against him because "a family cannot proceed against itself." In addition, the father, the perpetrator of the crime, is a nearer relative of his family than is his daughter, so his family would not take active steps against him. But he might be punished by the girl's mother's family on the ground that he had committed an offense against one of its members.[25]

Similar situations arise in political relationships, as I have described above. I hope I have demonstrated sufficiently that bung'a, ownership, is ascribed by the Barotse to anyone who has a masterful relationship of responsibility and demands on services over another in some situation. This masterfulness may arise out of property or not. Barotse jurisprudence sees every situation that arises out of status relationships as containing an essentially similar element which it calls bung'a. They distinguish relatively few forms of bung'a, for the rights and duties involved in any particular kind of bung'a are defined by the status relationship involved in dispute, and the main further clarification lies in the multiplying of names for different kinds of property. Suits in court may raise questions about rights, but the courts tend always to lay stress on obligation. This situation arises from the fact that Barotse society is dominated, as Maine said of all early societies, by status. We can appreciate therefore why Malinowski in 1926 insisted that the "ownership and use of the canoe [in the Trobriand Islands] consist of a series of obligations and duties uniting a group of people into a working team," and concluded that "ownership, therefore, can be defined neither by such words as 'communism' nor 'individualism,' nor by reference to 'joint-stock company' system or 'personal enter-

25. Barton, *Ifugao Law* (1919), p. 1ᢣ

prise,' but by the concrete facts and conditions of use. It is the sum of duties, privileges and mutualities which bind the joint owners to the object and to each other." [26]

I have examined the significance of property as a medium in extant social relationships and touched on the role of property in establishing a marriage. It remains to discuss briefly further examples of the importance of property in constituting new relationships.

Just as established relationships contain rights and duties as essential elements in respect of property, so as new social relationships are established they will contain this type of right and duty. Marriages, new allegiances of incoming subjects of the king, the birth of new children to parents—all these relationships of their very nature involve a reallocation of property rights and the vesting of fresh persons with rights in property. These steps are initiated by transfers of material items which symbolize transfers or creation of rights.

There are many reasons for this, and some will be considered in a later chapter. Relevant to the argument here is the fact that rights over property in Barotse society always involve rights over and obligations to other persons, and all rights over and obligations to other persons have a property element. As we have seen, the Barotse state all social relationships in terms of the handling of land and things. Therefore whenever a new social relationship is established it involves a redistribution, immediate or potential, of existing property rights; and it is usually accompanied and accomplished by an exchange of goods, which is equivalent if the relationship is of equals, but is uneven if one side is getting the greater rights. Thus blood-brothers give each other equal gifts, but a man who is entering the nation gives a gift to the king. The suitor for a woman's hand pays her guardian to begin discussion, and he pays for marital rights in his wife. He pays his wife to pass each crossroad on her way to his home and for the first night of intercourse. She makes a countergift for the latter. But as against the marriage payment which obtains the wife for the husband, he and his wife's kin each provide the other with a beast or food for the marriage itself, since both sides gain equally new kin and continuity from the children of the marriage. (To continue my comparison with early European law, note here that there were similar multiple payments at marriages in Anglo-Saxon times.) In the past, on the death of a spouse, the survivor's kin had to pay a beast, but this

26. Malinowski, *Crime and Custom in Savage Society* (1926), pp. 18 and 20–21.

due was abolished by a recent king as "theft," since God had taken the deceased. When a boy or girl attains puberty, the parents and other kin make gifts to recognize puberty and the new status this involves.

Not all gift giving in these kinds of situations is related to changes in the distribution of property rights. For example, all who attend a funeral, the installation of a headman, a puberty ceremony, or a wedding make gifts to the central figures in the ceremony. But wherever changes in property rights are involved in a change of status, some gift must be made to effect or symbolize transfers of rights.

In some respects it is of course true to say that in our own society there are always restrictions on the use of property under claims and rights of others. Clearly, the manner in which these claims operate in a tribal society produces a radically different situation. For the interweaving of status and property rights with us is mainly duplicated only within the family. In tribal society this interweaving spreads throughout social relations. The high importance of property in defining relationships may indeed be aggravated by the relative paucity of goods, as was argued by Evans-Pritchard in 1940 in a passage which I have cited in several books to draw attention to the problems he poses in it. He argues that the poorer a society be in material goods, the more symbolic functions these goods have to serve. In his account of the Nuer of the Sudan, a people who have little besides cattle, he writes:

> I risk being accused of speaking idly when I suggest that a very simple material culture narrows social ties in another way. Technology from one point of view is an oecological process: an adaptation of human behaviour to natural circumstances. From another point of view material culture may be regarded as part of social relations, for material objects are chains along which social relationships run, and the more simple is a material culture the more numerous are the relationships expressed through it. . . . Herds of cattle are nuclei around which kinship groups are clustered and the relationships between their members operate through cattle and are expressed in terms of cattle. A single small artifact may be a nexus between persons, e.g. a spear which passes from father to son by gift or inheritance is a symbol of their relationship and one of the bonds by which it is maintained. Thus people not only create their material culture and attach

themselves to it, but also build up their relationships through it
and see them in terms of it. As Nuer have very few kinds of
material objects and very few specimens of each kind, their social
value is increased by their having to serve as media of many
relationships and they are, in consequence, often invested with
ritual functions. Moreover social relationships instead of being
diffused along many chains of material links are narrowed by the
meagreness of culture to a few simple foci of interest.[27]

Ownership becomes the cement holding together the fabric of society in these circumstances. A study of the situation among the poorer
sections of our own society might be most profitable.[28,29]

27. *The Nuer* (1940), p. 89.

28. As this book is going to press, I am able to draw attention to Biebuyck's discussion of
how the Nyanga use the word *mine* in various contexts, which he gives after citing the first
published version of this chapter (Biebuyck, "Problèmes d'analyse et de terminologie," editorial
Introduction to *African Agrarian Systems* (1963), pp. 4–9).

29. After I had delivered this lecture in the Yale Law School, a member of my audience,
learned in medieval law, said that my analysis of the Barotse use of *bung'a* (ownership)
seemed to clarify implications of early English law. I have therefore looked at that situation
as well as I am able. Cheshire, taking "ownership" as a word of many meanings, but in the
present context as signifying a title "good against the whole world," concludes that the
"doctrine of tenure as developed in England made it difficult, if not impossible, to regard either
[the tenant] or his lord as owner of the land itself. The land could not be owned by the
tenant, since it was recoverable by the lord if tenurial services were not faithfully performed;
it could not be owned by the lord, since he had no claim on it as long as the tenant fulfilled
his duties." As against Roman law, English law directed its attention not to ownership, but to
possession or, as it was called in the case of land, *seisin*. "All titles to land are ultimately
based upon possession in the sense that the title of the man seised prevails against all who can
show no better right of seisin." Cheshire quotes Plucknett to the effect that " 'seisin' . . . is
an enjoyment of property based upon title, and is not essentially distinguishable from right.
In other words, the sharp distinction between property and possession made in Roman law did
not obtain in English law; seisin is not the Roman possession and right is not the Roman
ownership. Both of these conceptions are represented in English law only by seisin, and it was
the essence of the conception of seisin that some seisins might be better than others." After
this quotation, Cheshire states that "the English actions for recovery of land, called in early
days *real actions*, have consistently and continuously turned upon the right of possession.
Moreover, their object throughout has been not to enquire whether the title to possession set
up by the defendant is an absolute title good against all persons, but whether it is relatively
better than any title that the plaintiff can establish. English land law is committed to the
doctrine of relative titles to possession. Thus the issue raised in the most ancient and solemn
remedy, the *writ of right*, was not whether the demandant (plaintiff) could prove an
absolute title good against third parties, but whether he or the defendant could establish the
better seisin." [Cheshire, *The Modern Law of Real Property* (1962, 9th ed.), pp. 27–28,
quoting Plucknett, *A Concise History of the Common Law* (5th ed.), p. 358.]

Clearly, there are similarities between this legal situation and the situation of claims for bung'a, which I have called ownership, among the Barotse. The difference seems to be that in Barotseland, determination of who was *mung'a*, owner or possessor, was also made in suits between lords and underlings, holding rights over the same parcel of land, and in suits between a trespasser, who disseised a seisor, and the earlier holder. It may be that my commentator was suggesting this possibility, which does seem to clarify some of the complications considered by Maitland in his exposition of "The Mystery of Seisin" in early feudal times. (In *Law Quarterly Review*, 2, 1886, reprinted in *Collected Papers*, 1, 1911, 481 f. See also his essay on "The Beatitude of Seisin," ibid.) The problem is exceedingly complex, and I dare not venture an opinion; I only raise a point that was made to me rather than let it slip into limbo.

It may also bear on the emergence only in 1583 of the use of "ownership" as "the fact or state of being an owner; property, proprietorship" (*Shorter Oxford English Dictionary*, 2d ed. 1936, 2, 14–19). "Own" as "to have or hold as one's own, possess" is Old English, but after early Middle English it is scarcely found with this sense until the 17th century, "owe" being the usual word in the 14th–17th centuries (cf. Chap. 8 below on debt and obligation). "Own" in the sense of "to make (a thing) one's own; to seize, win, gain; to adopt as one's own" passes out of use at the end of Middle English (c. 1450), but 1815 is the last recorded use of "own" as "to claim for one's own." "Owner" was Middle English. Skeat (*An Etymological Dictionary of the English Language*, 1910, p. 420) says in Anglo-Saxon the equivalent of "own" in the sense of "possess" was "to appropriate, claim as one's own"; in Icelandic, "to claim as one's own"; and in Gothic "to make again of, lit. make one's own, from *aigin,* one's own property." He concludes that "it is thus evident that the verb is a derivative from the adjective." I cite these details, because they suggest a situation in which "owning" was defined in a situation of conflicting claims. Diamond's bare treatment (see p. 141 n. 3) of the appearance of "ownership" in 1583, as evidence "that primitive law has no such conception as 'ownership,'" seems unsatisfactory except in a narrow technical definition. Cf., the Barotse often indicate rights over things and persons by possessive, grammatical constructions.

I may add here that Ellis on *Welsh Tribal Law and Custom in the Middle Ages* (1926, 2, 206) states that "the right of occupation was inviolate . . . The king was in practice the ultimate administrator of land, not the arbitrary owner." The "supreme ownership" of the king "meant nothing more" than that customary dues had to be rendered to the king and there was an ultimate escheat of land to the king.

Chapter 6

THE IMPORTANCE OF OBLIGATION IN CONTRACT

IN THE PREVIOUS CHAPTER we began to examine the rights of Barotse in land and chattels and saw that these rights were contained in the Law of Persons. Further, we saw that the Barotse extend their right of ownership to cover claims on other persons and on their property and their services. This is, on the whole, the manner in which Barotse state these rights. But they also describe rights against other persons and over property as obligations (*liswanelo*), so that had we started from "obigations" we would have been led to property. For the civic estate of a Barotse entitles him to hold land, and it is an obligation of the king to give him that land. The rules of the Law of Persons and the Law of Things are "inextricably mixed together" (Maine), and the same body of rules contains a Barotse's most important obligations to and rights against others.

This was even more marked in the past, when almost all transactions involving goods and services took place in the kinship and political systems. Before the abolition of serfdom, the Barotse made few labor contracts. They traded fairly widely with unrelated persons but frequently established pacts of friendship and bloodbrotherhood with regular exchange partners. Other goods to meet their deficiencies were circulated by giving tribute to the king who distributed it as gifts. Their other special, important contracts were loan of gardens, placing of cattle to herd, and certain forms of share fishing. But on the whole, most of a Barotse's transactions took place with his kin, in-laws, and neighbors or with his political superiors and underlings. He was obliged to render them goods and services and they were in turn obligated to him.

Even today this is largely true. It is shown in the paucity of cases I heard that arose out of transactions, and therefore for data on contracts with strangers I rely largely on discussion of cases stated. The Barotse in Barotseland still depends on his share of the nation's land and on the help of his kin and political fellows. I exclude from this statement the men's long absences while working for Whites in Barotseland or abroad, and their large purchases from and sales to Whites. Since relationships between Whites and Barotse, whether they arise out of contract or injury, have been controlled by British courts, they are marginal to my present analysis, which is concerned with the law administered by the Barotse courts. Therefore, though Barotseland would today find it hard to manage without that system's goods and employment, I shall neglect this field of relationships. Most cases at law coming before a Barotse court arise between in-laws and between kinsmen, and the court tries to settle these cases by old standards, though it changes the standards to meet new situations. Barotse conceptions of other transactions seem to me to be consistent with conceptions inherent in a system of kinship obligations.

Free contractual relations between persons not united by social position were thus relatively few and unimportant in Barotse life. In this respect a study of Barotse law, as of law in most tribal societies, validates Maine's most widely accepted generalization, "that the movement of progressive societies has hitherto been a movement *from Status to Contract*." The Barotse have now been brought into a world of contractual relations. Their own courts do not handle those with Whites, but the abolition of serfdom in 1906 and the long absences of men at labor have compelled Barotse to make more use of ephemeral employer–employee relationships with unrelated persons of their own and other tribes. Money has facilitated internal trade and it has also been increased by variable falls in production for different groups. The king—instead of claiming tribute and labor—collects tax, and the Northern Rhodesian and Barotse governments employ laborers for wages, instead of rewarding them with gifts. But, with the unbroken system of landholding, Barotse still live with their kin and are linked with their overlords, and the goods and money they earn flow into these established relationships. Barotse society on the whole is still a society dominated internally by status rather than contract.

I have argued that Barotse property law defines not so much the rights of persons over things as the obligations owed between persons in respect of things. Hence, except for extending a general protection against trespassers on others' rights, the law is concerned with the respective claims on one another's services and goods of persons related permanently by kinship or political bonds. In the previous chapter I abstracted the element of property from political and kinship bonds, and this led to an analysis of the obligations between lord and under-

ling and between kinsfolk. Had I analyzed the obligations between
these persons, I should have had equally to consider property. For in
Barotseland the Law of Things and the Law of Obligations are both
mostly contained in the Law of Persons, and each of these three is also
the others examined from a different standpoint. Barotse society is
relatively undifferentiated, and the different branches of its law are
intertwined.

The greater part of the Barotse Law of Obligations is covered by the
rights and duties which lie between kinsfolk and in-laws and between
lords and their underlings. Claims on the goods and services of others
inhere in these relationships. Transactions between previously unrelated persons—contracts freely entered into—are relatively few
among the Barotse, though they make an important contribution to
economic life. It is therefore understandable that the law of these
contracts has been markedly influenced by the major preoccupation of
Barotse jurisprudence, its concern with the law of status. This influence will now be considered.

Defaults in obligation of status are punished nowadays by reprimand or fine (previously also by inflicting physical pain) and ultimately by expulsion of the defaulter from his status with its rights
and obligations. The standard of what has to be rendered is thus set by
general norms, and within those by what can be reasonably expected
from a person of a certain age, strength, and wealth. That is, there is a
certain reasonable minimum which is enforceable at law, in the setting
of all his obligations. But the expectations of morality go far beyond
this minimum. All these relationships are marked by a public demand
for love and affection and generous mutual aid, and people are expected to express these sentiments through material goods and services.
The stress of morality is on generosity, helpfulness, cooperation, and
give-and-take in the vicissitudes of life. These values are publicly
stated in many cases between lords and their underlings and always in
cases between kinsmen. Thus in the land dispute cited in the first
chapter, the headman who demanded that kin come to his village or
stop using his fish dams, was reproved for his stinginess and told:
"Indeed, you ought, if you are rich, to add to the goods of your kin,
not to take things away from them." Trials over ownership of land
may become inquiries into how the kinsfolk concerned have dealt
with one another through long periods: whether the junior gave the
senior fish from his catches and money from his earnings in European

enterprises, or let him take poles, mats, and so forth, and whether the senior had contributed, for example, to his juniors' payments of cattle for brides.[1]

Since land, and to a lesser extent chattels, are principally held by virtue of status, the settlement of disputes over ownership may turn on whether the parties have fulfilled all the duties of their station; whoever has failed to do this generously will be severely admonished and may ultimately be expelled from his position. Here the stress of Barotse law is clearly on duty rather than on right. Even when the judges affirm that a particular person has a right to some thing or some service from another, they tend to stress that the defaulter should render the right, rather than that the abused shall receive the right. It is only by this generous rendering of obligations that multiplex relationships can endure and function; they are likely to break if either party tries to live by the letter of rights and duties. These virtues inhere in the relationships of parents and children, and they are extended not only to relationships with other kin but also to political relationships. The good subject is he who is generous as a child is to a parent; the good lord is he who is generous as a parent is to a child.

Since these are the typical relationships of Barotse society, their more ephemeral transactions involving previously unrelated people tend to be assimilated to the pattern of status relationships, and this influence permeates the Barotse law of transactions. In Barotse law individual parties had little liberty to make special agreements, for each transaction had particular and specific incidents. Hence I consider it is better here to follow Seagle when he says of certain archaic systems that "the law was still dealing with particular forms of transactions rather than with contracts." [2]

A noteworthy fact of Barotse life is the tendency to expand isolated transactions between strangers into multiplex associations that resemble kin relationships. This tendency is marked in their magical and religious beliefs, as in their secular life. For example, Barotse barter goods with one another. Many people with small surpluses or the products of specialized skills or particular environments travel through the country seeking to trade with others who have goods they lack, although

---

1. "The Case of the Biassed Father" in my *Judicial Process among the Barotse* (1955), pp. 37–45.

2. *The Quest for Law* (1941), p. 256. He quotes with approval Diamond, *Primitive Law* (1935) at p. 392: "In the primitive law we must speak not of Contract but of Transactions."

of late, British money has provided a medium of exchange. But once a couple has made several bartering exchanges of this kind, they consider they have entered into a pact of friendship (*bulikani*, literally, the quality of being equals). Thereafter they do not barter item for item, but they are under a general obligation to help each other and to outdo each other in generosity, rather than to seek a good bargain. They thus obtain hospitality, protection, and an additional home in an area where they lack kin. These pacts of friendship, if of long standing, may then be sealed by the pact of bloodbrotherhood, which makes them quasi-kinsmen; now they cannot marry into each other's family. These pacts had additional importance in the past when the parties lived in different nations, for they enabled safe travel across boundaries. Thus when David Livingstone traveled with Barotse carriers outside Barotseland in 1855, he recorded that his people made compacts of bloodbrotherhood with Lunda so that they could later exchange cattle for canoes. The French missionary Coillard made similar notes on his journeys. Here the pact provided a protecting friend in a foreign land. Within the Barotse kingdom these pacts are very numerous, and people constantly make them with others with whom they have entered into regular exchanges. The Barotse court in 1942 had to consider a case in which two bloodbrothers had quarreled because one had committed a gross breach of obligation by refusing hospitality to his fellow. The court totted up the extent to which the injured party had given more than he had received and made the defaulter pay him double, thus treating the case as theft.

Similarly, if a Barotse employs a servant, places cattle to be herded with another, or lends another land, once the relationship has endured for a few years, it approaches that of lord and subject or father and child.

The tendency is marked in the linking of persons through mystical beliefs. If a Barotse employs a leech to treat a serious disease, their relationship endures beyond the cure. The patient may be compelled to become a pupil of the leech, and have to learn to treat the disease. Doctor and patient become permanently linked; and if the patient defaults in payment, the doctor's medicines will turn against him and make him ill again. The doctor must also respect his tie with his patient, for if he defaults in an obligation, the patient's condition may worsen. One night an old man fell suddenly ill. The diviner he consulted held that his illness was the fault of an old woman who had cured him the previous year of a dreadful disease in whose treatment she specialized. She had passed his village without entering to greet him, and the disease became angry and struck him again. Sometimes the patient's failure to follow rules may threaten the doctor's well-being.

Other mystical beliefs, in a corresponding way, set up relationships between persons who have some contact or shared experience. Thus there are some diseases which link together all who suffer from them or have suffered, so that when a patient is being treated by drumming, all other patients feel the effects and are seized with paroxysms.

And men who wrong one another, like men who contract with each other, become expansively linked. If you wound a man, you can aggravate his wound by working with magical substances on the weapon. If you kill an enemy in battle, you enter into a personal relationship with him: you must rip up his stomach lest it swells where he rots on the battlefield, and your stomach swells in sympathy. His spirit, like the spirits of certain big game, is liable to drive you mad unless you are treated ritually. Like transactions, delicts thus tend to establish expanding relationships between persons who were previously unrelated. The obverse of this situation is exhibited in other beliefs. Many misfortunes that we ascribe to natural causes are ascribed by the Barotse to witches or sorcerers, personal enemies who have harmed them by mystical means. While for us, delicts and criminal charges arise only when another is patently responsible for a misfortune, among the Barotse every mischance, through beliefs in sorcery, may produce a delictual or criminal case. (It is worth noting here that among the Tiv of Nigeria, even litigants enter into a wider relationship: they call each other "partner." [3])

Within the framework of the Barotse law of status there are three general characteristics which, I consider, directly influence the Barotse view of transactions. First, all relationships are ideally relationships of generosity and the utmost good faith, *uberrimae fidei*. In disputes, the court emphasizes obligation rather than right. Similarly, all transactions tend to be contracts of the utmost good faith, with obligations emphasized.

Second, within the general demand for faithfulness and generosity, each specific type of kin relationship is marked off from others by the observance of a special etiquette and special conventions of behavior

3. Bohannan, *Justice and Judgment among the Tiv* (1957), pp. 20 n., 28.

and taboos. So each transaction is regarded as a specific complex of rights and obligations, and there is no general model of contract, which is not surprising, since the Romans failed to attain a general theory of contract even in their later jurisprudence, and in England only in the fifteenth century did a general remedy for breach of agreement begin to be supplied.

Third, the fulfillment of obligations in kin relationships is measured by what is done with property, and almost all these relationships involve property elements. In addition, new relationships are established by handing over gifts, as for example in marriage; indeed, there are some half dozen transfers of gifts in a proper marriage. Similarly, kin establish their relationship with a newly born child or an initiate at puberty by making gifts. People who do not share in these property exchanges may deny liability—i.e. they may deny that they have obligations. If a bride's father gives none of the marriage payment to the maternal kin or his own kin, they will say, "We knew nothing of the marriage." Finally, to re-establish relations after any affront to a kinsman or in-law, some gift must be given. So in transactions, transfers of property are critical.

We can now examine this situation in detail as it affects the interpretation of some Barotse transactions. Direct barter and sale, completed on the spot, are simple transactions out of which disputes for failure to perform cannot arise. In fact, the only disputes I recorded arose where one party alleged that the other had delivered to him goods to which the seller did not have title, or goods of an inferior quality (a cracked pot, improperly reduced poisonous cassava, inadequately seasoned paddles, etc.). In these cases, and on cases stated by me to the courts, the general maxim was that the seller is responsible to the buyer. If a seller had not a good title, the true owner could reclaim his goods from the buyer, and the seller had to recompense the buyer. Barotse describe the seller's action as theft, and they also call it theft if the seller is aware of a flaw in the goods he sells. They may then apply the punishment for theft—payment to the wronged party of double the value of the property, and a possible fine. If the seller did not know of the flaw, he would have to replace the shoddy with sound goods, or refund the goods or money given to him. But this obligation on the seller to take care he renders sound goods emerges most clearly if the goods develop a defect some time after the sale. Thus if a dugout springs a leak after some period of use, the buyer will not be held responsible because he did not use more skill in testing the wood's seasoning. The seller must give him another dugout or repay the price, even if the flaw had not been detectable. More surprising to us, probably, is the rule that if a purchased beast dies some time after the transaction, the purchaser can claim refund of the price on the grounds of what we might call latent defect. (The Barotse would not fix for me what period "some time" covered, but I recorded one case in which it was four months.) Here then we meet with a marked characteristic of Barotse transactions: each party must look to his obligations rather than to his gains. Every transfer of goods contains an implied warranty, which is extended severely. The obligation on the seller to provide eminently satisfactory goods is like the obligation on a man to be generous to his kin beyond the demands of the law.

Where a seller fraudulently, or sometimes even innocently, delivers poor goods, it is held to be a theft. For instance, if a hoe is purchased for money, and the hoe breaks because of a flaw which was not observable on the surface, the court may accuse the smith, denying his liability to replace the hoe, either of stealing the hoe or of stealing the money. That is, the court holds the injured party to be robbed equally of what he had given and of what he had received. If the court decides that the wrongdoer knew of the flaw, he pays double, as if for theft. The implication of this Barotse view is that in transactions, fraud and even innocent mistake are not treated as a breach of agreement but as taking or spoiling a man's property. In Barotse, as in Roman law, barter and sale are considered as reciprocal conveyances of property: both parties have proprietary rights in both pieces of exchanged property, and the deliverer retains some rights, with corresponding obligations, after delivery. Both are *beng'i*, owners, of both pieces of property, and the case is argued in these terms.

The Barotse word for barter is a reciprocal verb, so that both parties are said to change goods, or goods and money, with each other. The legal problems arising from this process involve not merely what the parties agreed or promised to do, but what property they exchanged and what rights each has in that property. This is quite clear if we consider the transaction which we know as a conditional sale, a sale on credit, and which students of early law call "credit-barter," [4] the true incomplete conveyance, in which only one party delivers the property. In technical terms, this is an agreement to barter and sell which

4. Seagle, *The Quest for Law* (1941), p. 52.

is completed on one side and is *executory* on the other. Where this transaction is recorded on ancient tablets in the Near and Middle East, it involves two tablets. The first records the sale or barter as if it had been completed; the second records the property or money which has not been delivered as a loan from seller to purchaser. That is, two transactions are involved: barter or sale, and loan.[5] Lacking both money and writing, the Barotse had not achieved this sophistication, though in discussing cases arising out of this kind of transaction they speak of it as they do of a straightforward loan: it establishes a debt.

In two cases I heard tried one after the other in a Barotse court, fishermen had ordered gill nets from two netmakers. One paid the full price in advance, the other paid part. When the netmakers had each made a net, the king's steward in charge of royal fishing, holder of the title Mukuba, came to the netmakers and wanted to buy the nets for the king. The netmaker who had been partially paid alleged that he protested his net was already bought, but that the steward swore that the king would stop the netmaker from taking roots to make nets unless he sold him the net, and would also stop the fishermen from fishing in public waters. The netmakers sold the nets to the steward. Both fishermen sued for delivery of the nets.

These cases created great public excitement because the steward's alleged threats amounted to stating that the king would take away certain land rights from his subjects. All Barotse declared that the king, who was almost speechless after a stroke, would never threaten this. In effect, the first part of the hearing became a trial of the steward for "spoiling the king's name." He satisfied the court that he had not uttered the alleged threats, and the maligning netmaker had to pay him damages for false accusation. The court then considered whether the nets belonged to the king or to the fishermen who had ordered them. The judges held unanimously that the fisherman who had paid the full purchase price had a sound claim on the net he had ordered, and must be given it, while the netmaker must refund the king's money. All the judges up to the senior judge then sitting in court held that the fisherman who had paid part of the purchase price was also entitled to the net he had ordered, and the steward could not buy it. (Note that they spoke of the steward's buying the nets, and neglected his acting as king's agent. The king, like any other Barotse

5. See Diamond, *Primitive Law* (1935), p. 412 f., and Seagle, *The Quest for Law* (1941). p. 57.

master, bears no responsibility for the actions of his servants.) The senior judge that day was number eight in the hierarchy on the right, a brother of the king's favorite wife, a member of a subject tribe living far from the metropolitan heart of the country and, to boot, a notoriously bad judge. He overruled all his juniors, since final decision is not by majority but by seniority. He held that the net belonged to the steward, and the fisherman was entitled to refund of the installment he had paid. The fisherman told me he thought he would win the net if he appealed to the Barotse national appeal court, but he would drop the matter, since he had recovered his money and would now be suing in effect the king, his "father." He philosophically accepted the loss of his season's fishing.

I discussed the decision with senior councillors of the national appeal court, with rulers in other capitals, and with a large number of commoners. They all said that the fisherman would have won the net if he had appealed. Indeed, they said that if the king had been able to speak properly, and had not depended on his queen, sister to the final judge, to interpret his sounds, he would have overruled the final judge and supported the junior judges. They said it was a typically bad judgment from this judge.

At that time I also discussed with judges what the position would have been had one of the fishermen not paid any part of the purchase price. High authorities told me that this would not have mattered; they would still have considered that the fisherman could claim any net made. This statement was made to me in 1942, and I first published this case in 1943.[6] Mr. (later Justice) E. G. Unsworth, then Crown Counsel in Northern Rhodesia, told me afterward that he had found no trace that executory contracts were enforced in Northern Rhodesian tribes, so I decided that I must check on this information. I did so when I returned to Barotseland in 1947, and I was then told that unless some payment was made by the fisherman, he acquired no rights in any net that was made. This discrepancy of statements exemplifies how Barotse courts apply their legal propositions within the context of specific relationships of status. When I first questioned a number of judges, they were concerned about the king's involvement in the case, even indirectly, and they were in effect telling me that the king would not enter thus between manufacturer and purchaser to the detriment of the purchaser. They had not detached themselves

6. In my *Essays on Lozi Land and Royal Property* (1943), pp. 15–16.

from the issue before the court. Later, when I asked them again, considering it as an issue between commoners only, they ruled that unless the buyer paid something, he got no rights. Unhappily, in his book *The Nature of African Customary Law* (1956, p. 154), Dr. T. O. Elias took up my first report and gave it as the only clear instance in Africa of enforcement of an executory contract, where no deceit was involved. It is significant that he found no other example in his survey of African law.

In discussion, the Barotse laid down the following rules for me, with different rules for different types of property:

1. Generally if a man orders something and does not pay the price, he gets no rights in anything the manufacturer may make. That is, a transaction which is executory on both sides will not be enforced. The manufacturer is not bound to make the article, and no damages will be levied against him if he does not; nor is the purchaser bound to accept the article if it is made.

2. If a man orders an article like a net or a dugout, only one or a few of which can be manufactured in a season, and he pays the purchase price but the manufacturer does not make the article, the purchaser can sue only for return of what he paid. If the manufacturer makes the article, it belongs to the purchaser and he can claim it from either the maker or a third party to whom it has passed, even if this party is innocent. The purchaser can only reject delivery of the article if it does not come up to common standards. That is, in orders for goods which can be individually distinguished, where the purchaser has delivered some part of the price, the Barotse consider that his ownership vests in the goods provisionally as soon as they are made. But if the goods are destroyed (as by fire) before the purchaser takes them, he can reclaim the purchase price. He does not bear the risk: although he is called the owner, and he can claim the goods against the world, including the maker, risk remains with the maker.

3. Should the manufacturer not deliver ordered goods like pots, hoes, axes, or food, which cannot be individually distinguished and which he is producing continually, the purchaser has no claim at all if he has not paid the price. If he has paid, and the seller does not produce the goods, the purchaser can claim refund. He cannot follow goods that are made and sold to another, if the manufacturer then ceases to make goods. The manufacturer cannot turn away trade because the purchaser does not collect his order in reasonable time. A

purchaser who has not paid can reject the goods offered to him; but if he has paid, he can reject only unworthy goods.

4. If purchaser and seller agree on the goods to be exchanged and point them out, but nothing is transferred by either party, no obligations are created. Neither can claim the goods from the other, nor can they follow the goods if these are transferred to another person.

5. If one party has fulfilled his part of the bargain by transferring goods against property indicated on the other side, he can claim the goods from the seller or from an innocent third party to whom they have passed. But should the indicated goods deteriorate or be destroyed, or if they be cattle which die, the risk remains with the seller till actual transfer. Increment, such as a calf to a cow, however, accrues to the purchaser. But if, after a period which is not defined in advance by the law, the purchaser still neglects to take delivery of a beast, the court will consider that he wished the seller to herd it for him under agistment. Then risk passes to the purchaser under conditions I shall discuss later. This is the only situation I know where Barotse courts find an implied contract.

These were the rules given to me in 1942, when I was in Barotseland. In 1946 the Barotse authorities passed a law stating that they would enforce promises to do anything (to make something, to cut a garden, to join a fishing team, etc.). They told me that they passed this law when they read in a published analysis of mine that they did not enforce agreements of this kind, and they saw that this produced considerable hardship for innocent people. With the increasing importance of free contractual relations in Barotseland under modern conditions, the need for enforcement of executory contracts is aggravated: yet the bias of the law against this enforcement is shown by the fact that the Barotse decided to pass this law only after an outsider had drawn attention to resulting difficulties. I heard no cases under this law, so I cannot say how the courts would punish breaches. The judges told me that defaulters on promises were like thieves and should be punished. They said they would order specific performance or levy damages. I asked how damages would be assessed. Would they be fixed, or would the court make a defaulter pay the other party for losses from inability to fish or to plant a garden? The judges said they had not thought about this and would decide when cases came up. Barotse law up to that time had allowed no claims for damages flowing from failure of another person to carry out an obligation. In Zululand I heard a court reject a jilted teacher's claim for loss of earnings in a suit for breach of promise of marriage, since she had left her employment to prepare for her wedding, and also for damages because she had lost time when she might have become betrothed to another.

That Barotse law did not enforce executory contracts may be partly related to the comparative unimportance of free contracts in indigenous Barotse life. In the past, where a man entered into such a transaction, there was also little point in his seeking to evade fulfillment. But this attitude is also consistent with their whole conception of what a transaction is, and with the remedies they provide for breach of a transaction.

The Barotse do not divide contracts into undertakings entered into by each party to do a particular thing for the other. I have never heard a court, or Barotse in discussion, formulate transactions in this way. They certainly do speak of agreement (*tumelano*) to barter, to enter into service, to arrange a marriage, and so forth, but they do not argue that a man who has promised to do something ought therefore to be compelled by the courts to do it or to pay damages. They condemn people who evade their promises, but they do not consider promisors to be bound in law. In effect they assert, with the Romans, *ex nuda pacta non oritur actio* (no action at law arises from a bare agreement).

In cases of barter and sale the dispute is always argued in terms of rights in property. Hence if no property is involved, there can be no obligation. There must be some transfer of property to create rights and obligations, and establish a *vinculum juris* (a nexus at law). Therefore problems of valid offers and acceptance, or of voidability, do not seem to arise. Thus a man cannot have a right in a net which is not made, and if he has not delivered the purchase price he does not get rights in a net which is made. If he has paid at least part of the price and the net is made, his rights in the net vest because in all these transactions the two items of property involved are regarded as equivalent.

This stress that some property be transferred before obligations are created undoubtedly conflicts with the idea that social life is a process of utmost good faith, *uberrimae fidei*. The judgment of disapproval on the breaker of a promise is severe but is not armed with legal sanctions. A promise to do something for another, having no reference to specific property rights, could not create an obligation. Here transactions differ from the obligations and rights created by birth into a kinship group, which is regarded as a person's main grounds for claims on the goods and services of others. But even these kinship claims may be referred to specific transactions with property in the form of gifts ceremonially given to particular persons at critical periods of life.

This gift giving is more marked in the establishment of in-lawship. To open discussions with a woman's guardians about betrothing her requires a small gift called "opening the mouth" (*vula'mlomo*). The bride must be enticed to leave home to go to her husband by a gift, and paid to pass each crossroads instead of going to someone else's, while her acceptance of a gift signifies her satisfaction with the consummation of the marriage. At the marriage feast there should be an exchange of beasts (each called "eating of porridge") between the two sets of kin. On one occasion, the bride's father generously offered an extra beast to the groom's kin; the groom's kin refused it on the grounds that it would be like a return of the marriage cattle, thus canceling the transfer of conjugal rights over the woman to the bridegroom. They said this was different from the beasts "to eat porridge," which are exchanged to establish kinship between the two groups.

Ceremonial gifts are thus property which conveys rights from one party to another in amending status relations. That the marriage agreement and ritual alone cannot achieve this is made clear by the rule that if a man agrees with a woman's kin to marry her, and all the marriage ritual is performed but he does not transfer the marriage cattle, there is no marriage. He cannot proceed against adulterers, and the court describes the woman as "a wife of the country." Some transfer of property is essential to create any rights and obligations.[7] There was a similar stream of gifts in early European marriage.[8] Kroeber states of the Yurok, that transmission of property is transmission of status.[9]

Barotse law is here like all early law. In archaic legal systems, said Maine, "conveyances and contracts were practically confounded," and "a *Contract* was long regarded as an *incomplete Conveyance*." [10]

---

7. There is an excellent theoretical discussion of this situation by Fortes in "Analysis and Description in Social Anthropology," Presidential Address to the Anthropology Section of the British Association for the Advancement of Science, 1953.

8. Wessels, *History of the Roman–Dutch Law* (1908), pp. 461–63.

9. Hoebel, *Law of Primitive Man* (1954), p. 59, cited from Kroeber.

10. *Ancient Law* (1861, in 10th ed.), pp. 324 f. See also Potter, *The History of the Common Law* (1932), p. 366.

Barotse sales are reciprocal conveyances, rather than contracts creating obligations. But Barotse law arms with its sanctions not, as Maine said of early law, "a promise accompanied by a solemn ceremonial" [11] (the public weighing of copper in Rome), but the yielding of property, which in some situations should be set in a ceremonial context. I do not here cite Maine to deny the validity of his statement about early Roman Law but to emphasize that Barotse look at the property rather than at the ceremonial.

The conflict between this view of contracts and the idea of social life as a process uberrimae fidei is resolved in this way. A transfer of property is essential to create a legal obligation. But once an obligation is created, once a valid relationship is established, then it is uberrimae fidei. Each party is generally expected to look to his obligations rather than to his rights; the seller gives an extensive implied warranty. But the lack of property (of *causa* or *consideration* defined by material goods alone) to establish a *vinculum juris* (nexus of obligation) overrides the general demand for generous fulfillment before valid transactions are established. There is a demand for what Stone speaks of as the "outward and visible sign of a bargain." [12]

The basic importance of property in Barotse law runs through all their contracts. I exhibit this in a case I heard tried by the national appeal court in 1947.[13] A man called Kamandisa bought cattle while he was working in Mongu, the main British township in Barotseland. He sent the cattle to his father's village. His father placed the cattle for herding under agistment with a neighbor as *mafisa* cattle. This is a very common transaction, by which a rich Barotse spreads his surplus cattle and gets them herded by others who in return get the use of milk and manure. Or a man acts thus when he is pressed for someone to herd his cattle, or wants to conceal them from his kin lest they take the cattle under the custom of privileged theft. An important effect of this contract is that it enables a man to establish friendship with others; some men thus disperse most of their own cattle and themselves herd the cattle of others. If one of the herded cattle dies, the herder must take meat and hide to the owner, or if this be impossible, he should sell them and take the money to the owner. The owner can

11. *Ancient Law* (1861, 10th ed.), p. 327.
12. See Stone, *Province and Function of Law* (1947), p. 538, and on Roman–Dutch *causa*, p. 540.
13. Reported also in my *Judicial Process among the Barotse* (1955), pp. 109–10.

reclaim the cattle when he pleases, provided he gives reasonable notice to enable the herder to find other cattle; but he must then leave one heifer with the herder as reward.

Kamandisa approved of his father's action in thus having his cattle herded. Kamandisa was later sentenced to several years in jail for manslaughter. After some time his father took back from the herder all the cattle except two heifers; he left one heifer to be herded for his son and said that the other was the herder's reward, though this reward is not customarily given until the whole relationship is broken. The herder objected that when Kamandisa came out of jail he would claim the reward heifer and its progeny. They therefore called in the Sambi, the chief councillor of the southern capital, to be witness. The Sambi, giving evidence, said he warned them that Kamandisa would object and advised that Kamandisa be consulted, though he was still in jail. Kamandisa's father and the herder both died.

On his release from jail, Kamandisa found that his father and elder brother had disposed of some of his cattle. He went to claim the others from the herder's sons, and they showed him the heifer left with them and its progeny (altogether 10 cattle) as his, and the reward heifer and its progeny (7 cattle) as theirs. He sued for these as well, offering them one heifer, and lost in the local subordinate court, but was successful in the local capital, whose chief's judgment read: "Herders, I have found out that you ought to take one from the 7 cattle, because the cow did not belong to Kamandisa's father who you say gave it to your father. He gave away a cow which did not belong to him. Now the owner of it ought to take it, because he was not the one who gave it to your father. . . . I have satisfied myself through the witnesses that the cow belonged to Kamandisa and not to his father as you say."

The herders appealed to the national appeal court, and there Kamandisa objected to the appeal on the grounds that it is not customary to reward the herder of mafisa cattle until all the cattle are taken from him. He pleaded: "The old Barotse law says that when mafisa cattle are taken, the herder takes one cow, not an ox, and he is not paid for his work. He is given the cow when the cattle are taken back. If now in the times of the White men the law is changed so that the herder is paid, let the chief councillor announce this law so that we may know."

It is worth noting that Kamandisa under cross-examination by the judges did not blame his father and elder brother for killing and selling some of his cattle: "I know that the cattle of my father are my cattle, and that if I am in trouble I can spend my brother's cattle, and he in trouble can use mine. But my father wasted my cattle by paying the herder."

The appeal judges were divided. Some found for the herders. Thus one prince said: "Kamandisa, it is your father's fault. He gave away your beast. He gave it because you were his child . . . as you said, what is your father's, is yours. You cannot sue for what was given by your father . . . because your cow is your father's." But he hedged somewhat on the general principle by saying that he was convinced by the evidence of Councillor Sambi, and he did not believe that Kamandisa, in jail, was not informed by his father about what he had done. Another judge followed this line of argument, stressing the strength of the evidence that the father had given the heifer: "Your father gave it to the herder. If your father had taken something belonging to a stranger, this stranger could follow it and say it was his. You cannot, because your cattle are your father's. Your quarrel is with your father. . . . You know that your father gave it: you cannot deny it."

On the other hand, most of the senior councillors found for Kamandisa. Here is a typical judgment on this side: "Kamandisa: . . . if a man takes a thing and sells it, without the owner knowing, the owner can sue for it. A man's father is owner of his thing, but the son can sue the father and the father can sue the son if he does badly with the other's thing . . . But your father sent only your beasts to be herded and not his own. The parent does not judge for the child. So I see that the cattle are yours and you give them one." The other judges, up to the most senior, followed this analysis: they stressed that the father could take his son's cattle for himself, but as he did not own the cattle, he had no right to give a beast to the herders in the middle of the herding, against customary rules. The herders were entitled to one heifer only.

This case arose in circumstances created by British occupation and it therefore confronted the court with a new problem. All the judges, whether they supported the appellant or the respondent, discussed the issue in terms of what were the father's proprietary rights in his son's cattle. Even those who held that he could give an agistment (mafisa) cow, against common practice, in the middle of the transaction of herding, defended their ruling by assuming that Kamandisa, in jail, had been informed of the action. But their main argument was that the father had rights of ownership in his son's cattle, and hence he could—maybe foolishly and unnecessarily—give away a cow. The others restored the cattle on two grounds: first, his father had the right to take cattle for himself, but his right did not entitle him to give them away. Second, they held that this action involved a variation from customary rules in the transaction concerned, and this was unreasonable at another's expense. For Barotse tend to see each type of transaction as specific to itself, with its own rules, just like a status relationship.

None of the judges considered the problem in terms of whether the father was acting as an agent for his son in caring for his cattle, and in arranging for them to be herded had exceeded his powers, though several stressed the father's wisdom in selecting such good herders and praised the herders for the way in which they discharged their obligations. Nor did they think of him as a kind of *negotiorum gestor,* as Middle Roman law might have done, acting for his son in the emergency of the latter's imprisonment. The judges, in stating "your father did wrong," in effect emphasized their view that Kamandisa was suing his dead father for the beast, and that his suit against the herders was to assert a title against the world. One judge regarded the father's unnecessary reward to the herders—which the herders themselves knew to be against custom—as unreasonable without his son's agreement; and therefore he considered that the son could not be bound by the gift.

It is striking that no judge considered whether the father's action had created an obligation between him and the herders, by which they could claim against his estate in which Kamandisa had shared. Rights of ownership in a particular cow were in dispute, and the court as a whole held in effect: a son now has primary ownership in his own earned cattle; his father and brothers can take of these cattle only for their own needs, in difficulties; they can take steps to secure the proper herding of the cattle under the mafisa transaction, but cannot dispose of cattle outside customary practice; the son is bound by the rules of this transaction to pay the herder one beast. This last ruling was made by all the judges; and had the father, before his death, taken back all the cattle from the herder, he would have been compelled to leave one heifer.

I state these findings in terms of rights of ownership over the cattle, for the Barotse looked at the problem thus, within the setting of a specific transaction, "placing cattle to be herded." There was no reference at all to a general conception of agreement or contract.

I heard only one trial involving anything like agency, and this from another point of view shows that for Barotse judges rights and obligations are established by conveyances of property. In this case, heard in 1942, a man sued another for the purchase price of a beast bought some twenty-two years before. The defendant admitted he had made the purchase, but said it was on credit for a White cattle buyer, who died after receiving the ox but before he had given his "agent" the money for it. The plaintiff said he knew the ox was bought for, and delivered to, this buyer. The court held unanimously that nevertheless he had had nothing to do with the White man, and his dealings were only with the defendant, who had received the ox and must pay for it. I omitted to inquire whether the plaintiff could have claimed possible progeny if he had sold a cow; he claimed no interest on the money. In Barotse law, an agent does not establish any obligation between his principal and the man he deals with on his principal's behalf; and correspondingly, a man is not responsible for the delicts of his servants, although he is for the delicts of his children.

This statement of the law was confirmed by Epstein in a report of a case heard in the Urban African Court at the mining town of Chingola. Here a Barotse was sued for damages by his neighbor whose house was burned as a result of a fire started in the defendant's house by the defendant's servant. The Barotse sought to evade liability on two grounds. First, in Barotseland no suit lies for damage caused accidentally by fire or water which, say the Barotse, "are other chiefs"— i.e. the damage they cause is considered to be an act of God. (Arson and deliberate drowning are punishable.) Second, he pleaded that, since under Barotse law a man is not responsible for the acts of negligence of his servant, if the court held the plaintiff entitled to compensation, it should be against his servant. He argued further that ultimate responsibility for negligence must lie with the builder of the house because of defective construction of the chimney. The court, composed of representatives of several tribes, held for the plaintiff. The absolute denial of responsibility where damage is caused by fire or water seems peculiar to the Barotse among the Northern Rhodesian tribes; Epstein does not say specifically what the law is in other tribes about the responsibility of masters for servants. He concludes that "Starting from the general concept of Injury [the judges] were enabled to affirm that the plaintiff's claim was good not only in terms of the Copperbelt practice, but the validity of such claim was indeed recognized in the law of nearly all the tribes of Northern Rhodesia." Houses in towns, he adds, are more difficult to replace than houses in the tribal areas, and hence the injury was greater than in tribal areas.

For the reasoning of the judges, which was supported by Barotse judges in the Urban African Court at Livingstone, to whom Epstein put this as a case in conflict of law, was that "when a man injured his neighbour in that way the case must be settled according to the custom of the party who was injured." Epstein considers they would have been at cross-purposes if he had put the issue in terms of Barotse law, since the law of the plaintiff disclosed no wrong. A man had suffered damage and was entitled to compensation: the master and not the servant had means to pay recompense. The courts worked from these general principles, and considered that the principles were part of their customary law. Hence the judges did not seem to be aware in any sense that they were establishing new law.[14]

I have already reported that Barotse did not mortgage or pledge land in return for money, or lease land for rent. And they did not pledge chattels, or have any suretyship.

In Barotse law, then, the maxim is strongly *caveat vendor*, for the seller gives a powerful implied warranty that his goods are sound and are his own. Latent defect is widely interpreted. The buyer can reject a cow which falls ill some time after transfer, and an owner can pursue his goods against an innocent purchaser. An agent is personally responsible, and does not bind his principal to the third party, but must himself recover from the principal.

It is difficult to assess what the indigenous Barotse doctrine was on the question of fair and proper exchanges of goods, or of a fair price when money came into common use. During World War II, in 1940 to 1942, inflation of prices led British and Barotse governments to attempt to control prices, and hence in the Barotse courts the charging of prices beyond those set became a criminal offense. In the past, when goods were traded by barter, more or less set standards of exchange seemingly persisted over a long period. When money was introduced, prices were also standardized. These, according to records in the Dis-

14. Epstein, *Juridical Techniques and the Judicial Process* (1954), pp. 26–27.

trict Notebooks, rose very slowly until 1940, when typical prices were twelve fish for 1 shilling, a normal-length sleeping mat for 1s., a hoe for 2s. No cases arising out of barter occur in a set of court records given to me and covering cases heard around 1920, nor did I hear of any in 1940, my first year in Barotseland. Barter was always in direct transactions settled on the spot, apparently with standardized prices. Moreover in 1940 I noted no differences in prices of products at their source of production and points of sale from the plain into the forest up to thirty miles away, or down the Zambezi River below the plain. Indeed, in that year a series of incidents indicated that Barotse did not put a money value on the time and labor involved in transporting goods from one place to another.

By 1942 these valuations had become important. The war caused a sharp rise in the price of goods in European stores. It also led to a sharp rise in the number of Barotse men away at work, which produced a fall in home production of grain and fish and an increasing importation of cassava and millet from the Lunda and Lubale to the north. Shortage of imported axes, spades, nails, etc. caused the government to purchase articles of this kind made by Barotse smiths. The control of bovine pleuropneumonia, and the reopening of cattle purchases for distant towns, raised the price of cattle, milk, and meat. All food prices, and prices of utensils, etc., began to rise steeply. Wages of Whites' employees were raised. By 1947 the end of the war had allowed Government to begin large-scale building: demands for local labor and locally produced food increased while home production continued to fall. Increased supplies of money from labor in Barotseland and abroad accelerated this inflation.

In 1942 the position of the court was not yet clear. A fishmonger was caught by a Northern Rhodesian Government (Barotse) sergeant of police selling fish to people at a price of four small fish for sixpence, and was sent by the Provincial Commissioner to the court. The court found that this price was "just stealing the people's money," and several councillors said the price ought to return to earlier prices, when 1 shilling bought 12 fish. The head of the court, the private Ngambela of the king, said:

> If the court wishes to inform the whole country of Barotseland of the price of fish set by the court I have not power at this time to summon the whole nation to the court because the Ngambela

[the chief councillor] is not here. When the Ngambela arrives I will report this affair to him because we all know very well that reeds, grass, and poles are no longer bought at the decent prices agreed to in the past; and if the prices of fish are increased greatly thus, why is it? If the owner of the country [the Ngambela] agrees in this affair as we have spoken, it is easy for me to gather the country and tell the people the prices set. [He scolded the council, saying:] All prices are ruined by you of the capital. The year before last you began to sell your sacks at a higher price—a sack of cassava meal we sold for ourselves for £1, of millet for £1.2s.6d., of maize for 19s. And by this custom the Lunda [trading meal and grain from Balovale District] took these bad prices; and afterwards when you failed to find food which you could sell, and had yourselves to buy from the Lunda, you complained greatly. The fault was not the Lunda's but yours —they saw it in you of the capital. When you began to complain of the prices of the Lunda, you asked me to discuss the matter with the District Commissioner, and indeed I carried out your request. Now a basket such as we set to be the scale of the whole nation has been sent by the District Commissioner—now we have no complaint.

He then instructed the fishmonger to go away with his fish, since he had committed no offense under existing legislation.[15] (Notice the clear distinction between the judicial and the legislative functions of this multipurpose council.)

That same year the national council, with representatives from all the capitals of the country, debated whether they could control prices.[16] All were agreed that some rise was inevitable, since wages paid by Whites, as well as prices of European goods, were rising, but most considered the actual rises were too great. The debate concentrated on difficulties in enforcing control. In their discussion some councillors argued that it was impossible to fix prices for Barotseland as a whole, since a man must be paid "for his shoulder" and his time in moving goods from one place to another. Also variations in supplies and demands of different goods in different places and months must affect prices as well as variations in supplies of money at various cen-

15. Reported in my *Judicial Process among the Barotse* (1955), pp. 69–70.
16. See my "Lozi Price-Control Debate" (1943).

ters, according to their distance from the towns where Europeans offered employment. (There was, in fact, a range in tax rates for Barotse under British laws according to this distance.) Finally they said that if prices were regulated by law, all trade would be driven from public centers where need was greatest into out-of-the-way places. The council decided it could do little, but the Ngambela, concluding the discussion, maintained: "We are the Government. We must rule and enforce our laws." Prices were then set on various goods.

Peddlers and hawkers continued to increase in number, gaining their living by charging for their labor and time in moving goods, where in 1940 no purchaser considered this an argument. Incidents of the following kind began to occur. A clerk agreed to purchase a certain quantity of fish for 2s. He asked the fisherman who was passing his village to carry the fish there. When they arrived the fisherman demanded 2s.3d., the extra 3d. being "for his shoulder," the work of carrying. The purchaser paid, and then grumbled to his fellows that the good days were gone. He had bought at a price above the controlled price and feared to go to court, lest they both be fined for breach of the price-control laws. The court, I think, would have allowed the 3d. for carrying, as a separate transaction.

Barter and purchase in practice had ceased to be exchange of conventional quantities, and haggling over quantities and prices became common. The council as a court did not react to this development by arguing, "they made an agreement which we will enforce," since it had attempted to apply price control, stimulated by the British Government's efforts to carry out a price-control policy. In the few cases that came before the council out of these exchanges, all involving nonpayment of the purchase price, the court in fact enforced payment of the legislated price and fined at least the seller, and sometimes the purchaser, for breaking "the laws of the nation." The court had begun to move tentatively, with the change in economic conditions, to a recognition that barter and sale were not set transactions with all conditions determined, but were transactions influenced by the agreement of the parties within the limitations of legislation and public policy.

The data thus indicate that probably, as might be expected, the Barotse had a concept of fair price, and therefore in the case of the exorbitant fishmonger they described him as "just stealing the people's money." I suggest that here, as everywhere, the concept of a fair price fitted with the doctrine *caveat vendor*.

In practice therefore I heard of only one case that in any sense produced a situation in which the court might be described as applying a doctrine of relief from overcharging, and as it happens this case also involved problems of public morality. A man told me that the court upheld his suit to recover part of his payment to a woman because she had not allowed him a commensurate number of acts of intercourse. The number had not been determined in advance. The court assessed a price and ordered the prostitute to refund the balance. The court confirmed this to me, but replied to a question I put that they would not allow a suit by a prostitute for her fees as against decency and public policy, and they doubted if any woman would have the courage and shamelessness to bring such a suit.

There is here a double standard at work, which rules out the strict application of the rule that *in pari delicto potior est condito defendentis* (in equal guilt the position of the defendant is stronger). In other circumstances, as I have shown in my study, *The Judicial Process among the Barotse* (pp. 204–05), the court applies this doctrine. The male judges regard an alleged increase in adultery, and the certainly new phenomenon of prostitution, as due to the vicious nature of women, not of men. Therefore prostitutes do not in any way merit the protection of the law, but their clients are protected against exploitation by something akin to the Roman and Roman–Dutch law doctrine of *laesio enormis* [17] (I draw this parallel, because laesio enormis also seems to be a doctrine fitting the stress on obligation). But it is important to note here on the other hand that as prostitutes have begun to appear, the courts will not allow men even to seem to make money out of their wives' adulteries. For when a husband has recovered damages for adultery by his wife against two or three co-respondents, the court will say either that she is really a prostitute, or that her husband refuses to divorce her in order to make money out of her peccadilloes, and will declare her "a wife of the country," with whom any man may cohabit.[18] These cases also show how the Barotse look at what they consider to be public policy and interest in dealing with transactions of all kinds.

17. See my *Judicial Process among the Barotse,* p. 215, and Schapera (1938), p. 267.

18. Epstein reports this attitude of Urban African Courts, and says they may apply penal sanctions against the husband (*Juridical Techniques and the Judicial Process,* 1954, p. 28).

We ourselves speak of a marriage contract, but clearly marriage is a contract of quite a different kind from a commercial transaction.[19] Barotse will also speak of the agreements between buyer and seller, and between bride's kin and groom's kin, as *litumelano,* but they do not think of them as therefore requiring similar treatment. Hence while they were trying within the law to apply a doctrine of fair price to sales, allowing some rise with inflation, they did not do this to marriage payments given by a groom to his bride's kin to obtain conjugal rights from them. The amount of payments had been limited by the council, but many brides' fathers demanded and obtained more from eager grooms. In the event of a divorce the court would enforce return only of the statutory sum, holding that anything above that given by the groom was "his wealth," the measure of his wish for the marriage and the relationship with his father-in-law. Daughters and wives are not goods in exchange, but persons with status in kin relationships, so that the court resisted pressure on it to let the marriage payment rise in the inflationary spiral, though it attempted to reduce adultery and abduction of wives by raising both the fines imposed on erring wives and the fines and damages imposed on their lovers.

I have had to build my analysis of the Barotse law of transactions mainly out of a few cases like Kamandisa's and the case of the fishing nets. Since these transactions are relatively rare in Barotse life, few cases involving them come to court. I have records of other cases arising out of agisted cattle, a few straightforward cases of sale, and some cases of employers failing to pay their servants. Most of my records are of cases arising from breach of status relations. Therefore I can only add that even when servants sue their masters for their wages they tend to argue not in terms of the agreement to pay them wages but in terms of what has accrued from their work, as if they have proprietary rights in this product, which the employer has filched. A man herding cattle in the owner's village claims his milk, a fisherman employed for wages claims his fish, and a man who has staked his cattle in another's garden to fertilize it claims the manure. Owners of fishing nets, and of fish dams in which traps are set, may arrange with a fisherman to do the fishing in return for the catch on alternate days. Here disputes are also argued in terms of rights in the fish and obliga-

19. Lewis overlooks that contract has several meanings in using his excellent account of political contracts, or treaties, among Somali to comment on Maine's dictum of the movement from status to contract ("Clanship and Contract in Northern Somaliland," 1959, p. 292)

tions arising from this ownership. Transactions lead to debts, not to agreements.

The manner in which Barotse law lays its emphasis on obligation is also shown in the absence of any doctrine of limitation or prescription of suit. In the case I cited of a Barotse who had bought a cow on behalf of a White man who had died, twenty-two years had elapsed between the original purchase and the suit. Barotse say "a debt and a case never die"; both are inherited by the heir of a dead man. But this last rule was changed almost casually in 1942 when, on a case stated from a minor district court, the court at the capital ruled that a dead man's kin are no longer responsible for his debts and cannot be held liable for a judgment in damages against him if he dies. The court here, as in the case of the father who put his son's cattle to be herded, seemed to be altering customary law partly to accord with changed economic and social facts in Barotseland, and partly in deference to what it believed to be the rulings of the Northern Rhodesian Government that people should retain their own earnings and should be personally liable only for their own faults.[20] Clearly, there was no prescription of action in the past among the Barotse, or as far as I know any other tribe. The position in general is beautifully stated in a maxim given me by Richard Werbner from the Kalanga of Southern Rhodesia: "Meat rots but a case never rots." Schapera (1938, p. 286) had reported the same maxim from the Tswana: he discusses prescription.

It is less clear how far stringent definitions of warranty, latent defect, fair price, and possibly even *laesio enormis* apply in other tribal systems, or what in these systems determines delivery of goods and transfer or gain from increment or loss from risk. Unfortunately few writers on these systems have looked at these problems. I have searched many, but obviously not all, accounts, and I have found mostly blanks. A few records show that the Barotse are not unique, for example, in holding the seller responsible for death of an animal some time after the purchaser has taken it. Among certain Plains Red Indians, when a horse was stolen within a day or two after its purchase, or was lamed in the first race it ran for its owner, a part of the purchase price was refunded.[21]

Among the Kalinga of the Philippines if a water buffalo, horse, or

20. See my *Judicial Process among the Barotse* (1955), pp. 243, 287.
21. Quoted by Herskovits, *Economic Anthropology* (1952), p. 205.

ox died within the year after its sale, the purchaser could demand the refund of the purchase price.[22] But the present practice, according to Barton's later work, is that buyer and seller agree on a point on the homeward journey of the buyer "when the sale becomes irrevocable— that is to say, a point beyond which, should the animal fall over a cliff, the buyer will bear the loss and inside which the purchase price will be refunded." If the two parties are of different political districts, this point will usually be the boundary line between the districts. However, in one of their districts accident is not thus taken into consideration, but there is sometimes a provision against death by pest for a number of days.[23] Barton noted also that when he was first in Kalinga in 1916, if a landslide or other force of nature badly damaged a field before its delivery to the purchaser, then the purchaser might refuse to accept it and require refund of the price. Later the rule changed, and the seller was liable only if the field were washed away or otherwise destroyed. Barton considered the seller was more favored by the later rule, which stated "there must be a field to deliver." [24] But in his earlier book on the neighboring Ifugao he had noted that both among them and the Kalinga, if a rice field after delivery to the purchaser was subject to an unusual number of slides in the terrace wall, or in part washed away by a freshet, "the purchaser may at any time within the year following the purchase, relinquish the field and demand the return of his purchase price. This is on the ground that the seller may have put a curse on the field when it left his hands, or that, at least, he did not relinquish his hold on its welfare and fertility." [25]

We are here entering into some of the mystical attributes of land, and perhaps chattels, which identify them with the owner and his spirits. For example, among the Akan of Ghana the buyer had to provide a sheep for sacrifice to the spirits or gods of the land lest he not thrive on the land, or the seller not profit by the purchase money.[26] To understand this mystical association we need to examine tribal concepts of injury, for under these concepts to alter any social

22. Barton, *Ifugao Law* (1919), p. 50.
23. Barton, *The Kalingas* (1949), p. 113 and n.
24. Ibid., p. 115.
25. *Ifugao Law* (1919), p. 49.
26. Danquah, *Akan Laws and Customs* (1928), p. 217; Obi, *The Ibo Law of Property* (1963), pp. 54–55. See also Ter Haar, *Adat Law in Indonesia* (1948), p. 131 (orig. Dutch, 1939).

arrangement, even by transferring goods, is a wrong. Ideally a tribal system is stationary. Here I am emphasizing the extent to which *caveat vendor*, and not *caveat emptor*, was the rule.

In general, this rule is shown by the fact that increment but not risk may pass to the purchaser even if he does not always take immediate delivery of a cow. Schapera records this of increment for the Tswana, but does not state whether risk passes simultaneously.[27] In other tribes it is not clear whether there was the same stringent favoring of the buyer. Among the Sukuma of Tanganyika nowadays (i.e. 1953), once a beast has been transferred to the buyer he cannot have the sale declared void unless the vendor has given before witnesses undertakings about the beast which afterward prove to be false. And nowadays Sukuma hold that if a beast dies or becomes sick while awaiting transfer the loss falls on the buyer. But this rule was enacted by the chiefs, where formerly the rule was uncertain, and some courts held the seller liable till actual transfer, as the Barotse do. The investigator did not say who had rights in calves, but if a man buys a female calf, which has yet to be produced by a particular cow, the law favors him rather than the seller in various contingencies.[28]

The problem of when delivery passes, or when indeed a valid transaction is completed, is also overlooked in most studies, but again there are some statements indicating that some transfer of property on both sides is usually necessary to establish rights and obligations. In the adat law of Indonesia, says Ter Haar's authoritative summary, the "mere agreement in words does not obligate anyone to anything. This is accomplished only by the presentation of a small coin or some other object." With the exception of a report on one Indonesian tribe, Ter Haar says that there must be such "a material binder." This rule is applied also to labor contracts, for upon taking employment the worker must be given a trifling payment by his employer, a payment which is later deducted from his wages. He goes on to describe "numerous other customs [which] are based on the idea that the transfer of some tangible goods effects a desired connection between the two persons at the time of transfer." [29] The rule is not universal. Among the Ifugao if a seller takes the initiative in making an offer to one person,

27. *Handbook of Tswana Law and Custom* (1938), p. 243.
28. Cory, *Sukuma Law and Custom* (1953), pp. 147 f.
29. Ter Haar, *Adat Law in Indonesia* (1948), pp. 140 f.

he is liable for damages if he then sells to another party. By implication he can withdraw his offer if he retains the property.[30] Here too we are told that agents do not bind their principals.[31] In general the problems of sale and barter cannot be discussed in terms of offer and acceptance, etc., apart from transfers of property. One is reminded of "God's penny" which sealed bargains in early English markets.[32]

Obviously the Barotse law of transactions in these respects appears to correspond with the early law of Europe. Vinogradoff reports that throwing a stick and handing over a sod symbolized the transfer of a field.[33] Maitland states generally that in early English law "without transfer of a thing there is no transfer of a right," and that it seems to him that "the law of an earlier time required a change of possession on the one side or the other, delivery or part-delivery of the goods, payment or part-payment of the price." [34] Similarly Holmes in *The Common Law* (1881) stresses that debt throws most light upon the doctrine of consideration (p. 253); that originally debts were not conceived of "as raised by a promise, but were a 'duty' springing from the plaintiff's receipt of property, a fact which could be seen and sworn to before proof of writing" (p. 264); and that only since Edward III have debts arising from a transaction without writing been said "to arise from contract, as distinguished from debts arising from an obligation" (p. 267). He stresses generally that "before consideration was ever heard of, debt was the time-honoured remedy on every obligation to pay money enforced by law, except the liability to damages" (p. 269).

I have also described how the Barotse tend to speak of the defaulting party in a transaction as a thief, stealing the other's goods; or at least the judges say he spoiled the other's property. Breach of transaction is a wrong. Again, in Holmes' words, when the doctrine of consideration developed, "the notion of tort was not at once abandoned" in breach of obligation. Even at the beginning of the reign of Henry VII "it was said that the action would not be for a failure to keep a promise, but only for negligence after the defendant had entered upon his undertaking" (p. 284). Stone puts it that "the gist of the

---

30. Barton, *Ifugao Law* (1919), p. 46.
31. Ibid., pp. 57 f.
32. Hamilton, "The Ancient Maxim Caveat Emptor" (1931), p. 1160, n. 189.
33. "Transfer of Land in Old English Law," in *Collected Papers*, 1 (1923), 150–51, 157.
34. "The Mystery of Seisin," in *Collected Papers*, 1 (1911), 377, 384 n.

action of *assumpsit* was rather a tort claim for loss due to reliance on the defendant's undertaking, at first available for damage caused by misfeasance in performance, and only later extended to his simple failure to perform." [35]

Finally I draw attention to a Barotse estate holder's claim for the return to him of land, discussed in the third chapter. If he is not to be barred in his claim, he must give the borrower notice in time for the latter to acquire a new field for the next planting season and to make use of his improvements, such as fertilizing the field. Similar rules are reported from other tribes, e.g. from the Tswana.[36]

Among the Ifugao, a man can enter on the use of anyone's abandoned land, and he is entitled to continue to cultivate it for as many years as the field was abandoned by the holder. Thereafter it reverts to the holder. The latter has to pay for the labor expended if he wants the field earlier, or he can demand that the user purchase it, "but he may not take advantage of the labour that the other has spent on the land in making rice fields, to demand an exorbitant payment. To take such a course would invite danger to himself." Generally here it is up to the owner to warn people if they take over the use of his land that he will require it: they need not seek his permission. If he does not warn them, he is not allowed to profit from their labor.[37]

In attempting to generalize from the Barotse to other tribal systems, I have to rely on odds and ends of information of this kind. I have therefore concentrated on my own data from the Barotse. My thesis is that in tribal systems the law has to stress obligations, rather than right, in its handling of disputes between kin, since only thus can these relationships, which are full of strains, be helped to endure.[38] This doctrine of relationships uberrimae fidei is extended to other transactions, in which the emphasis is on obligation rather than right. Again, few students of tribal law have looked at these problems. But there are some illuminating statements. Ter Haar writes that the central thought in adat law runs,

> "I give somebody something, or I work for him. For this I am
> to get a return in services at the proper time. And then—if

35. *Province and Function of Law* (1947), p. 537.

36. Schapera, *Handbook of Tswana Law and Custom* (1938), p. 204.

37. Barton, *Ifugao Law* (1919), p. 42.

38. See e.g. Gibbs, "The Kpelle Moot. A Therapeutic Model for the Informal Settlement of Disputes" (1963).

explicitly agreed in the transaction—he gets an expectation of a
return from me, upon demand by him at the suitable time. . . .
An over-balance accrues to the advantage of the person who
gives more than he receives. Therefore, giving more than you
receive comes to be a desire, a duty, or even an act of preservation
of your own respectability. . . . The obligation to respect the
interests of the other fellow with whom a legal deed has been
made, the obligation of good faith, places the solution [of problems arising from fraud on creditors] beyond the range of doubt,
in many instances.[39]

More striking is a fairly bare statement in Bohannan's analysis of
Justice and Judgment among the Tiv of Nigeria:

Tiv . . . use both the institutions of self-help and the *jir*
[court] to enforce their rights. This is not, however, the way
they put it. Their emphasis is on means of making others carry
out their obligations. They discuss social acts by comparing them
with what one "ought" to do or to have done. Both the *jir* and
the institutions of self-help are used for the same purpose, that of
making people carry out their obligations towards one.[40]

In this way it is reported from both the Ifugao of the Philippines [41]
and the Tallensi of Ghana [42] that a creditor in an independent group
can enforce his claim for debt on another by seizing a beast belonging
to a man in the debtor's group. This thrusts the obligation of meeting
the claim of his close fellow onto the debtor, while the man whose
beast is seized takes no action against the creditor. The Tallensi regard
the discharge of this debt to a fellow-clansman as so heavy a moral
obligation that they may pawn a child to redeem it.

Bohannan reports an interesting development of this emphasis on
obligation among the Tiv. A party to a dispute must pay something to
an independent witness to induce the latter to give evidence on his
behalf. This does not mean that Tiv "sell themselves as witnesses, but
rather that they seek to establish a relationship with the man to whom
their testimony is advantageous so that they will not be charged with
interfering in affairs not their own." The defendant appreciates that a

39. Ter Haar, *Adat Law in Indonesia* (1948), pp. 131–32, 139.
40. 1957, p. 131.
41. Barton, *Ifugao Law* (1919), p. 57.
42. Fortes, *Dynamics of Clanship among the Tallensi* (1945), p. 245.

kinsman or someone paid by the plaintiff will support the plaintiff but for some unrelated persons to do so is to be "guilty of an act of aggression." [43] Being put under an obligation exculpates the witness from this charge.

I have picked out these few explicit statements to emphasize what is implicit in many monographs. Firth alone has given his attention directly to the doctrine of *caveat emptor* in his study, *Primitive Polynesian Economy*, on the admittedly very small island of Tikopia. Of it, he writes:

> Concerned for some centuries only with an internal market, the personal relations of producer and consumer enter into their economic position and condition the evaluation of goods and estimate of requirements. The essence of a modern price economy is its impersonality. An essential feature of the primitive system is the control of the good faith of the giver by manifold relations with him, and his endeavour to keep faith in view of these relationships. Our commercial system is characterized on the whole by the want of concern for the satisfactions of the other party to the contract, once it is concluded. The principle of caveat emptor would not function well in a primitive society. [44]

This states the position succinctly. On the other hand, I have found only one clear statement in a monograph on these sorts of societies that caveat emptor applies. Miner states that in the market in Timbuctoo this is the rule, for the vendors cheat without even public disapproval. He lays stress on the difficulty of bringing suit, but he does not follow up problems involved in the doctrine, beyond the question of selling shoddy goods. [45] He is not using the phrase in the legal sense and he does not state what would happen in a suit in court.

I hope that this analysis may focus the attention of anthropologists on this problem and its relationship to ideas of law, particularly where there are no courts armed with enforcing powers. For against the general thesis I have presented stands the following statement by

43. *Justice and Judgment among the Tiv* (1957), pp. 39–40.

44. 1939, p. 349. Oliver (*A Solomon Island Society*, 1955, p. 82) draws a contrast: "Native moralists assert that neighbours should be friendly and mutually trustful, whereas peoples from far-off are dangerous and unworthy of morally just consideration. For example, natives lay stress on honesty in transactions involving neighbours while holding that trade with strangers may be guided by *caveat emptor*."

45. *The Primitive City of Timbuctoo* (1953), p. 52, and Chap. 13.

Evans-Pritchard on the Nuer of the Sudan: "The Nuer has a keen sense of personal dignity and rights. The notion of right, *cuong*, is strong. It is recognized that a man ought to obtain redress for certain wrongs." A man's kin will support him only if he is in the right, and threat of force is the main sanction by which a man secures his rights.[46] But quarrels within a village or camp about ownership of cattle concern obligations of kinship or affinity, and those, Evans-Pritchard observed, "have eventually been settled by one party giving way on account of his relationship to another," i.e. from obligations of status.[47]

Tribal law as I have observed it, like early European law, thus emphasizes that responsibility rests heavily on the seller. In a learned and witty examination in the *Yale Law Journal* (of 1931) of "The Ancient Maxim Caveat Emptor" Professor Walton H. Hamilton showed that the doctrine did not exist in Roman law, canon law, or the common law or law merchant of England. It does not appear until well along into the sixteenth century, and then almost by accident, and it was only firmly established in the seventeenth century. It has been given a much longer pedigree, but Hamilton lampoons this by heading his essay with what he designates as an Old Simian Proverb: "A doctrine is like a family that is coming up in the world; it fits itself out with an ancient lineage." He says caveat emptor was alien to Roman law up to the time of Justinian,[48] while in the law merchant, "credit, not distrust," was the basis of commercial dealings under most exacting standards.

Hamilton stresses that in the days when commercial dealings were restricted, goods went directly from manufacturer to consumer, so that the manufacturer could justly be held liable for defects. At fairs and markets it was in the interests of merchants themselves to maintain high standards, and Hamilton shows how in various ways this was

46. *The Nuer* (1940), p. 171.

47. Ibid., p. 165.

48. The position in Roman law was in fact not quite clear. Jolowicz (*Historical Introduction to Roman Law*, 1939, pp. 305 f.) considers that in the early stages of Roman law the seller was not bound to transfer title and was not responsible for latent defects of which he had no knowledge; these responsibilities, he writes, developed later. Responsibilities for defects in slaves was established by a praetorian edict of at least the first half of the second century B.C., and those for defects in cattle by a later edict. Problems of handing over title arose partly from lack of clear conception of ownership, partly perhaps from the fact that sale is a contract in the *jure gentium*, and hence it would be impossible to bind foreigners. But sale in this form was a later contract.

exploited to maintain monopolies. His hypothesis (p. 1163) seems to be that the doctrine caveat emptor emerged in the byways of social life away from marts of organized trade. In these byways were the palmers and peddlers, strangers with whom men traded at their own peril in stolen goods and in trinkets and charms. He says there is no record of the emergence of the phrase, caveat emptor, and that perhaps it was the sad reflection of a man who had bargained in the horse trade once too often, or a lawyer reflecting that a client had no redress. But being the perfect pithy legal maxim it caught on when conditions altered. Coke first took it up.

I have tried to show here, however, that there is a very ancient lineage indeed for the opposing maxim, caveat vendor, and to suggest that it states an emphasis on obligation and good faith which is characteristic of societies dominated by kin relationships. Then, as with the common law, offenses "such as petty larceny, conscious deceit, and plain negligence are not clearly separated," to quote Hamilton on early English law (p. 1152), nor even accident to a cow or horse. Doubtless out of a similar kind of tribal situation in Europe caveat vendor flourished through a long period of economic and social development, sustained by other communal requirements even when the kinship basis of society had disappeared. When caveat emptor emerged, a freer commerce was blossoming. Freedom of contract developed in the eighteenth century, says Stone,[49] and the new maxim prospered.

One of the key problems for lawyers and anthropologists in the developing countries must surely be a study of the situation that will arise there when new commercial conditions begin to favor this parvenu doctrine against the truly ancient doctrine *caveat vendor*.

49. *Province and Function of Law* (1947), pp. 533-35.

Chapter 7

INJURY, LIABILITY, AND RESPONSIBILITY

WHEN I COME to analyze Barotse jurisprudential ideas about injury and wrong, I am short of data on certain types of cases. Some 80 per cent of cases tried in Barotse courts while I was there were suits by husbands against adulterers or abductors of their wives or suits by women seeking divorce. I heard very few cases arising out of a variety of wrongs committed by people on others previously unrelated to them. Trials for murder, rape, major assaults, and thefts of large amounts of property had been shifted into the courts of the British protecting power. Cases involving suspicion of witchcraft—i.e. accusations of witchcraft—were reserved for the same forum. On the two occasions when "witchcraft" was mentioned while I was recording cases in Barotse courts, the head of the court immediately stopped the hearing and ordered it to be remitted to the British District Commissioner.[1] My data on the Barotse for this chapter come mainly from a different category of situations.

Wrongs in Barotse society arise out of aggressive actions by outsiders, or out of failure to fulfill obligations of familial life or between persons in specific status relationships.[2] I have plentiful information on wrongs arising from breach of status obligation. I shall argue that general ideas of wrong are again best understood in terms of reactions to these wrongs arising in status relations. To demonstrate my argument I begin not from the Barotse, and their governmental system with its courts, but from the societies where redress was secured by self-help and where vengeance for the killing of a man was enjoined on his kinsmen.

1. This was not done by all tribal courts under the British in modern Africa. For example, among the Yao of Nyasaland the court moved out of the courthouse and tried witchcraft cases in the open—they shifted symbolically out of the area of political and juridical relations with the British (see Mitchell, "The Yao of Southern Nyasaland," 1948, and *The Yao Village,* 1956, pp. 100 f.). Tswana courts tried witchcraft cases and looked for tangible evidence (Schapera, "Witchcraft Beyond Reasonable Doubt," 1958, pp. 100 f.).

2. Howell, *Manual of Nuer Law* (1954), p. 22, has a similar statement for the Nuer, a Sudan tribe which, before the establishment of Anglo–Egyptian rule, had no courts.

The operation of rules of vengeance brings up in sharp form key concepts in the law of wrongs: recognition of intention to kill as against killing by negligence or accident, questions of responsibility and liability, and provisions for restitution or punishment. Maitland concluded an essay on "The Early History of Malice Aforethought" in English law by speaking of "the utter incompetence of ancient law to take note of the mental elements of a crime." [3] This statement undoubtedly applies to certain aspects of tribal law. If one injures a man, even accidentally, one may be liable for damages. There are even records of cases in tribes lacking governmental systems under chiefs, where blood money was demanded by the deceased's kinsmen and yielded by the kin of the killer, when the killer (among the Pokot) had "committed" his crime in fighting against a common enemy. Kikuyu stated that payment would be due if the man killed in attempting to save his victim from a lion.[4] There is in these records undoubtedly the implication that whatever the motivations of the killer or the circumstances surrounding the deed, blood money had to be paid if a member of one grouping of kinsmen was killed by a member of some other group. The mental element seems to be irrelevant. What is important is that "murder" is committed within social relationships where blood compensation is due.

Absolute liability has here to be set in the particular context of established social relationships. It is one of the incidents of the relations between discrete vengeance groupings in feuding societies. In his discussion of this "rule of law" among the Nuer, Howell constantly emphasizes that the purpose of the payment is to restore "the equilibrium," as he puts it, between the groups of killer and killed.[5] A killing, even unintentional or accidental, disturbs the balance of blood due between the groups, and this has to be redressed, since the social description of the groups is that they take vengeance upon each other for all killings. This is part of their rights against each other. We

---

3. First published in *Law and Magazine Review* (1883), and then in his *Collected Papers*, I (1911), 304–28, at p. 327. But see Potter, *The History of the Common Law* (1932), p. 317, citing Winfield "The Myth of Absolute Liability" (1926). I continue to use absolute liability, rather than strict liability, as these authors suggest, in contexts where it seems more suitable.

4. Peristiany, "Pokot Sanctions and Structure" (1954); Kikuyu law quoted by Dundas, "Native Laws of Some Bantu Tribes of East Africa" (1921), p. 239. Dundas has a valuable report here on "manslaughter and accidents," and problems of liability.

5. *Manual of Nuer Law* (1954), pp. 41 f.

have to think of a particular killing in these societies not as an individual offense but as one of a series of offenses occurring over a long period of time. Each offense is relative to its context of social relationships, and the chances of securing redress for a wrong in the absence of a governmental organization depend on the social relations between offender and injured. If a killer is a member of a Nuer tribe other than that of his victim, the victim's kin are unlikely to secure compensation. Theoretically it is due, but since the parties live far apart there is no pressure on them to reach a compromise, in which the one will offer and the other accept compensation. If the two vengeance groups live sufficiently close together for them to have to reach a modus vivendi in order that they may go about their business in some peace, various social mechanisms and pressures induce such a compromise.[6] In these circumstances the kin of the deceased have by custom to express "a conventional vindictiveness," and are induced to agree to settlement by a ritual mediator.[7] But if a killing occurs within a vengeance group itself, the payment of blood money has to be made by the very people who are due to receive it. No redress is then possible, and the killing may be regarded as a sin, subject only to ritual or religious sanctions.[8] At this extreme there is no legal liability, while at the other extreme compensation is not likely to be paid. In the middle range compensation may be offered and accepted. Within the social organization, operation of the law is relative to the relations between disputants. Strangers may be outside the law but protected by ritual beliefs. Inside the tribe we have the paradox that where a man injures a close relative the offense is greater, and yet it is less in that no redress is possible.

In these circumstances reaction to a killing therefore only appears to exclude attention to the mental elements of the offense. It is assumed if a man kills a member of a group with which his own group is at feud—i.e. where a past record of killings exists between them—that he must have done so deliberately. The injured parties look mainly at the fact of the deed, and rule out attention to the killer's will. They

6. Ibid., pp. 39 f. I have analyzed the kinds of pressures and mechanisms that operate on the two groups in these tribes in my *Custom and Conflict in Africa* (1955), Chap. 1, and *Politics, Law and Ritual in Tribal Society* (1965), Chap. 3 and 5, where I cite studies of various tribes.

7. Howell, *Manual of Nuer Law* (1954), pp. 42, 45–46, 59.

8. See Schapera, "The Sin of Cain" (1958). Cf. Wallace-Hadrill, "The Blood-Feud among the Franks" (1961).

operate with a legalistic psychology in which intention is presumed from action.

In practice, the Nuer do look at actual circumstances, and though they always require compensation, the deceased's kin are readier to accept compensation if the killing was not intentional. For instance, killing with a fighting spear signifies deliberation, and in some tribes a murder with this weapon entailed higher compensation than if it were committed with a fish spear, or stick. These weapons seemingly suggested that the killing had been by chance. Howell states that "theoretically the question of intention does not enter into the assessment of compensation [after homicide] because the principal object of the payment is to restore the balance [between the groups] which has been disturbed, but Nuer do in fact take it into consideration." He continues to explain that before the Sudan Government instituted courts which had some power to enforce peace and payment, there were set scales of compensation for various injuries, but these were in practice a basis on which compromise could be reached. "In the case of unintentional homicide the indignation of the dead man's kin will be less than in cases of intentional killing." Negotiations were carried out between relatively independent parties under the aegis of a spiritual mediator, who in the end could exert pressure on the recalcitrant party, resisting payment or acceptance of compensation, by threatening to curse them by invoking failure of their enterprises based on the land. This enabled the dead man's kin to accept the mediator's pressure not to insist on the debt of blood for blood, but instead to accept the proffered compensation, "without great shame." [9] Howell does not state whether killing in self-defense affected compensation. Nowadays in the newly instituted courts Nuer "chiefs" have held that half the compensation is due after an accidental, as against an intentional, killing.

Certain social relations are thus denoted by the payment of compensation for injury and death. "There are certain extreme cases," says Howell, "where the principal is held to be liable in theory, even though no compensation is necessary. For example, if a man who is thatching another's house falls and is killed or is seriously injured, the owner must pay . . . a purely symbolic payment in bundles of grass and ropes accompanied by appropriate ritual." [10]

9. Howell, *Manual of Nuer Law* (1954), pp. 41–42, 52, and passim.
10. Ibid., p. 17.

Seemingly, among the Nuer the issue of guilt for a particular killing was unlikely to arise. It was a heinous breach of moral duty for a
man to conceal that he had killed another, since killing set up a spiritual
barrier between the two sets of kin. For example, if they ate together
illness would assail them. The killer himself had to be cleansed from
his spilling of blood.[11] Hence there was no problem of fixing guilt.
This ritual "detection" of blood guilt is reported from diverse parts of
the world.[12]

The Nuer evidence shows that even where liability is absolute, in
that compensation must be paid, attention may be paid to the mental
elements of the killing insofar as this may determine whether the
liability is discharged by blood for blood, or by payment of cattle.
The fact of killing requires adjustment: the circumstances of killing
and the mental elements which the wronged read from those circumstances determine discharge of the liability that inheres in these specific relationships. Thus killing from ambush, as against killing in fair
fight, is "an offence against Nuer standards of chivalry" and rouses
great "moral indignation." But no additional compensation is paid for
killing from ambush, "though a feud arising in such circumstances
might well be harder to settle than one arising from straightforward
homicide or single combat." But if killing from ambush is done in
pursuit of vengeance, "the circumstances are considered to be miti-
gated." [13]

Another circumstance that aggravates a homicide among the Nuer
seems to be a breach of the period of the truce in which a compromise
is negotiated. If the two parties are threatening to fight, the ritual
mediator draws a line between them which neither should cross. On
one occasion:

> A few of the more hotheaded warriors did cross the line and
> were condemned by public opinion afterwards, principally be-
> cause by doing so they showed an excessive determination to join
> battle with the other party in a situation where the majority
> wanted peaceful settlement. In fact, the final result of [the ritual
> mediator's] action was to provoke a much more serious conflict
> than would have otherwise been the case, because the side opposed
> to the youths who had rashly crossed the line were so incensed

11. Ibid., pp. 44 f.
12. See e.g. Barton, *The Kalingas* (1949), pp. 241–43.
13. Howell, *Manual of Nuer Law* (1954), p. 55.

that they found a way of renewing the fight next day in another part of the area, well removed from the place in which the line had been drawn, and in greater force than before.[14]

Howell's careful study of demands for compensation among the bellicose Nuer gives us a series of cases which show that ameliorating cirumstances, from which less guilty intention is assumed, do mitigate the absolute liability that is stated by the rules of law.[15] The principle of liability is not evaded, but those who are wronged are readier to agree to accept material compensation, in place of blood. Furthermore, they may even agree to accept a reduced compensation, either altogether or as "down-payment." They are more likely to do so, the closer they live to the offending group, since this situation puts a premium on attaining some kind of concord. Both the possibility and the manner of settlement are influenced by social distance. Yet, since the two parties live close together, there is also a greater chance that new offenses will be committed and old animosities reawakened. Indeed, every offense may rankle, despite surface composition, and as memory of the mitigating circumstances fades and only the killing is remembered, a new score may then be added to the tale of feud. For between groups of this kind feud is a permanent state of hostility, in which each injury can only be temporarily compensated.

This is not to assert that there are no feuding societies in which liability is absolute and regard is never paid to extenuating circumstances. Yet I cannot help suspecting that adequate case records would show that this is unusual. For example, I have already cited a case from the Pokot of East Africa where compensation was demanded when a man of one clan killed a man of another clan during fighting at night against a common enemy. The deceased's clan mobilized and demanded payment. The killer's clan agreed that they were liable but argued that in the circumstances they should pay little, and neutral elders sided with them. But the claimants insisted on, and obtained, heavy compensation. This rankled with the offenders, and Peristiany,[16] who recorded the case, described how they brought suit after suit, sometimes in futile situations, to even the score. It is surely significant that this was apparently the best-remembered tale of feud

14. Ibid., pp. 43–44.

15. See also Colson, "Social Control and Vengeance among the Plateau Tonga" (1949), reprinted in *The Plateau Tonga of Northern Rhodesia* (1962).

16. "Pokot Sanctions and Structure" (1954).

which Peristiany was able to collect, sixty years later; and I am prepared to suggest that the claimants were adamant because of some un-
balanced score farther back in the relations of the two clans.

A dramatic instance of this kind of absolute responsibility occurs in
Chinua Achebe's novel, *Things Fall Apart,* which deals with the Ibo
before the White men came. Okonkwo fired his gun at the funeral of
Ezeudu, of his patrilineal clan. The gun exploded, and a piece of metal
killed a son of the dead man.

> The only course open to Okonkwo was to flee from the clan. It
> was a crime against the earth goddess to kill a clansman, and a
> man who committed it must flee from the land. The crime was of
> two kinds, male and female. Okonkwo had committed the fe-
> male, because it had been inadvertent. He could return to the
> clan after seven years.
>
> That night he collected his most valuable belongings into head-
> loads. His wives wept bitterly and their children wept with them
> without knowing why. Obierika and a half a dozen other friends
> came to help and to console him. They each made nine or ten
> trips carrying Okonkwo's yams to store in Obiereka's barn. And
> before the cock crowed Okonkwo and his family were fleeing to
> his motherland. It was a little village called Mbanta, just beyond
> the borders of Mbaino [the village of his father's clan].
>
> As soon as the day broke, a large crowd of men from Ezeudu's
> quarter stormed Okonkwo's compound, dressed in garbs of war.
> They set fire to his houses, demolished his red walls, killed his
> animals and destroyed his barn. It was the justice of the earth
> goddess, and they were merely her messengers. They had no ha-
> tred in their hearts against Okonkwo. His greatest friend,
> Obierika, was among them. They were merely cleansing the land
> which Okonkwo had polluted with the blood of a clansman.

But they had to act as they did, since "if the clan did not exact
punishment for an offense against the great goddess, her wrath was
loosed on all the land and not just on the offender."

I have discussed the question of liability for homicide in several
societies where self-help and feud were the standard reactions to this
offense, in order to raise concepts of intention and responsibility in
tribal law more sharply than I can on my own material about the

Barotse kingdom. Stirke,[17] one of the early administrators in Barotseland, wrote that there was no fixed penalty for homicide before the
arrival of the British, and no difference was made between murder and
manslaughter. The kin of the victim had the penalty in their own
hands, and could kill the offender, or fine him, or take him as a slave,
or let the matter drop. He states that only a very poor man, and one
who would be possibly useless as a slave, was killed, while the matter
was dropped when it was "politic to do so." Compensation was nearly
always settled by the court. A village was held responsible for the
killing of a man whose corpse was found near it, unless evidence could
be produced to identify the slayer; and in some circumstances this
evidence might be sought by divination. The accused was then generally fined.

Stirke adds that theft was punished frequently, and more severely,
than homicide. He states that if the stolen goods were of little value, a
first offense was occasionally punished by fining, but for a second
offense the punishment was severe: "The guilty party had all his
possessions seized by the aggrieved party and a clay pot was smashed,
portions of it were made red hot with fire and the thief was seized and
his fist tightly closed round one of the red hot pieces and firmly held
there. This generally resulted in his being maimed for life, as the
burnt hand festered and rotted away in most cases," and at best it
never returned to its normal condition. An incorrigible thief was
killed.

This period of severe punishment, before the advent of the British,
was fifty years before my own work in Barotseland. Stirke's account
of the punishment of theft does not accord, of course, with the tradition (cited in Chapter 1), that King Mulambwa ruled that all except
recidivist thieves should be rewarded for their courage! My own
informants, some of whom were alive before the British Protectorate
was established, told me that Stirke's statements were not quite correct
—though I assume they were. These informants said that an incorrigible thief was maimed or killed, but that isolated acts of theft were
punished by levying a fine and compensation in double the amount of
stolen property. This was the rule operated for damages in the 1940s,
when serious thefts were tried by British courts.

My informants also stated that before the British came murders were

17. Stirke, *Barotseland* (n.d.), pp. 108–10.

tried by their courts; and a court might either award compensation, or allow the victim's kin to enslave the killer, but not to kill him. They said that the court did take note of the mode of killing and the extent to which it was done deliberately. But this may well be a later gloss, and Stirke's statements are more likely to be correct. Unfortunately, I did not collect sufficient cases on these points, but I recorded one good case which, however, raised also the issue of defiance of the king's authority. I was told of a killing in the 1880s, in which the king intervened and ordered the dead man's kin to accept compensation of two cattle, since the killing had been accidental. The dead man's father, who was the headman of a village, tried to kill the wrongdoer. The king thereupon ordered the father to be executed, and all his villagers, freemen and serfs, to be sent as serfs to royal villages throughout the plain. The father and some of his relatives escaped to the chief-of-the-south, and she kept him in sanctuary from the wrath of the king for many years before he secured a pardon from the king for his defiance of the royal orders and was allowed to return to the north. But his village was never re-established.

In some African tribes, like the Zulu, every man "belongs to the king"; hence if one man slew another, compensation went to the king who might out of generosity give something to the deceased's kin. Among the Zulu the liability was absolute, for death robbed the king of a "war-shield." In other kingdoms, as among the Bashango, the punishment for murder was hanging, while for accidental killing compensation might be paid to the deceased's kin. There is great diversity of law on this point. But if these kingdoms may be assumed to have developed by the establishment of royal authority over offenses previously redressed by groups of kin, it may well be that liability for the killing of a king's man was likely to remain strict, and possibly even absolute. The terms would be the same, since liability of the murderer, or one of his kin, to be killed in return tended to be absolute in the period when vengeance was enjoined. The offense of killing was set in a particular matrix of social relationships which defined rights and liabilities between the parties, including liability to vengeance. A presumption was therefore made that all killing was deliberate, but in some circumstances this presumption could be rebutted, by demonstration that the killing was accidental. Barton gives a number of cases to illustrate this rebuttal among the Ifugao and the Kalinga in the Philippines, but he emphasizes that the legal situation is of this type.[18] For example, among the Kalinga a man accidentally wounded a cousin to death at night; the cousin told his "injurer" to call his kin so that he could assure them before he died that it was accidental. On another occasion a policeman was held to have accidentally hurt a comrade from another group, and clearly he *had* done it accidentally. Later he boasted of the blood he had drawn without retaliation; this showed the wounding was malicious, and he was attacked. Accidental wounding among the Kalinga required that the injurer provide means of sacrifice to help the cure; accidental killing required that recompense, though less, and a contribution to the funeral feast, be rendered. And always an accidental injury or killing of this kind might be regarded as, "the debt is not yet paid," [19] despite the apparent settlement, and revengeful killing might be resumed.

In my opinion it would therefore be a misinterpretation to say that no note is taken here of the mental elements of the offense, even if a death for a death is insisted on. Intention—the motivation or mental elements—is presumed to be what a reasonable man in those social circumstances would have felt. Feelings and motives are interpreted in terms of stereotypes. If one kills a man with whom one's group is at feud, one must have intended to kill him. This presumption can be rebutted in many tribes, but there must be cogent evidence to do so. This does not absolve one from liability to provide compensation, but the compensation is more likely to be accepted by the deceased's kin. And since the relationship of retaliation is set between groups, and not between individuals, any member of one's group is vulnerable to attack, while the group is responsible for indemnification.

If this view is correct, does it give us clues to an understanding of early English law on this point? The view of vengeance and feuding in early English history is colored by the fact that we have to draw on epics which deal with noble houses, between whom feuding is part of the form of political relationship. If they were separated by some distance the parties—as among the Nuer—could wage armed feud. It is less likely that they could do so when they lived close together, and it is unlikely that less prominent people living close together could evade the fact that proximity and other social ties exerted pressure on them to reach a settlement—a situation clearly analyzed among the Nuer, the Ifugao, and the Kalinga. Historians and historical jurispru-

18. Barton, *The Kalingas* (1949), pp. 219 f. Cf. *Ifugao Law* (1919), pp. 75 f.
19. *Ifugao Law* (1919), p. 77.

dents have pointed out that the very constitution of the early Anglo-Saxon vengeance grouping entailed that a man might be at once required to exact vengeance and be subject to vengeance. Each vengeance grouping consisted of the cognatic kin of the deceased to a certain genealogical distance. Hence the grouping of avengers centered on an individual, or at most on a group of full brothers and sisters. Therefore, as Bloch puts it, "when two families clashed it might very well be that the same individual belonged to both—to one of them through his father and to the other through his mother. How was he to choose between them?" A contemporary writer ruled that he should "side with the nearest relative, and if the degrees are equal, . . . stand aloof." [20] Anthropological analyses of feuding societies indicate that those men who were under pressure of conflicting loyalties tended to press for offer and acceptance of compensation, rather than for insistence on blood for blood.[21]

It is certain that the pressures were not always successful. Maitland has a significant passage in a discussion of the blood feud among the early Welsh:

> It is plain that since every manslaughter involved four kindreds in the feud, some nice questions might arise from the mutual interference of family obligations. A man might be called on to support his mother's kin in a feud against his father's kin. Such a case is actually provided for, and in the strangest fashion. If a man slays another of his own kindred he has to pay to the kindred the *galanas* (= wergild) of the slain, and in this case he alone is liable, for the kindred cannot pay to itself. He also forfeits his patrimony, and doubtless the law affords him but little protection against the justice more or less irregular of a domestic forum; but lawfully he may not be slain "since the living kin is not killed for the sake of the dead kin." Now if a man in avenging the death of a maternal relation kill one of his own kindred and thereby forfeit his patrimony, he is to be allowed an inheritance from his maternal grandfather. Perhaps there is no more striking example of the queer mixture of barbarism and logic which characterises these Welsh laws. One of the few exceptional

20. Bloch, *Feudal Society* (1961), p. 138 (orig. French, 1939–40).

21. I cite these analyses and discuss this problem more fully in my *Custom and Conflict in Africa* (1955), Chap. 1, and *Politics, Law and Ritual in Tribal Society* (1965), Chap. 3, where I also consider the Anglo-Saxon situation.

cases in which a woman can transmit inheritance to her son is where that son is a murderer.[22]

This appears to provide for a situation where the processes of settlement, often effective, broke down. Here in Wales the kindred was an agnatic group, but at least two kindreds, of father's and mother's side, had claims on the blood compensation and a duty to contribute to its payment. It would seem better in this hypothetical Welsh case to see the avenger as being exiled from his paternal group which could not slay him, and adopted into his maternal group, whose interests he had pursued. It also seems anachronistic to speak of him as a murderer.

In Wales galanas was payable for every death, including, said Maitland, deaths which "a modern coroner's jury would be inclined to refer . . . to misadventure, or to the Act of God."[23] This was the compensatory payment, to balance the debt of blood, as tribal peoples put it. The Welsh had an additional payment, *saared*, payable only for injury willfully inflicted. It was not paid, as galanas was, where the slayer was an idiot or an infant. In most homicides payments were made. But the payment of saared, for willful injury, was paid or received by a smaller circle of relatives than the main blood wealth, as in old English law *heals-fang* payment, though different from the Welsh saared, was also paid to a smaller circle of kindred.[24] (It is worth noting here that in 1928 Kroeber stated of the Yurok Indians of California: "Damage must be fully compensated for even though inflicted without the shadow of intent; but if the infringement is wilful, or malice evident, added compensation is due for intent." He here corrects a statement made in 1925 in *Handbook of the Indians of California* that the fact and amount of infringement are alone considered, not the intent.[25])

I cannot here follow up these complications in old English and Welsh law; I cite them to emphasize that in those systems of law many injuries were regarded as specific to particular contexts of social relations, and hence modes of redress and restitution had a similar specific character. This must have tended to establish presumptions

---

22. "The Laws of Wales—The Kindred and the Blood Feud," first published in *Law and Magazine Review* (1881), republished in *Collected Papers*, 1 (1911), 226–27.

23. Ibid., p. 220.

24. Ellis (*Welsh Tribal Law*, 1926, 2, 99), states galanas to be a kindred. My concern is motive.

25. Kroeber, "Yurok Law" (1928), pp. 511–16.

about motivation, according to the previous relationship between the wrongdoer and the wronged. As royal power increased, we know that in England it extended its jurisdiction by operating also in specific, though now different, social relations. Foreigners, presumably having no kindred, were under the direct protection of the king, and a fine was levied on a "hundred" if a foreigner perished accidentally. The blood wealth, so to speak, went to the king,[26] and Maitland shows elsewhere that this arose in Canute's time to protect Danes, the "foreigners to whom the king was 'a protector and a kinsman.' "[27] But the same rule is found in some tribal societies, since chiefs did not have detectives; and where murder remained a "tort" the kin of the slain man brought suit; strangers, and particularly traders, were under the king's protection—his peace—and liability for their deaths was absolute.[28] In England it fell on a locality even if the death was accidental.

The English king thus seems to have stood in a special relationship to foreigners, as later he stood in a special relationship to the victim of manslaughter "because of the circumstances, place, time and the like, in which it was perpetrated." The king cast his protection against killing on his highways, and particularly against killing by "foresteal," ambush, or premeditation. By these special circumstances, and fictions, the king intervened to claim rights at the death of a man which overrode the claims of kinsfolk and landlord, or the protests of slayer or slayer's landlord against the king's jurisdiction and intervention.[29] Liability to the king for killing, as in feuding systems, apparently was so strict that as late as the seventeenth and eighteenth centuries in England and France it was necessary to obtain a formal pardon from the king to avoid the penalty even after excusable homicide.[30]

I have attempted to abstract a few, if authoritative, summaries of these complex problems to emphasize that in early European law, as in tribal law, the circumstances of killing in particular social relation-

26. Maitland "The Early History of Malice Aforethought" (1883), in *Collected Papers*, 1 (1911), 305 f.

27. "The Criminal Liability of the Hundred," first published in *Law and Magazine Review* (1881–82); republished in *Collected Papers*, 1 (1911), 246, citing laws of Ethelred, Canute, and Henry I.

28. E.g. among Zulu and Barotse, on information given to me.

29. Maitland, "The History of Malice Aforethought" (1883), in *Collected Papers*, 1 passim.

30. Ibid., pp. 320, 327.

ships created liabilities which in themselves raised presumptions about intentions and determined the penalties. Certain objective circumstances in a killing (or other injury) led to reasonable conclusions on basic motivation: actual motivations might influence the ease of settlement of feuds, but even accidental killing might not avoid the demand for restitution. As cited, excusable homicide later required a pardon. I hope this way of formulating the problems illuminates them. It does not entail that we deny to early lawyers, any more than to tribal lawyers, an insight into the complexity of human action. The killings that were not compromised by settlement because of mitigating circumstances are more likely to have been remembered, and especially those cases where one party refused to accept a mitigation that was appropriate, as in the Pokot feud cited above. Hence what has tended to survive are the waged feuds, and the harsh letter of the law.

It would be as dangerous, however, to assume that these show the full operation of social control and adjustment, as it would be to describe modern married life, or commercial operations, from the disputes in those relationships that are not adjusted and therefore enter the records of the courts. To understand feuding, we must look at more than vengeance. To grasp how the law regarded intention, we must include in the objective circumstances the social relationships in which injuries were committed. It apparently takes a long period of development before, theoretically at least, intention in the form of malice aforethought, of *mens rea*, is assessed independently of a particular context of social relations, and the nature of most offenses becomes the focus of legal investigation outside the pre-established status relation between wronged and wrongdoer.

If there is some illumination to be gained by this approach from the data on tribal studies, it is nevertheless strange that strict liability should persist so long after status ceased to dominate society. But that there is some connection between the dominance of status and the legal view of intention, and between offenses in status relationships, absolute or strict liability, fixed responsibility, and presumed malice aforethought, is suggested by the conclusion to Maitland's essay, "The Early History of Malice Aforethought." He had examined the development of the idea of murder, and the loss of sanctuary for murder, considered as premeditated waylaying and concealment. I quote at length from his concluding paragraphs.

It is not impossible that the texts in the Vulgate about *insidiae* are the root of the whole matter, the cause why the old notion that murder is slaying in secret, or slaying with concealment, was after the formation of the Canon Law replaced by the theory that the differentia of the worst homicide is guet-apens, premeditatus assultus. I imagine, however, that at least a co-operative cause was the fact that waylaying, "force faite en real chimin," was an infringement of the king's own rights, "un cas royal," an ancient plea of the crown, for that highway was the king's, and they that walked therein enjoyed his peace.

This may seem a superfluous attempt to explain the sufficiently obvious. We are wont to think, or to speak as if we thought that premeditated manslaying is the worst type of manslaying, and are perhaps rather surprised when Sir James Stephen [in his *History of the Criminal Law*] points out that this is no universal truth. But whatever may be natural to us, we ought not to suppose that in the eyes of our remote ancestors the fact of premeditation would naturally have aggravated the guilt of manslaughter. The curious agreement between French and English law as to the necessity of obtaining a pardon in a case of excusable homicide, must suggest that this usage, for which Hale and Blackstone make half-hearted apologies, and which may have owed its long continuance partly to texts in the Old Testament, partly to the fees payable by those who sought a pardon, had its origin not in any accident, or in any desire to extort money, but in the utter incompetence of ancient law to take note of the mental elements of a crime. Of this incompetence there is plenty of other evidence. The rank of the slayer, the rank of the slain, the rank of their respective lords, the sacredness of the day on which the deed was done, the ownership of the place at which the deed was done—these are the facts which our earliest authorities weigh when they mete out punishment; they have little indeed to say of intention or motive. When they do take account of intention or motive, then we may generally suspect that some ecclesiastical influence has been at work, as when, for example, the compiler of the Leges Henrici borrows from Gratian and St. Augustine the phrase about *mens rea* which has found a permanent place in our law books. Secrecy, or rather concealment, it may be allowed, was from of old an aggravation of manslaughter, so was the taking of an unfair advantage. Of this we see something in the definition of foresteal already quoted; it is foresteal to lie in wait for one's enemy and to attack him on the flank; it is not foresteal to call him back and have a fight with him. But in the days of the blood feud, such days for example as are represented by the story of Burnt Njal, mere deliberation or premeditation cannot have been thought an aggravation of the crime; a man was entitled to kill his enemy provided that he was prepared to pay the price or bear the feud, but he was expected to kill his enemy in a fair, open, honest manner, not to take a mean advantage, not to fall upon him like a thief in the dark. In the fact therefore that premeditation became an element in the definition of murder, there is, it seems to me [Maitland], something that requires explanation, and towards such an explanation we have made some advance when we see that ambush or waylaying is an offence against the King, and that the book of Exodus excepts him who has slain another *per insidias* from the privilege of sanctuary.[31]

I am suggesting that we may make a further advance in understanding if we follow the clues in Maitland's own analysis and see that intention in injuries—like transactions—was interpreted in terms of the specificity of status relationships. A particular matrix of social relationships defined the rights and liabilities attaching to an offense, including liability to redress. The added wrong of concealment may be due to the fact that unwittingly the kindred of the slain may eat with the kindred of the slayer, which is what Nuer and Kalinga fear. Intention becomes determined by general circumstances, which give clues to mental elements, only when killing is handled independently of a specific social setting.

Howell gives an example from Nuer law, as applied to the injury of adultery, which emphasizes this point. To escape physical injury a Nuer adulterer pays one beast ritually to enable the wronged husband to sleep with his wife, since it is dangerous for a man to do so after she has had intercourse with another man. Husband and wife will suffer misfortune unless expiation is made by the guilty party. Five other cattle are paid as compensation. But if a child is born as a result of the adultery, these five cattle should be returned to the adulterer. Adulter-

31. Ibid., pp. 327–28.

ine children, like all children born to a woman, belong to the man who became her husband by giving marriage cattle for her. The man who impregnates an unmarried girl can obtain the child by giving five cattle if it is a male, six cattle if it is a female. If an adulterer pays compensation and there is a child, the compensation might be held to be a legitimation fee attaching the child to him. To avoid the confusion, the Nuer logically therefore in these circumstances return these cattle. That is, to maintain clarity in social relations, the liability for restitution is lifted. Similarly, if a man marries a girl who had a child out of wedlock, which has been legitimated by cattle, the husband may insist that her kin return these cattle and he claim the child. The status of the woman's children must be kept clear.[32] With a change in the matrix of social relationships the nature of the offense—or at least of redress for offense—has to be altered. If the adulterer is a near kinsman of the husband he pays only the beast for ritual killing; he is a member of the agnatic group to which the child is attached by the husband's payment of marriage cattle.

Another type of absolute liability is reported by Kroeber from the Yurok of California. If one man gets another to ferry him across the river, and while the ferryman is away his house burns down, the traveler is liable to pay for the house. Had he not employed the ferryman the latter might have saved his house. This liability is set in a situation in which no one can refuse ferriage.[33] It should be remembered from Chapter 6 that the Barotse give absolute immunity to accidental loss by fire or water.

I have argued that in the situation of feud, liability thus attaches, to some extent irrespective of intention, if killing is committed within a certain range of social relationships. The same kind of absolute liability may also be attached to breaches of certain taboos or conventions which are of critical importance for a particular social status or relationship. For example, in Chapter 2 I cited that it was treason to usurp any of the privileges of kingship. In kin relationships there are also certain defining conventions which are regarded as so important that any breach is punishable, whatever the circumstances.

This ruling is most definite where breach of the taboo threatens mystical danger to the society or to the other party. The only case of this kind I recorded from the Barotse was of a man ordered by local

32. Howell, *Manual of Nuer Law* (1954), pp. 131 f., 154 f.
33. Kroeber, "Yurok Law" (1928), pp. 511–16.

councillors to send his daughter, recently bereaved of a baby, to wait on a princess. He refused to do so because "her breasts of death" would harm the princess. His fellows refused to listen to him, and threatened to bind him. He ran away and took his gun to shoot himself, but his wife prevented him. She urged him to go to the king, though it was night. Early in the morning he entered the capital and, instead of approaching the king through his councillor or steward, went straight to the Palace and insisted that the royal attendants take him to the king, to whom he reported what had happened. The king praised him and ordered that he be fed. When his fellows came to the capital to report his refusal to help "the child of the king," and his disappearance, the king summoned the accused to the council and upbraided the astonished neighbors for risking death to the princess, and he rewarded the alleged wrongdoer with gifts of cattle and honey. The latter shared his feast with his neighbors.

Records on other tribes give many instances of the inherent liability and responsibility that fall on those who even inadvertently commit breaches of sacred rules or ritual prescriptions. An excellent example is reported by Meggitt from an Australian Aboriginal tribe of a woman who by accident saw the men preparing sacred paraphernalia for a circumcision ceremony. The woman had, quite properly, gone to look for a little girl who had wandered away from the place where the women were dancing. She had inadvertently come upon the men at their sacred task and, horrified, fled unseen. In a couple of days she went insane, and wasted away till she almost died; indeed, at one point she was pronounced dead. But she never recovered her senses. Meggitt concludes: "Men with whom I discussed the affair said that [her] 'trouble' did not surprise them. She had broken an important dreamtime[34] law, the automatic punishment for which should be death; therefore everyone expected her to die. The fact that she had seen the [sacred] shells accidentally while acting like a good 'mother' to help her 'daughter'[35] was irrelevant. She knew what she was doing; she knew the law; consequently, she must have intended to act in that way."[36] This graphic incident involves self-punishment by mental stress after breach of a sacred taboo, though the breach was

34. The Australian "dreamtime" was the period of Creation, when the world in its sacred as well as its secular aspects was established.

35. "Mother" and "daughter" are in quotation marks because they were classificatory, and not "own" mother and daughter.

36. Meggitt, *Desert People* (1962), p. 260.

committed while fulfilling another duty. For my present purpose I stress that here again the absolute liability for breach arose in a particular set of social relationships within the tribe, those ordaining that men have their sacred mysteries which no woman may gaze on. While the men practice these sacred mysteries on which the well-being of the tribe depends, women participate by dancing apart; the two complementary spheres must not be brought together.

There are many reports from various tribes of this type of absolute responsibility. If a Cheyenne killed another Cheyenne, the sacred Arrows had to be renewed by ritual cleansing. White Bear killed his mother accidentally while drunk. He was not at first exiled as required by law for a homicide, but was asked to leave when the Soldier Societies feared bad luck at the beginning of the hunting season.

> In the fall when the hunt season was over, it was decided that because White Bear's misadventure was accidental, he could be permitted to rejoin the community. . . . The real legal problem, which was the tribe's source of perplexity in this situation, was the question of the personal culpability of the drunken man. Could a drunkard who has revealed no malice aforethought be excused for an accidental homicide? This was a new problem to the Cheyennes. In this case the chiefs apparently deemed banishment unnecessary. The Arrows, however, were renewed for White Bear's mother almost immediately. Manslaughter, intentional or not, was a sin to be cleansed; at least any doubt there might be was too grave to let continue.

This cleansing seems not to have been necessary when an alien was killed by accident. Again, suicide, when carried out by a girl in foolish protest against nothing, was held not to be killing of a Cheyenne by another Cheyenne: hence the Arrows were not cleansed. When a mother so beat her daughter that the girl killed herself, it was held that the mother had committed homicide; she was banished and the Arrows were renewed. Finally, when a girl killed her father who was attempting to rape her, she was not banished, but the Arrows were renewed.[37] There was room for adjustment over the nature of homicide in terms of varied offenses in special social relationships: absolute

37. Llewellyn and Hoebel, *The Cheyenne Way* (1941), pp. 137, 149, 179, 316 f. See also for other examples Fortes, *The Dynamics of Clanship among the Tallensi* (1945), pp. 100 f., and Goody, "Fields of Social Control among the Lodagaba" (1957), pp. 81–84.

liability of the tribe for the sin of homicide was inescapable. And mystical pollution demanded strict ritual adjustment. This form of ritual liability did not exist in all tribes.

Meggitt, as cited, says the Aborigines presumed from the woman's action that she had an intention to break the sacred rule and hence was bound to suffer. I have no similar case of as serious a breach as this from Barotseland. There are breaches of ritual rules which are believed to bring down automatic punishment, even if the breach is apparently inadvertent. I did not ask the people whether they ascribed implied "guilty *intention*" to the wrongdoer in these circumstances. They spoke of the defaulter as "doing wrong," and they did not seem to me to show any concern with the motivations that lay behind the wrongdoing. My impression was that ritual arrangements were often most strongly emphasized, and derived a specific character and authority, when absolute liability attached to any breach.

This type of absolute responsibility and liability attaches in Barotseland also to breach of certain important prohibitions and prescriptions in important relationships of status. Again, I did not inquire carefully enough into whether the Barotse thought about the motivations of defaulters and, if they did, how they formulated these motivations. I heard cases suggesting that they are prepared to accept the defaulter as completely innocent in a mental sense of any guilt, but nevertheless as liable to punishment for the offense. For example, in Barotse, as in most tribal societies, there is a general postulate that if a man and woman are alone together they have in effect had sexual congress. A man should never place himself in such a position with his sisters, or with distant female cousins in all lines whom he may not marry. On one occasion a young man thus sat in a hut alone with a sister. His kin demanded that he provide a beast for a cleansing sacrifice. When he refused to provide it on the grounds that he was innocent, they took him to court. There again he protested that he had merely talked with his sister, and had not touched her. The head of the court assured him that the judges believed him, but he had done wrong in being alone in a hut with his sister and must provide the sacrifice.[38] These conventional offenses are damaging in themselves.

Similar absolute liability attaches to aspects of marital relations. A Barotse husband with more than one wife must never act in such a

38. "The Case of the Incestuous Action," in my *Judicial Process among the Barotse* (1955), p. 154.

way that his sexual relationship with one wife touches his relations with another wife. A drunken husband slept with one of his wives and in the middle of the night he rose to go outside to urinate. In his drunkenness instead of going out of the door of the house he entered the room where his other wife was sleeping and urinated on her. Both wives sued for divorce and were granted it: no payment could efface the wrong done to each wife though it was accidental. Since he came from congress with his first wife he had confounded sexual relations with both wives.[39] But it would be a sufficient offense if a husband took a blanket from one wife to another.

In Barotse, where the divorce rate is high, absolute liability of this kind attaches to many actions of the husband. In Chapter 5 I cited a case in which a man's wife secured divorce because he had broken the rule that a man must not look into his wife's granary, though he pleaded that it was in her interests. He had taken grain from her granary to feed her visiting kin in her absence, and had sold some grain profitably for her. Furthermore, I was repeatedly told that, since a man can divorce his wife by sending her home, if a man pushes his wife out of his hut, or says "go home" or "get out" to her, he was formerly held liable to have divorced her, however much she had provoked him. More recently the courts have been less ready to grant a divorce in these circumstances, particularly if the husband was drunk. They hold that it was the drink, and not the man, who spoke.

Taboos and conventions of this sort attach to most relationships, but vary in strictness. They are said to be enforced most strictly where women with whom sexual relations are incestuous are concerned. All conventional behavior to senior female in-laws is strictly enforced. Informants said that a man must never be alone with his mother-in-law, and if he meets her on a path he must go off it into the fields or woods. The sanction is that his wife can claim a divorce. I have seen men dodge their mothers-in-law thus, and daughters-in-law avoid their fathers-in-law. In the only case involving these relationships which I heard tried in court, a wife, on top of other complaints, alleged that her husband had committed adultery with her mother's brother's wife (in Barotse terms, a "mother" to her). The husband admitted he had seen this woman naked but said in defense he had only done so when helping her to cross a ford where he wished to protect her against crocodiles. The court did not in fact immediately grant the divorce, as I had been led to expect, but spent some time in

39. "The Case of the Urinating Husband," ibid., p. 140.

destroying the husband's story and establishing to its satisfaction that adultery had occurred. Since the Barotse are polygamous a man cannot commit adultery in relation to his wife, but this particular adultery involved a confusion of relationships. Hence divorce was granted. The view the Barotse judges take of these wrongful actions is shown in the following judgments addressed to the husband. One judge:

> You were wrong in not going to your wife to mourn the death of your parent-in-law [her father]. Then I would increase your fault with sleeping in the Mawiko village with your small mother-in-law, and crossing a ford with your small and your great mother-in-law. You have entered the huts of two mothers-in-law. As for the girl, you just fight her. You drove her out, so you brought a pot [to redress the offense] to her father. Above all, no one marries a girl and then her mother. You, girl, when you look at this man he is your father. You may be returned to him by your lords [the senior judges]: for me, you are free.

Another judge:

> The taboos between parents-in-law and children-in-law are not made by government, but come from the beginning of our people. I believe there was adultery with your wife's mother's brother's wife on the journey. How can an innocent man go on a journey with the wife of an absent man, and carry her dress and cross a ford together with her? No one crosses a ford with a woman. If you see a woman crossing, you turn back and hide till she has gone. This is an old law made by our government. . . . Long ago you drove out your wife, and when you returned to the village you came to your liaison with your mother-in-law. You did not go to your wife's father's illness—how did you love him? You knew you were wrong, and it is shown by payment of the pot. No one just pays—it shows you had a fault. On top of that, then you went into the hut of her mother . . . I see that she is not your wife, she is the child of her father.[40]

The statement, "you, girl, when you look at this man he is your father," brings out the confusion of status to which the Barotse object. I repeat, a woman cannot divorce her husband if he has had

40. For a fuller report, "The Case of the Man Who Helped His Mothers-in-law Cross a Ford," ibid., pp. 148–50. Cf. in last phrase the statement of rights of "ownership" over a woman by husband and father, Chap. 5, p. 164.

intercourse with another woman, or claim payment (as an Ifugao woman can, for example). Normally the judges grant an immediate divorce to any woman whose husband marries one of her kins-women.[41] Again, I must note that some tribes encourage a man to marry two kinswomen, while others forbid this. But here it is an absolute fault, in denial of the marital relationship.

The judges' statements also bring out the importance of making a payment to a related person in order to redress a breach of convention, if this convention be not an absolute requirement for maintenance of the relationship, and also to redress default in meeting an obligation or exhibiting the appropriate sentiments. Each such default is a "fault" as I have translated in the judgments the Barotse word *mulatu;* but mulatu also covers "a debt," so that debts are constantly created by kin and in-laws when they wrong one another. These debts have to be paid not only with apologies but also in material terms. Such pay-ments are frequently made by husbands and wives to each other, and this appears in several of the divorce cases cited in my full study of the Barotse judicial process. If a husband has committed a serious but redeemable wrong against his wife, the judges consider whether they should grant her a divorce or persuade her to accept damages.

A husband and his wife came into court.[42] Namunda-Katanekwa (a title), eleventh councillor-of-the-right, who was head of the hus-band's political sector, explained that the husband had broken his wife's teeth and he, Namunda, had first sent the woman to hospital. He asked them if they had returned with a letter from the doctor. The husband replied: "We have just returned; here it is." The wife said her husband had just kicked her; they had had no quarrel or fight. Her husband admitted this; he pleaded that he had tried to kick his wife on the shoulder but by mistake (*kaziezi,* accident, bad luck) kicked her mouth. He complained that she had given his blanket to a stranger to sleep with. Another senior judge asked the wife: "What do you want?" She replied: "I want a divorce. If I stay with him, my life will be bad. If he just did this, when he is angry he will kill me." Namunda-Katanekwa specified: "There are two cases here: the first,

41. See "The Case of the Prudish Wife," ibid., pp. 145–47.

42. I heard this case in the Saa-Katengo Court at Lealui (see ibid., p. 14 and preceding pages) on 19 October 1942. When the case was brought into court, the head of the court, Solami, private Ngambela to the king, rebuked the councillors who were chatting among themselves: "Look at this case. We sit with a White man [myself], and he will think our cases are bad."

of the teeth; the second, of their marriage." A junior judge urged: "Your husband still loves you—he loves you a lot. We cannot enter there." To the husband: "If you still want her, to be her husband, I think you should give her something. How many teeth were broken?" Another judge, related to the parties, told him, "Two teeth," and he continued: "I think you should give her £1 or a fat cow, because this is the law we work with everyone. Also, it is a bad custom [*mukwa omaswe*] to hit a person who did not do anything. You admitted this. So I say £1 for your fault" [*mulatu*, also: debt]. Since the facts were clear, a prince consort interposed: "I will not say much. You must pay £2 or two cattle."

Another judge was more lenient: "Husband, you fight without reason [*sibaka*, also: cause, grounds of argument, permission], to hurt a person thus. You must pay £1." The judge who was related to them emphasized: "This is not a case: they just ask the price." The head of the court, Councillor Solami, thereupon asked his fellows: "How much do you think?" Namunda-Katanekwa cited a precedent: "I know the case of X was one tooth, and he got £1." The prince consort, supported by the princes in court: "So here are two teeth, and it is £2." Another senior judge, as judgment moved to the head of the court, ruled: "I said the case should go to the District Commissioner. Now it has returned to us. The wife does not complain of her marriage. She said she was hurt when she had not committed a fault; she did not know it was a blanket of *solume* [the husband's own possessions, as against the wife's; see Chapter 5] because it was in her place. So I say £1—but, you, husband, as your wife says, if you return and fight with her, it will be a big fault [or debt, mulatu]. This £1 or beast is to go to the wife's home. You, husband, be careful of what you do." (Notice he orders that the beast is to go to her home, so that it will clearly be hers.) Solami, the head of the court, concluded: "Husband, I think you have done wrong [*ufosize*] greatly. If your wife refuses you, and goes to marry again, she lacks teeth. Teeth come from God, and their loss is a great thing. If they are teeth of people [artificial teeth], seven shillings and sixpence is enough, but the teeth of God cost more. However, your lords have reprieved you [literally: caused you to live]—I think it is a big fault. Today I begin to see this affair of teeth, and in the past I would have said £1 for each tooth. With £1, they have reprieved you—I wanted to coerce [*hapeleza*, also: force] from you a cow which would bear for her, in her heavy

trouble. However, I enter into the words of the Malozi—it is £1."
Solami told a junior councillor to report the case to the Ngambela, the
Chief Councillor, and stressed that he must retail the prince consort's
judgment recommending £2 or a fat heifer (in fact, two). But the husband thereupon agreed to bring a heifer for his wife into the court.

This is a fair example of how the court handles disputes when one
spouse has wronged another. Each fault, or debt, between them must
be paid. Here, and in other tribes, though there are some common
rights in some property, husband and wife have separate sets of property rights.[43] This is clear when property is divided between them on
divorce or widowing, as described in Chapter 5. Therefore from their
properties they can recompense each other. The divorce rate is high,
for recompense is not always possible. Had the wife in the above case
insisted, she would have been granted a divorce.

While husbands cannot commit adultery in relation to their wives,
they must render each wife regular conjugal rights; and the wife can
sue for these if the husband neglects her to fornicate with other
women.[44] On the other hand, if the wife has intercourse with another
man, the adulterer pays £2 or two cattle as damages to the husband,
and the wife pays £1 or one beast to the court. In assessing whether a
woman has committed adultery, the court will accept as proof of adul-
terous relations any unaccustomed familiarity with an unrelated man.
There is a judicial presumption that men and women do not have
platonic relations. To eat an orange at an unrelated woman's hut in
her husband's absence is highly suspicious.[45] In one case, a member of
an immigrant tribe where cross-cousins marry each other—among the
Lozi themselves these count as brother and sister—had given a
woman a mat and a basket of meal. When her husband sued for
adultery, the defendant pleaded that she was his cross-cousin and it
was proper for him to give her presents. The judges countered that
had they been Lozi he would have been acquitted:

> For were you a Lozi she would be your sister indeed, though
> even a Lozi makes gifts to his sister in public. But we know you
> Mbunda do not call the daughter of your mother's brother "my

43. See Barton, *Ifugao Law* (1919); Schapera, *Handbook of Tswana Law* (1938), pp. 153,
228 f.
44. See Chap. 5, and "The Case of the Libertine Husband" in my *Judicial Process among
the Barotse* (1955), p. 66.
45. See "The Case of the Schoolboy Adulterer," ibid., pp. 130–33.

sister," and you can marry her. If you can marry her, you can commit adultery with her. If you were making presents to her because she is your relative, you should have given the things through her husband. Then he would have thanked you, for you would have been giving them to him. But you gave them on the side: you gave to her as your mistress. You will pay him £2, and she will give us £1 to send to the court.

This shows how each action in these societies is considered in a setting of specific relationships: the moral man acts towards everyone in cognizance of all ranges of relations.

Debts similarly accrue between blood relatives, as shown in the cases about gardens and fish dams cited in the first chapter. But here the relationships are not so frangible as those between husband and wife. The situation has to be very serious before people will break with their kin, even if a kinsman commits adultery with one's wife or assaults one, or attempts to sell one's life in order to acquire particular magical powers. The judges are reluctant to agree to a final breach of relationships if a case comes before them. Yet kin also constantly redeem their faults with payments, and among the Barotse it is generally held that the closer the relationship the more important it is to have adequate recompense for breach of obligation. This is not a general rule among all tribes. Howell reports that among the Nuer other associations mitigate the wrongdoer's offense, so that if a man commits adultery with a kinsman's wife, the "moral indignation [is] much less . . . social equilibrium has not been disturbed." The cuckold asks only for the beast to cleanse ritually, and not the compensation cattle (p. 24). But here, as with homicide, we have a situation where the recompensing group is the receiving group; and, since kin contribute to a man's bride cattle, the bride is also "their wife" though they should not commit adultery with her.

In practice, the problem which a man has to solve in order to avoid default of obligation to some among his many kinsmen is a straight economic problem: How is he to direct scarce resources to many ends? For all kin and in-laws make demands on his poverty, and he is bound to offend some. Hence if disputes between kin come before a Barotse court, the judges consider carefully all the demands on a man before they will hold that he has defaulted in his obligations to any kin. They set up reasonable standards for a man of his status, age, strength, wealth, and connections, and ask no more than that he do his best.[46] They apply similar standards to his dealings with his lords.[47] If a man meets these standards the judges hold him to be a good citizen;[48] if he more than meets them, he is acclaimed an upright man.[49] In these kinds of disputes the judges, as always, speak in terms of "doing wrong" and "doing right": they concern themselves, even when they state the law's rules, with internal moral states. But the cases I have quoted in my study of the judicial process, and the few I have been able to summarize here, show that these internal moral states and motivations are inferred from the actions of the parties. Motives follow logically from action. And motives are seen in legalistic terms. The Barotse view of human psychology admits ambivalence in human action and feeling in the words of one of their songs:

> He who kills me, who will it be but my kinsman;
> He who succors me, who will it be but my kinsman.

In court this awareness is used to assess evidence and, when possible, to mitigate punishment. But guilt and innocence of motive are determined from the facts. In this respect judicial psychology is an "ethical" psychology. It is not concerned with an objective assessment of why people act as they do, even when the judges see this. It judges their actions and presumed motivations in comparison with legal and moral norms. Here the judges work with both a legalistic ethical psychology of a generally reasonable person, who has a general ethical psyche, and with a set of psyches specified for the various categories of persons who come before them—fathers, children, husbands, wives, and so forth. They even have standardized pictures of wrongdoers of specific kinds: i.e. they argue that certain deviations in behavior, which are nevertheless standardized, can be understood only by referring them to the psychical motivations of a wrongdoer. Here the judges in their cross-examination, as I show in my study of the judicial process, probe into motives inferred from actions in order to trap the wrongdoer. Where they are concerned with maintaining a relationship between linked persons who have quarreled, they bring wrongful motiva-

46. See my *Judicial Process among the Barotse* (1955), Chap. 1 and 2.
47. See ibid., p. 152.
48. Ibid., p. 205.
49. "The Case of the Good Son-in-Law," ibid., pp. 151–52, and pp. 125 f., 155, 177, 187, 201, 267.

tion under open examination, to exhibit even to the wrongdoer where he has erred. Barotse judges are concerned with *mens rea*, emotional and intellectual guilt, even when the absoluteness of an offense compels them to decide "guilty and liable" through accident or negligence, and not by malice aforethought.[50]

The critical point is therefore the fixing of responsibility for actions in terms of the specific relationships within which these actions are set. Some are automatically offenses. They make the actor liable. This liability establishes a very strong presumption of guilty motivation, which however can itself be rebutted, even if this does not enable the wrongdoer to escape liability and he has to make restitution or be punished in other ways. From this extreme there is a range of situations where mens rea has to be established, though always the specificity of tribal relationships with their particular customs establishes a presumption of liability for breach. But here it is easier to escape liability if the accused can show that his intentions were not malicious, but good.

It is thus possible to range injuries and wrongs from situations where liability and responsibility for breach are absolute, either between groups or by custom in a particular relationship, and mens rea is investigated only to see whether its absence mitigates an offense, to situations where there is careful assessment of the nature and degree of wrong. The absoluteness of responsibility is shown in punishment in many societies of the deodand. Otherwise at every point in this scale we have to consider the specific social background. The less close the relationship (and among the Barotse, relations of spouses are not legally close in many respects) the more absolute the liability, and the less the regard paid to intention. Or rather, the more do the circumstances warrant an assumption of guilty intention, and the more is the question of actual intention irrelevant. Thus if a man brings a prima facie well-founded charge against a stranger for adultery or theft, but it is not sustained, he may be ordered to pay the accused damages for wrongful accusation (*kutanta*). I have seen a plaintiff ordered, and cheerfully agree that he ought, to pay £1 damages to a defendant whom he had summoned to court as an adulterer, having mistaken him for another on good grounds. The defendant did not have to prove malice.

The cases I have cited in this book and in my book on the Barotse judicial process indicate that the Barotse impose on the individual a

50. Ibid., p. 154.

stringent duty to take care in his dealings with his fellows. A man must avoid doing anything which reflects on another's reputation, harms his person, or damages his property. He is also responsible for damages done by his related dependents, and by his stock or dogs, but not for damage done by his servants or agents. The latter are themselves liable. The liability arising from this stringent duty imposed on a man toward others is always strict and sometimes absolute. Only damage caused by fire and water is excluded from this liability, unless such damage can be proved to have been done deliberately. Otherwise, damage by fire and water are, as we would say, acts of God. This particular law is not reported from the other tribes of the region; it may be a reaction to the Lozi's habitation of the flood plain.

Unfortunately I did not record a rich enough variety of cases tried in court for me to illustrate how Barotse judges handle in practice problems of damages arising from negligence or accident, or from damages committed unintentionally through ignorance or when drunk. Nor do I have adequate cases on how far provocation reduces damages. I realize now that my attempts to fill in these gaps in court records by putting hypothetical cases to Barotse were not searching or subtle enough to illuminate adequately the tricky problems involved. But I can state definitely, on the data I have, that the Barotse consider that if one man suffers through the action, even if it be inadvertent, of another, the latter must recompense the former. The Law of Wrongs starts from the fact that damage has occurred, and damage has to be redressed; and the person responsible must make amends. In short, the law imposes a duty on all not to harm their fellows; the injured does not have to demonstrate that the other party owed him a specific duty in those circumstances. That is, the injured party does not have to establish that he has a right. Here, as in the Law of Transactions, the emphasis of the law is on duty rather than on right. I refer again, as in Chapter 6, to Epstein's case of the man whose hut was burned by the fire which started in his neighbor's house. He had suffered damages, he was entitled to be recompensed, the case had to be tried under his own tribal laws; and therefore the Barotse defendant's plea that he was excused under the Barotse rules excluding liability for damages by fire and liability for the acts of one's servants was not accepted. The court, says Epstein, started from and developed the general concepts of Wrong and Injury.[51]

51. Epstein, *Juridical Techniques and the Judicial Process* (1954), pp. 25 f.

Having accepted that damage suffered establishes a strict liability against him who caused the damage, the Barotse then enquire into matters like deliberation and intention and provocation, accident and degree of negligence. If the damage was deliberately done, or caused by gross negligence, they may add penal damages and possibly fine the wrongdoer. They do not lessen the damages for accident. Drunkenness excuses only one particular offense, and that under a recent enactment; a drunk man is excused for an action that would otherwise entitle his wife to divorce. I stress again that in the case of the wife whose teeth were kicked out by her husband, the wife could clearly have insisted on divorce; the judges, led by the husband's kin among them, pleaded with her not to insist on her right to divorce because her husband loved her. And it is public policy to try, within the limits of the law, to maintain marriages.

In *The Nature of African Customary Law*, Dr. Elias (now the Honorable the Minister of Justice and Attorney-General in the Federal Government of Nigeria) has argued in his chapter, "Principles of Liability for Legal Wrongs," that "there is a notion of *mens rea* in African law." He points to distinctions made in various tribes between murder and manslaughter, and to variations in the scale of damages for injuries where the damages are caused by accident, or at least not intentionally. Nevertheless he states that liability is generally strict, and cites a writer on the Kamba: "Kamba law does not distinguish between murder, manslaughter or a death caused by accident. The blood-price is payable in each case. If a man were to fire an arrow at an animal and hit a man beyond, not knowing that he was there, he would be held fully liable." Yet the same writer stated that the first of the eleven cows paid after homicide is known as the "cow of the accident," and Elias concludes that most killings must therefore be by accident or must lack premeditated malice and occur in brawls. He thereupon writes:

> This seeming paradox can be resolved if it is frequently borne in mind that here, as elsewhere with some other writers, there is a confusion between *liability* and the quantification of *damages*. There are varying degrees of liability as well as of damages in almost all other cases of injury to the person outside the category of fatal ones. In homicide cases, however, the elders naturally regard the consequences of the children and other dependants of

the victim being suddenly left destitute as more important than the *manner* of the encompassing of the death by the killer.

With all respect, I suggest that it is more accurate to see the law as applying a strict liability arising out of duty to avoid harming others, and that the extent of liability can be reduced if the defendant can adduce mitigating circumstances. Here the onus lies on him. And as I have shown, certain social relationships, involving hostility, raise a presumption that the harm was done of malice aforethought.

I suggest that the general position I have stated for African law is similar to that in early and even medieval English law. Potter, dealing with the Middle Ages, cites Holdsworth:

> The general rule is that a man is liable for the harm which he has inflicted upon another by his acts, if what he has done comes within some one of the forms of action provided by the law, whether that harm has been inflicted intentionally, negligently, or acccidentally.

But Potter further cites Winfield's later conclusion that after the Anglo-Saxon period there is little to encourage the idea that a man acted at his peril, so that human action resulting in injury renders the doer liable in all circumstances. For Winfield went on to state that the liability was never absolute, though "it was in some directions stricter than it is at the present day. Certainly is was so where what was complained of was a positive act. But if it were a mere omission, it was a great deal less stringent than it is now."

Potter himself observed that the opinions of Holdsworth and Winfield are not really so far apart:

> Professor Holdsworth lays emphasis on what he conceives to have been the general rule, admittedly subject to exceptions, and Professor Winfield upon exceptional circumstances which may exclude the application of the general rule, but his contention is that the existence of such exceptions implies a recognition of some regard to intention on the part of the alleged wrongdoer.[52]

Among the Barotse, omissions which led to damages to others founded a suit only where inadequately herded stock damaged property, or improperly drained channels on a man's land caused flooding

---

52. Potter, *The History of the Common Law* (1932), pp. 321–23.

of his neighbor's gardens. Here, as generally in Africa, there was in this respect little development of liability for negligence—not surprisingly, since in Britain this development occurred on a large scale only in the nineteenth century, when liability of master for servant was also enhanced. Winfield states in the "General Historical Outline" that introduces his *Province of the Law of Tort* (1931):

> But injuries to real property bulk more largely in Blackstone's "private injuries" than in our law of tort. Chap. X to XVI cover them, and here it was impossible for him to escape from the domination of remedies. If we are better off than he was in this respect, we seem to be just as far from deciding the relation of the law of property to the law of tort, chiefly because we cannot make up our minds whether the main basis of law is Right or Duty. [p. 26]

If we apply this statement more generally in the light of data on tribal societies, where remedies did not found rights, may we see this as one aspect of the general shift from a situation dominated by status relationships in which the law emphasized duty to others, with strict liability in transaction and injury, toward a situation, dominated by ephemeral social relationships, with onus on the plaintiff to prove that he had a right to expect a duty from the defendant?

I have now to consider a class of wrongs which stand in apparent contrast to those at the extreme where mental states seem to be most irrelevant. The contrasting wrong is that of which Kroeber speaks, when he says of the Yurok that even harboring injurious thoughts is injurious and an offense.[53] (Perhaps we should note here that apparently in England "it became settled that mere intention unaccompanied by an act could not be criminal," only in the sixteenth century, for in the fourteenth and fifteenth centuries "the will might be taken for the deed." [54]) But what we have to consider for our present purposes is that in tribal societies alleged injurious feelings are believed to lead to witchcraft and sorcery. The offense of harming others by witchcraft is believed in some tribes at least to flow from the mere feeling of malice, envy, spite, hate, anger, jealousy, or greed, without the volition or action of the alleged witch, provided that he has the

53. "Yurok Law" (1928), pp. 511–16.
54. Potter, *The History of the Common Law* (1932), pp. 307–08.

power of witchcraft in his body. The classic exposition of how these moral beliefs operate was by Evans-Pritchard in his book, *Witchcraft, Oracles and Magic among the Azande of the Anglo-Egyptian Sudan* (1937).[55] Briefly, it may be asked of any misfortune: "How did it happen?" and also "Why did it happen?" If I am knocked down by a motorcar and killed, it would be clear to an African who believed in witchcraft that I died because my body was crushed by the car. But this does not explain why I, going about my legitimate business, should happen to have been struck by the car of a motorist going about his legitimate business. Why should I have had an accident with his car and not another car, at that moment and place and not at another moment and place? Witchcraft explains this particular aspect of a misfortune: why one man's crops fail when others prosper, why one man is ill when others are well, why one man is killed by an elephant on a particular hunt, and so forth. The beliefs in witchcraft ascribe this coincidence of events, this occurrence of particular misfortunes, to the malevolence of a person having the power of witchcraft, who sets this power in him to work harm to those he has grudges against; and he can be detected only by some means of divination.

What these beliefs entail is that ill feeling itself becomes endued with mystical power to harm the witch's enemy. Hence legally, so to speak, any misfortune suffered by a tribesman whose society holds these beliefs can be converted into a tort or crime. He can bring action in some form or other against another. Under these beliefs "mental elements" of malice are delictual or criminal. This seems to stand in apparent contradiction to the situation in which responsibility fixes guilty intention, irrespective of actual mental states. I believe it can be referred to the same social factors. But before I do so, I must emphasize that I am not able here to consider the full range of these beliefs as they vary among tribes, or the situation in tribes where beliefs in witchcraft are unimportant or nonexistent, but where there are beliefs in other types of mystical agents to explain the particularity of misfortunes.[56]

This type of belief gives a close and personal moral dimension to everything that happens to people. If there is a misfortune, it is due to

55. I have provided a summary of his analysis of how these beliefs operate in *Custom and Conflict in Africa* (1955), Chap. 4, and have analyzed several more recent studies in a more complex way in *Politics, Law and Ritual in Tribal Society* (1965), Chap. 6. In the latter I also consider studies that attempt to explain why in some situations judicial action is taken and in others search is made for mystical and ritual "upsets."

56. See references in previous footnote.

a disturbance in the moral relations between the sufferer and his fellows. Though the belief is that an individual has vicious feelings, and therefore he harms the person who is their object, in social life the process starts at the opposite end. A man suffers harm, and it is referred to the vicious feelings of a fellow. In the case of a society practicing an ancestral cult, failure in amity, and feelings of hostility and unspoken grievances against one's kin, spoil sacrifice to the spirits and bring mystical retribution in the form of misfortune. Or misfortune may be ascribed to a breach of taboo or to a warranted curse by an elder who has been offended.

These are clearly the views of a small-scale society which sees the working of the "universe" as closely involved in the particularities of its own social system and the personal relationships this contains. As shown in Chapter 2 this particularism is expressed in the specific conventions and rules that are established to differentiate roles. It is therefore characteristic of these societies that their rituals and ceremonies demand that individuals act their prescribed and specific roles, perhaps directly, or in inverted patterns or by special symbolic actions, in order that they may receive the good things of life. The demonstration of the moral elements in social relationships affects the natural world, as we think of it, for social and natural relationships are inextricably intertwined. Under belief in witchcraft, a disturbance of social and moral relations, even if it be covert, can thus affect natural events. I suggest that this situation arises from the complex interdependence of persons which I have repeatedly stated to be characteristic of these societies. Groups of kin have to cooperate to achieve multifarious purposes of all kinds. The effect is that every action by any member of a group, which departs from norms, influences adversely many purposive activities. A quarrel between two brothers has wider effects than in our industrial society; it may imperil productive work, affect the solidarity of political action, or disturb the unity of a religious congregation. Hence each breach of norm has a spreading moral disturbance: many relationships and activities are affected. Conversely, if outside events do not run normally, this points to secret disturbances in the moral relations of the members of the group. Someone is not observing in his feelings the appropriate amity: hence he harms his fellow. In this relatively stationary society, with limited types of opportunity for personal advancement, to grudge your kinsman help or his success is to wish he may not have it, and he will suffer.

These beliefs thus confer a kind of absolute responsibility on immoral feeling, akin to the absolute responsibility that falls on a large number of actions. We are here looking at the other side of the same coin. Accusations of witchcraft or sorcery in various tribes fall in specific sets of relationships, which are determined by some of the tensions inherent in the particular social system. It is here part of the definition of specific relationships that they are liable to produce witchcraft attacks. This applies in some tribes to fellow-wives of one man, in others to the members of a matrilineal lineage, in others to members of an agnatic lineage or members of a village. Among the Barotse any close kinsman is liable to attack one thus. These variations can be related to other aspects of the social system. It is more difficult to show a connection where witches are always outsiders—but again they are specific outsiders, often in groups with whom one has a feuding relationship. The dominant point is that where ill feeling is inappropriate in the first set of systems, it produces harm; in the second set of systems, ill feeling is appropriate, and it is believed to achieve mystical ill and cause misfortune through witchcraft or deliberate use of evil magic in sorcery. Absolute responsibility attaches to feelings, as well as to actions. I remind you that a false accusation is per se damaging.

There is also considerable variation in reaction to witches. In some tribes a successful accusation of witchcraft or sorcery starts a feud. In others, it establishes a tortious relationship, for which compensation can be sought. In yet others, it is a criminal offense, which has to be confirmed either by public opinion and accepted by the witch's kin so that he may be safely killed, or confirmed by the chief so that he can be punished. But since no one studied these systems in full operation before the intervention of European governments, we do not know how a system in which theoretically every death was due to witchcraft and punished by possible execution, worked without eliminating much of the population.

The whole treatment of injury and tort is influenced by this situation. I have cited earlier that if one man wrongs another, he may come into a kind of permanent social relationship with the victim: if he stabs him, he can mystically operate on the weapon to aggravate the wound. Alternatively, he must provide payment and a ritual offering to help the severity of the wound abate.[57] In another form similar processes appear in the Nuer reaction to adultery.

I am tempted to go even farther and to suggest that in these relatively undifferentiated societies not only are the Law of Persons, the

57. See Barton, *Ifugao Law* (1919), p. 79, and *The Kalingas* (1949), p. 223.

Law of Things, and the Law of Transactions intimately intermingled but also the Law of Wrongs becomes involved in this single matrix. All of them involve the concept of debt: debts exist in the law of status obligations, are created in the Law of Transactions, and arise out of the Law of Wrongs. This single mode of considering all types of legal relations reflects a common element in all of them. This common element is that any departure from what is established or should be observed is an injury. It seems to me that if one examines the rituals and ceremonials of tribal society, which reflect the interdependence of social, moral, and natural spheres, one can see that any change is an injury to the social fabric. The birth of a child, a boy's growing up, a marriage, a death, the transfer of a beast or a field, all injure the social fabric by disturbing existing arrangements. This is, perhaps an exaggerated statement. But as one observes customs, one notices again and again how each such alteration tends to require the payment of compensation and the performance of ritual. These attach to transfers of property as to changes of status. Action on breach of contract is an action in wrong, and in debt. Debt is constantly applied to interpret all social relationships. Debts are owed to ancestral spirits and have to be paid in due course. Compensation for wrongs involves often an absolute ritual element. The highly personal character of wrongdoing, in specific relationships, prevents the development of a clear concept of crime, apart from tort. I shall discuss this further in my next chapter; but it was of course late in the development of English law that crime became clearly distinguished from tort.[58]

I have derived support for this thesis from studies of the adat law of Indonesia. We are told by Ter Haar [59] that "the adat responsibility of the headmen to give each thing its place . . . (to order the relationships of things and people) . . . extends over the entire fields of the law—in the form of preventive legal action, as well as the settling of actual disputes" (p. 74). When an individual reclaims land he "makes his personal sacrifice, alone or with the aid of a land soothsayer. He does this in order to remove the danger to his life that could magically result from upsetting the existing state of affairs" (p. 104). In the sale of land in Minangkabau some rice and utensils are involved to symbolize "the magical equivalence of the buyer's share in the land exchange" (p. 114). (We may remember the mystical tie between seller and land in Ashanti and Ifugao referred to in Chapter 6.) In transac-

58. Potter, *The History of the Common Law* (1932), p. 303.
59. Citations (pages in text) from Ter Haar, *Adat Law in Indonesia* (1948).

tions after transfer of the binding token payment, one feels bound to perform because there is a "magical bond" (p.141). Meanwhile in personal relations marriage payments are "the magical means of releasing the woman and effecting her transfer and that of her children, without disturbing the social equilibrium and the balance of the cosmos" (pp. 168, 180). These citations culminate in Ter Haar's introduction to the law of delicts:

> In the legal order of the small law-communities, a delict is to be considered as a unilateral disturbance of the equilibrium. . . . Such an action demands a reaction . . . by means of which equilibrium can and must be restored. . . . The above . . . takes for granted the possibility of a relationship in each community between people, invisible powers, land, goods and everything else, which, in the opinion of the community, is considered as normal and necessary for a successful and harmonious life. This relationship may be called an "equilibrium." Since the people and the community are the central point in a complex of relations, so that one may speak of the life-circle of a man or of a community, the "normal" condition is one of equilibrium between life-circles. The content of individual life-circles may be small compared with that of the community itself. The process of strengthening and enlarging the individual life-circle at the expense of that of the community has already been mentioned many times [in discussions of family, property and contract law]. The complexes which we here call life-circles include . . . complexes connecting man, land and goods in addition to those things to which man is related in other ways. Every usurpation by outsiders, every disrespectful transgression of or contact with the life-circle and anything connected with it, and even every disrespectful remark about it produces a feeling of shame . . . and a desire to be rid of the cause of that feeling.

Every relationship esteemed in the community, continues Ter Haar, has a certain value which can be compared with other values, so that material and incorporeal goods can be substituted for one another to restore the equilibrium. Each damaged value must thus be replaced by an equivalent under the idea of reciprocity.

When thought of in this way, the demand for fines for delicts is a part of the concern for recovery of the cosmic equilibrium. . . . The payment for a fine for delict in case of trespass is consequently, a magic relation most closely related to the cash transaction. The first restores, the second prevents disturbance of the equilibrium. In another way it bears a relation to the credit transaction, in which giving, taking, and returning are included as part of the equilibrium process.

On top of this, when the offense is within a group, the feelings of the injured person must be assuaged (pp. 213–14).

While I do not like this formulation, I am glad to acknowledge how this passage guided my own view of wrongs in Barotse life. When I was working in Barotseland, I saw the same ethos of identification of all branches of the law that Ter Haar found in Indonesia.[60]

60. I have concentrated mainly on how status influences the concepts "liability" and "responsibility." Fauconnet's classic *La Responsabilité* (2d ed. 1928; written 1914) poses many sociological problems. He argues that "la responsabilité" is a social fact, unintelligible if approached from the actor. After an offense "la responsabilité préexiste"; the deed creates responsibility (p. 244). "La peine se dirige vers le crime" (p. 234), and "la responsabilité, c'est l'aptitude à devenir *légitimement* le patient de la peine" (p. 254). The person or thing alleged to be responsible has a social role to play, more important than the role of victim (p. 273). Fauconnet thus approaches responsibility from procedures and sanctions, but I feel does not sufficiently stress the difference between liability and responsibility. This may be difficult because in French "responsabilité" covers both conceptions: "sanction restitutive" is used but has not the same force as liability. Perhaps therefore he does not develop clearly for tribal society the founding of "la responsabilité" in specific social relationships, though he stresses: "Des catégories de sujets passibles de la peine sont préconstituées" (p. 253). In line with this, he concludes that in modern times "la considération de l'état subjectif du patient est d'abord et surtout un facteur non de responsabilité, mais *d'irresponsabilité* (p. 346) . . . [et] la spiritualisation de la responsabilité . . . modifie et atténue la responsabilité" (p. 347). I argue that this process arises from the liberation of most offenses, objectively, from specific contexts in social relations. Where Fauconnet's analysis stemmed from "la responsabilité" in the feud, he had not the high quality of data available to me. As I correct page proofs, I have seen the best yet, in E. L. Peters' "Some Structural Aspects of the Feud among the Camel-herding Bedouin of Cyrenaica" (*Africa*, July 1965). In the ideology of this agnatic society, liability is fixed in some contexts. Mental states are presumed from social and political relationships. The killer of his father or full brother is expelled from his specific agnatic relationship: he must be an adulterine, not an honorably fathered child. A killer inside the smallest agnatic political section, within which vengeance cannot be taken, is likened to an animal without human reason. Between neighboring sections of this size a killing provokes immediate vengeful killing, or payment of blood-money only rendered in full if hostility is being shown. Otherwise "debt" is left to maintain friendship. Further killings are not linked to earlier ones, but are presumed to be brand-new misdeeds. Killings between larger sections (encapsulating the smaller sections) are presumed to be linked. A killer of his mother's brother is assumed to be mad and stupid. Killing of a woman is always assumed to be accidental. Peters shows that this ideology differs from real struggles over resources and power.

Chapter 8

OBLIGATION AND DEBT

I HAVE DESCRIBED how the Barotse conceive of all relationships, whether of established status or ensuing from either "contract" or tort, in terms of "debt," and I have made brief citations from authorities on early English law which show that this law also was based on debt. In his history of law, Seagle states that this is true of all early law. He comments on the transaction of credit-barter in archaic times, by which the credit granted was recorded as a loan, as follows:

> This rather curious way of concluding a credit sale illustrates as well as anything else the truth that archaic law knows not so much a law of contracts as a law of debts. Indeed, its creative power seems to be exhausted in devising machinery for recording or enforcing a debt irrespective of its cause or origin. The Babylonian law recognized the *i'iltum* or obligation note which could be employed to incorporate any cause of debt. Medieval English law developed a general action of debt.

He goes on to point out that Babylonian, Greek, and Roman law considered the letting of a house and the letting of services to be secured by precisely the same form of contract or transaction. In Rome, the contract of *nexum*, the earliest form of transaction after *mancipium*, "appears to have been a loan transaction." The four early Roman real contracts were *mutuum*, a formless loan; *commodatum*, loan for use, the thing being returned; *depositum*, deposit; and *pignus*, pledge.[1] I take it that Seagle is here stressing that all these early Roman contracts involve transfers of property and the idea of a debt; and he implies that the "literal" contract, an entry made by the creditor in the household book of accounts, also has this element. He contrasts this situation with the development of the four Roman consensual contracts—sale, hire, partnership, and agency—which were all bilateral contracts that were shaped in the second century B.C. as

1. Seagle, *The Quest for Law* (1941), pp. 260–61.

Rome's commerce expanded, although "sale and hire, were obviously of early origin." [2]

These brief citations must serve to emphasize that debt, obligations conceived in terms of property, may have dominated early Roman law, as it did early English law. With this conception goes the idea that a defaulting debtor is a wrongdoer, as Seagle again makes clear earlier in the same chapter, in which he discusses the rise of contract:

> The burgeoning of ideas of contract has to wait upon the rise of credit transactions—credit barter and loan. Yet even when this stage has been reached, it is still a far cry from the age of enforceable promises. It is possible but rather unlikely that the seller who had parted with his cow thought of the defaulting buyer in terms of broken promises. It is much more likely that he felt himself cheated and thought of the buyer as a thief. Under similar circumstances a modern farmer's or peasant's thoughts are very unlikely to run in terms of the broken promise: he will want, above all, to get his cow back. The existing courts which deal with personal injuries and the transfer of property will certainly try to assimilate the transaction in the known legal categories. They will regard the original transaction as a transfer or conveyance of property that has failed of completion, and the failure to pay the price as a wrong which the seller is entitled to avenge. Hence the great savagery of early law towards debtors, who were treated as befitted those who had secured, as we still say, property under false pretences. They had sinned against the great god of Property, not of Contract. The Hittite Code and ancient Chinese law imposed especially bloody penalties for what we should regard as mere breaches of contract. [3]

This statement brings out the connection of early contract and injury with property and ideas of debt. My description of the Barotse law of transactions and of injuries did not report an uncommon situation. Indeed, I feel that the evidence indicates this to be the general structure of all tribal law, though not all studies of tribes have dealt explicitly with this point. Strikingly, many studies of feud speak in terms of the blood-debt. For example Barton, as already cited, wrote of the Ifugao:

2. Ibid.
3. Ibid., p. 256.

The feud is an affair between families only. It consists of a
series of vengeances and "returning of vengeances," . . . each
killing in a feud is considered by the killers to be an entirely
justifiable execution in payment of crime. The deities of war and
justice are called to witness that the debt is not yet paid. Contem-
poraneously, the kin of the slain are calling on the same deities to
witness that their family is sorely afflicted; that no debt was owed
the other; that no chickens or pigs, or rice had been borrowed;
that no theft or other crime had been committed, and so on; yet,
that innocent, they are being slaughtered.[4]

I could multiply statements of this kind. These might well be misleading, since the word "debt" has many connotations and we cannot
be sure what particular ethnographers intended when they used it.
Barton is exceptionally clear. Moreover, it would I think be possible to
talk about any system of obligations in terms of "debt," proceeding
from the use of the concepts of "owe" and "indebted."[5] Yet clearly
from the passages I have cited from Seagle he, like other legal authorities on early law, finds something specific in the way the idea of debt
dominates early law and does not dominate developed law.

There are a few explicit discussions of the point in works on African law. Epstein, who had legal training including the study of early
English law, examined how African Urban Courts in Northern Rhodesia developed the general concepts of tribal law, including ideas of
equity, to meet new situations involving Africans newly settled in
industrial towns. He says the judges start from the fact that the
plaintiff has suffered an injury, which leads to a debt, particularly
where there has been some form of cheating. Again, claims are upheld
where they are alleged as a debt or where the facts disclose an element
of fraud or deceit. There is no "remedy in contract." The court con-
ceives of a debt, and the action is in debt; for one party owes a debt
only after the other has performed his side of the bargain because the
plaintiff has then, so to speak, suffered a legal "wrong." Hence if there
has been part payment, action founds, provided delay in completing
payment has not been unreasonably long. Similarly, he shows, as in the

4. Barton, *Ifugao Law* (1919), p. 77. Cf. his comments on "the debt of life" in blood feud
among *The Kalingas* (1949), p. 178. See also for an excellent implicit account of a society as
a "network" of reciprocities in the material form of debts, Malinowski, *Crime and Custom in
Savage Society* (1926), passim.
5. See Hart, *The Concept of Law* (1961), pp. 85, 85 n., 243.

case of the burned hut I have cited in Chapters 6 and 7, that where someone has suffered an injury the court considers he has been damaged, and this establishes a debt which someone must pay.[6] I was thus not the only observer who reported the domination of debt from Northern Rhodesian African law, and Epstein's report is particularly valuable, since the courts he studied were composed of representatives of several tribes.

Yet we are left with the problem: What is the difference between debt in these contexts, and the fact that any obligation establishes a state of indebtedness, in another sense of the word, while clearly obligation is basic in any system of law? When I looked through the data I had previously collected in Barotseland, in the light of Epstein's study of African courts in the towns of Northern Rhodesia, I saw how the Barotse stated legal obligations as *milatu* (singular: *mulatu*). Jalla's *Dictionary of the Lozi Language* (1936) defines mulatu thus:

> fault, offence, guilt, debt. *Mulatu o mutuna* [great mulatu], crime; *ya na ni mulatu* [literally, he who has mulatu], guilty or debtor; *ku tokwa mulatu* [literally, to lack mulatu], to be innocent; *ku tama mulatu* [literally, to bind mulatu], to accuse, accusation, delation (p. 171).

It would therefore be possible to write about Barotse law largely in terms of debt, whether one were dealing with transactions, obligations of status, injuries, or offenses. My own data covering the use of mulatu are not specific enough, since when I was in the field I was not adequately aware of the importance of marshalling facts around the point. In addition, Barotse social relations were largely organized by the state's power. Perhaps therefore I was not struck as forcibly by the organizing power of debts as were students of tribal societies without governmental institutions. For other anthropologists who have studied African states have also not given much detail on this point.

Two excellent analyses of debt come from societies in which chiefly authority is little developed; and I consider that full quotations from these studies will illuminate the problem far more than would the accumulation of incidental references to the use of the word debt in many studies of tribal law.

I take first Leach's study, *The Political Systems of Highland Burma* (1954), where ten pages are devoted to the discussion of *hka*, which is

6. *Juridical Techniques and the Judicial Process* (1953), pp. 28–29.

translated as debt.[7] I follow, but summarize partly in my own words,
the course of Leach's discussion. He introduces it by stating that
Kachin ideas of debt correspond with the anthropologist's conception
of a social structure.

"Almost any kind of legal obligation that exists between two
Kachins is likely to be described as a debt (*hka*)." Debts are stated by
informants in terms of so-and-so many *hpaga*, which Leach translates
as "trade or ritual wealth objects." There are fixed "lists" of how
many such objects should be paid after an offense. These lists are
precise and apparently specific to each type of offense. The objects on
a list cannot be interchanged. Eight ritual wealth objects are levied on
the man who gets an unmarried woman with a child, and each object,
or set of objects, goes to a specific person or persons. The girl's parents
get five—a small calf, one gong, one length of silk, one small iron
cooking pot, and one sword. The three other objects are paid to the
girl herself, but only if the child is claimed as a member of the father's
lineage. Each of these objects is devoted to a specific purpose: one
necklace "to wash the woman's face," one length of silk "in which to
wrap the child," and one cow buffalo "for the milk of the child."
Negotiations are carried out by what Leach calls "agents for the principals"; but as this may confuse the situation with modern contracts
of agency, I shall call them "go-betweens." The go-betweens meet, lay
sticks to represent the requisite ritual objects upon the ground, and
begin to bargain. Items are substituted, not between those due on the
list, but by replacing, for example, the cow buffalo, if the wrongdoer
cannot provide one, with a pig. The pig counts as a buffalo, although
there is a doctrine that pigs do not rate as ritual wealth objects. But
when a pig is thus substituted for a buffalo, the doctrine is not
infringed.

Leach then contrasts the hpaga, a material fact, with hka, "the
immaterial debt," before explaining that in one sense hpaga "simply

7. At pp. 144–54. Below I use "ritual" since Leach does, but the word seems inappropriate
to me. He states (pp. 10 f.): "Ritual, I assert, 'serves to express the individual's status as a
social person in the structural system in which he finds himself for the time being.' " He then
states "ritual" to be that aspect of action which is symbolic of social status. This obscures a
difference most anthropologists insist on, when they use ritual to cover objects and actions
effecting ends outside their immediate range by extra- or supra-sensory power, and "ceremonial"
or "conventional" for those which are significant as symbolizing status, but lack this power
(see my own discussion and references in my paper "Les Rites de Passage" in Gluckman, ed.,
Essays on the Ritual of Social Relations, 1962, pp. 100 f.).

means trade." In the less sophisticated areas, a traveling trader has regular partners with each of whom he runs a credit account. They record the debts due between them with notches on a tally stick; this is split, and each holds half. Each notch represents a separate transaction, and these varied transactions have to be settled separately; they are not reduced to a common medium and balanced off against one another in total: "Each debt or notch (*hka*) had to be settled on its own merits."

Leach states that the procedures in the two situations cited above are akin. "For the Kachin, legal claims and commercial claims are alike *hka* (debts). The only difference is that with commercial claims the items may be anything, depending on the circumstances of trade, while, with legal claims, the items are stereotyped according to a traditional pattern in traditional goods." Some fourteen traditional goods are listed, though nowadays other types of goods and even cash are used. But if this is done it is always in process of substitution for traditional goods. The traditional ritual objects themselves are sometimes dealt with in open market, but normally their exchange is confined to certain set occasions: marriages, funerals, payment of ritual services of priests or agents [go-betweens], on transfer of residence or the building of a new house, and as judicial compensation in settlement of any kind of dispute or crime.

"The formal payments due on any particular occasion are defined by an agreed tradition. For each kind of settlement the tradition specifies a number of *hpaga* and gives a title to each *hpaga*."

These ritual objects vary with the nature of the offense and with the status of the parties. Penalties for impregnating an unmarried woman vary according to the status of man and woman. If one commoner has stolen another commoner's buffalo, he must return this and another buffalo in compensation, and give three ritual objects—a gong to cover the tracks of the buffalo, a hundred-bead necklace as halter for the buffalo, and a sword to clear the path on the way home. Leach points out that puns are involved in these "titles": the word for gong, for instance, is a derivation of hka, for the debt has to be settled, while another pun covers the friendship that has to be restored. He discusses also similar emphases among the hundred ritual objects that have to be rendered to settle a chief's blood feud.

The system is made flexible by the principle that substitution is allowed, since a poor man can give pigs or chickens whereas a rich man gives buffaloes according to the code. The poor man's properties count as full ritual objects. But since "in theory, gift obligations are scaled according to class," and payment depends on the economic standing and not on status of birth of the wrongdoer, an aristocrat to maintain his status must meet the scales set for his class. "Paradoxically therefore it is often true, especially of the more enterprising individuals, that they pay as much as they can afford rather than as little as they can haggle for." Considerations of this kind also affect the amount of marriage payments. Theoretically the same list of objects is payable whenever a chief's daughter is married, since the status of the bride sets the amount. But an aristocrat who is not a member of a chief's line and marries a chief's daughter, in fact pays less for his bride than the chief's son may pay for a chief's daughter.

Leach cites a series of instances in one family to show that "In every case the scale of the bride price, as measured by the number of cattle, corresponds to the ranking status of the bridegroom and not that of the bride." He examines the relation of this fact to the political system: though the theory is that the bride price is adjusted to the standing of the bride, men in fact pay more to gain in status. This general fact is important for our analysis, but I need not cite the details he gives. It is sufficient to note that Leach concludes: "the concept of *hpaga* ritual wealth [quaere: the exchange of *hpaga?*] is of great significance, for it permits structural rules which have all the appearance of rigidity to be interpreted very freely, thus opening the way for social mobility in a system which purports to be a caste-like hierarchy." This is followed immediately by [what seems to be a disconnected] statement that hka is equally important, because "Kachins tend to perceive every kind of mutual relationships that may grow up between a pair of individuals as being part of a system of debts." If A borrows from B, steals from B, gets B with child, fails to complete the stipulated terms of a contract (only payment of bride price is cited), fails to render a due to Chief B—A owes B a debt. If two lineages A and B have a set relationship of intermarriage and A marries into C's group when he should have married into B's, A's lineage owes B's lineage a debt. If A kills B, intentionally or unintentionally, A's lineage owes B's lineage a debt. If B has an accident, fatal or otherwise, while working for A, A's lineage owes B's lineage a debt. If a man of lineage A dies leaving a widow of lineage B, and no other male of lineage A takes her in leviratic marriage, lineage A owes lineage B a debt. [The connection of debt with social mobility presumably is that such a move puts one in a new relationship with others which entails a new series of indebtedness.]

All debts should be settled, and if they cannot be settled they may lead to feud.

> In principle any outstanding debt, no matter what its origin, is potentially a source of feud. For a Kachin, feud and debt are the same thing—*hka*. It is especially debts between strangers that must be settled quickly, otherwise the owner of the debt has a legitimate excuse for resorting to violence; in contrast, debts between relatives, especially affinal relatives, are not urgent matters. . . . some debts are always left outstanding almost as a matter of principle; the debt is a kind of credit account which ensures the continuity of the relationship [similar to the situation in County Clare, Eire, classically described by Arensberg and Kimball, which I discuss below]. There is thus a kind of paradox that the existence of a debt may signify not only a state of hostility but also a state of dependence and friendship.

With few exceptions, debts among the Kachin are deemed to exist not between individuals but between lineages. An unpaid debt may be carried from generation to generation to generation.

Leach concludes the discussion of hka (but not of ritual objects), with this statement:

> The close correspondence between the Kachin concept of debts and the anthropologist's concept of social structure should now be apparent. Kachin tradition and ritual lays down what are the proper relations between individuals, that is to say, it specifies what obligations A has towards B and B towards A. Debts come into existence whenever anyone feels that these formal obligations have not been adequately fulfilled.[8]

8. This final citation is in Leach, *Political Systems of Highland Burma* (1954), p. 154. In "Aspects of Bridewealth and Marriage Stability among the Kachin and Lakher" (1961) Leach argues that the "continuity of the structure 'vertically' through time" is expressed adequately through names transmitted agnatically, while "the continuity of the structure 'laterally' . . . is maintained by a continued chain of debt relationships of an economic kind." In these tribes lineages are involved in "permanent" intermarriage, and it is of the very essence of these ties that some part of the bridewealth payments is left outstanding from generation to generation. "It is the existence of these outstanding debts which asserts the continuance of the affinal relationship," under severe sanctions (pp. 122–23). I note that since agnation is related to landholding, we have here perhaps another illustration of the role of movements of chattels in setting up cross-links between landed positions, as set out in Chap. 4.

I have given this fairly full summary because it shows how a tribe, geographically and culturally distant from the Barotse, has the permeating idea of debt which exists in Barotse law. Since the discussion is only part of a book devoted to different problems, it is inevitable that Leach has not distinguished various elements which might well be separated. Before attempting this separation, I must eliminate his comparison of the Kachin's idea of debt with the anthropologist's concept of social structure. An anthropologist describes a social structure partly in terms of obligations between persons and social positions. The Kachin think of the obligations involved in their relationships in terms of debts. Hence there is apparently a close correspondence between the two conceptions. It is superficial only. For the way in which the Kachin think about their social organization, or social structure, the conception of hka, provides part of the data out of which the anthropologist attempts to analyze what he calls "social structure." Only in the very widest sense of the word debt, as equivalent to obligation, is there really an appearance of correspondence. For the Kachin's concept of debt covers a variety of different obligations arising out of different kinds of relationships between persons related in various ways; and our problem is to ask why these should all be covered by the idea of "debt"—usually in a material sense. What for the Kachin is an intellectual answer, poses for us a problem. When we put this problem into historical perspective, as Leach has not done, it takes a clearer form.

Among the Kachin there is clearly a high degree of specificity in social relationships within an economically undifferentiated situation dominated by ties of status. Each relationship has specific attributes, marked by conventional (what Leach calls "ritual") modes of behavior; and each relationship tends to contain a linked series of debts which have to be discharged by payment of specific objects. To quote Leach again, "debts come into existence whenever anyone feels that . . . formal obligations have not been adequately fulfilled [in] the proper relations between individuals" as laid down by tradition and ritual demands. Again, dealings with property provide one measure to assess fulfillment. Payments of conventional objects then redress the default. When a new status relationship is entered into, at least one party moves into "debt," and sometimes both parties; again specific objects, some devoted to a specific purpose, have to be paid. Leach does not give the data, but presumably several items in the marriage pay-

ments are specifically named to effect specific purposes in the total
transfer of rights, creation of obligations, and adjustment of relationships. Finally, if one person or group injures another, a debt relationship is established, whose form depends on the nature of the injury
and the status of the parties. If the parties are in a feuding (debt)
relationship, liability is incurred irrespective of whether the injury was
intentional or not. Accident in another's employment similarly establishes debt. Injury thus either fits into a series of debts in existing
status relationships or creates a relationship that is akin to a status
relationship; hence I have suggested it is liable to be expanded by
mystical beliefs. This sets up debts, whose varied payments among the
Kachin—and elsewhere, as we have seen with Nuer adultery—involve
for redress the delivery of specific goods, many of which are specifically named in the context of dispute to effect specific purposes, ritual
and secular, within the total situation.

Here then, as among Barotse, we find that the emphasis of Kachin
law is on the conventions, both of behavior and in rights to property,
which distinguish each status relationship. High value becomes attached to dealings with property as indicative of status rights and
duties. Relationships arising from injury, and out of what commerce
there is, occur either within pre-established relationships with their
own tally of dues or set up relationships conceived on this pattern. My
suggestion is that it is the linking of specific status relationships with
specific pieces of property—the situation among the Barotse which I
described in Chapter 5—that emphasizes the importance of particular
payments, of debts, both to meet established dues and to redress injuries. It is this that is meant by debt in a tribal society.

Before I elaborate this suggestion, I examine a study of another
tribe where "debt" was the organizing concept in all relationships. I
have suggested that Leach has perhaps got this particular problem
somewhat out of perspective because he has not set Kachin concepts in
a wide enough historical and comparative background. This lack of
perspective, if one focuses on the cultural beliefs of a single people, is
more strikingly manifest in Bohannan's study, *Justice and Judgment
among the Tiv of Nigeria* (1957). Here again the dominance of the
idea of debt in a tribe's law is well described. But Bohannan concludes
that this gives the system a unique character which cannot be examined in terms of the concepts of Western jurisprudence. He begins
by insisting, rightly, that we describe accurately a people's own

ideas—what he calls their "folk-system." But he urges further (p. 69) that:

> The cardinal error of ethnographic and social analysis . . . [is] raising folk-systems like "the law," designed for social action in one's own system, to the status of an analytical system, and then trying to organise the raw social data from other societies into its categories. I [Bohannan] have also tried to avoid the equivalent error of raising the folk systems of the Romans or the Trobriand Islanders to the level of such a filing system for data which may not fit them.

This raises two separate problems: First, can we compare different legal systems at all; and second, if we can make comparison, in what language and terms can we do so without distorting any of the legal systems? For comparison clearly carries this danger. Bohannan constantly emphasizes the danger, and I have therefore to discuss his argument before I can proceed with my analysis of his data.

Tiv, he stresses, class wrongs for example by the types of counteraction and correction which they provoke. Any offense that is followed by ritual reparation is *kwaghbo:* all homicide is an offense against the fetish called *swende* so that ritual follows on it, and it is therefore kwaghbo. But any offense that comes before a court (*jir*) is called an *ifer:* so homicide is also an ifer. Finally any offense that is punished is called a *kwaghdang*, so homicide is a kwaghdang. Incest and adultery also fall into all three categories. Other offenses may fall into two or even only one of these Tiv categories. Bohannan therefore concludes:

> Tiv do not make the distinctions that Europeans make between wrongs which injure the entire community and those which injure individuals. Many of our own jurists have pointed out that there is no delict which is not in some sense harmful to the community, and no crime which does not harm some individual's rights. The distinction which Europeans draw is a folk distinction. The distinction which I have drawn between *kwaghbo, kwaghdang* and *ifer* is a folk distinction. We can compare the two sets of distinctions. But it is just as wrong and just as uncomprehending to cram Tiv cases into the categories of the European

folk distinctions as it would be to cram European cases into Tiv folk distinctions.[9]

Clearly this is sensible, but Bohannan does not proceed to discuss how we can compare, or what can be compared about the two sets of distinctions. In this case it is perhaps significant that European jurists do not in fact classify crimes and delicts by reference to whether an individual or the community is harmed, as Radcliffe-Brown, a social anthropologist, did.[10] In fact, Kenny specifically rejects this criterion, though it has been adopted by others. His emphasis is rather on procedure and remedy. Indeed, he points out that the distinction in Roman law between *delicta privata* and *delicta publica* [on which Radcliffe-Brown based his theory], was originally established because crimes in early Rome were tried by the public itself, i.e. by the whole Roman people assembled in *comitia centuriata*. And his final criterion for isolating crimes from other wrongs is that they are "wrongs whose sanction is punitive and is in no way remissible by any private person, but is remissible by the Crown alone, *if remissible at all*." [11] He looked at punishment or remedy and at procedure, rather than at who was wronged, in trying to classify suits. Similarly, lawyers distinguish suits in tort from suits over breach of contract not only by the type of duty breached, but also largely by the remedies sought and the procedures pursued.

Put into Tiv categories, an offense in Britain that falls under Kenny's definition of a crime would be *kwaghdang*, followed by punishment, and *ifer*, as coming before a court, indeed almost compulsorily. It would not be *kwaghbo*, requiring perforce ritual expiation or coming under ritual threat. But of course it might also be a sin. That is nowadays. However, ritual and religion were more significant in early English law. Offenses and suits then were classified into those which fell under ecclesiastical or secular jurisdiction, and those which were clergyable and unclergyable. Again, various types of offenders either received or did not receive privilege of sanctuary in church, or objuration, right up to 1623–24. There was a religious and ritual element

9. Bohannan, *Justice and Judgment among the Tiv* (1957), pp. 119–20.
10. "Primitive Law," in *Structure and Function in Primitive Society* (1952), pp. 212 f.
11. *Outlines of Criminal Law* (1929), Chap. 1. This is the best way of analyzing "wrongdoing" among the Barotse; see my *Judicial Process among the Barotse* (1955), pp. 81, 150, 217.

both in offenses and reaction to offenses. The problem set here is similar to the one concerning debt: in tribal and in early European law there is present for offenses this additional ritual category. Why does this disappear from organized sanctions in later law? Obversely, why is it present in underdeveloped law? I speak here of legal sanctions applied by the state, for obviously there is still a religious judgment on wrongdoing, and in religious subgroups there may be organized punishment of such offenses. Indeed by order of the state's court the executed murderer is still not buried in consecrated ground, but in the prison where he is is executed, and in the past his very body was destroyed.

In my own opinion, this multiple Tiv classification of wrongs and the introduction of the ritual element show a process exhibited in Leach's discussion of Kachin offenses, and in my more general treatment in earlier chapters. Each offense tends to have multiple specific connotations, within several ranges of social relations, some of which emphasize the ritual concomitants which are believed to permeate social life. In our own history, the differentiation of social relationships has tended to restrict ritual elements to subgroups within the total society.[12]

Bohannan also gives warnings [13] against forcing Tiv concepts into Western categories, in dealing with the distinction between civil and criminal law (p. 70), speaking of the Tiv as having a body of law, a *corpus juris* (pp. 96–97), discussing sanctions (p. 101), dealing with tort and contract (pp. 111–12, 212–13), and considering the notion of courts and of law itself (pp. 210–14). These warnings are important; but the insistence on the cultural uniqueness of folk systems seems to me continually to distract Bohannan's attention from those similarities within differences that enable one to formulate more clearly both the problems of a single society's law and those of comparative law. He states the need of comparison (pp. 120, 214), but he does not explain how one is to compare what on the surface is unique, because he fails to look at Tiv law in the light of very early English law. It is seen as a system in equal right with that of the Roman; hence he can call Roman law, like Tiv and Trobriand Island law, a folk-system. Tiv law is entitled to independent respect but, like Barotse law, it undoubtedly

12. Durkheim, *De la Division travail social* (1893), passim.
13. Page references in this paragraph are to his *Justice and Judgment among the Tiv* (1957).

has parallels with an early phase—I do not say worse phase—of European law.

The insistence on uniqueness constantly obscures problems. The following example illustrates this clearly. When the Tiv conduct an autopsy on a man to see if he had practiced witchcraft, guilt is shown by the presence near the heart of colored sacs—presumably collections of arterial and venous blood. Hence Tiv speak of innocence as "empty-chested" which, Bohannan says, in Tiv means two things:

> a man of no talent and consequence, if he is alive and healthy. Applied to a dead man, it means a person who died for some reason other than his own evil propensity [his witchcraft bringing his doom through the operation of good ritual]. It resembles our own word "innocent" in that it has connotations of good, but in other usages the derogatory connotations of lack of experience are dominant.[14]

There is of course nothing unique in this Tiv idea that to be innocent is to be guiltless, and therefore in some way to be "guileless" —naive, simple, and foolish, as any dictionary shows. The existence in such widely separated societies of this feeling that the guilty are somehow clever, and the weak and poor are somehow innocent, while the innocent are also somehow foolish, poses a general problem. The same identification is found in Hebrew, Arabic, Greek, Latin, and at least some Bantu languages.

Bohannan's approach to all Tiv phenomena of social control appears to me to raise a bar to sociological and jurisprudential analysis, and I have therefore dealt with other examples before moving to a summary of his statements on debts, contracts, and torts. He has a chapter dealing with cases in debt. He concludes his analysis of seven cases of this type by saying that he wanted "to present the Tiv notion of debt in such a way that its unity becomes apparent, . . . We have discovered that Tiv use a single concept, 'debt' (*injo*), to cover instances and cases which we, in our folk system, classify into several different categories." In cases that we might classify by contract, Tiv "see the debt aspect rather than the contract aspect as the most important." The comparative jurist might see a contract between a man who owns a goat and the man who herds it, or a contract between a pledgor and pledgee. "Tiv agree with such statements if made and explained to

14. Ibid., pp. 199–201, especially p. 199 n. 1.

them. But they do not use this aspect of the relationship for purposes of classification. In their own folk system, the idea of contract takes, for purposes of classification, a subordinate position to the idea of the debt involved." Similarly if a man's livestock damage another's crops, a right is infringed. "But Tiv classify this idea also under debt: if a man's livestock injures a farm, he falls into debt to the farmer. Debt is an aspect of both this sort of contract and this sort of tort: it is an aspect on which Tiv classify. Needless to say, our categories of contract and tort are not coterminous with the Tiv category of debt." [15]

The similarity between this Tiv situation and that of Kachin and Barotse law is manifest in the discussion of the Tiv word *injo*, which Bohannan translates as debt. He says it "covers a wider range of phenomena and social relations than the English word 'debt' usually does." You are in debt if you borrow and do not repay, if you herd stock for your kinsman, if your animal damages your neighbor's crops, if you marry a woman from another group without return [and presumably if you assault another]. The phrase "flesh debts" is important in the necrophagous beliefs of Tiv about witchcraft: if another witch provides a corpse of a relative for you to feast on, you owe that witch a corpse. In addition, "many personal relationships are expressed in terms of debts." Damages awarded in court are called debt. Hence Bohannan states that: "Rather than fit Tiv cases into European cases like tort, contract, property rights, etc., thus hiding the most important thing about them, I have organized the cases in such a way as to illustrate the Tiv notion of debt or *injo*," while attempting to make finer distinctions within the Tiv folk-system.[16] In his conclusion to the book as a whole, he states even more emphatically:

> [Though] we found it possible to say that Tiv "have" actions which resemble tort, contract, or the like . . . were we merely to do that, we should miss the organising concept which contains several English categories. This categorising concept is debt . . . Many torts have debt aspects; most contracts have debt aspects. Tiv "classify" on the notion of debt, as it were, not on the notion of "tort" or "contract." [17]

15. Ibid., pp. 111–12.

16. Ibid.; citations mainly from p. 102, also from p. 106. Note, however, that the Tiv dictionary gives words for "to agree" and "to hurt."

17. Ibid., p. 212.

This is obviously sound as a first step in presenting Tiv ideas. Yet, somehow, despite this emphasis on how the Tiv classify by "debt," what is involved in this notion never becomes clear. I suspect that this is because Bohannan makes a further step, and this step seems to be in the wrong direction:

> It is not for us to say that Tiv do not understand tort or contract; neither is it for Tiv to say that the English do not understand debt. We must realise that the same general type of material can be classified in several ways. It is, in the long run, the folk classifications that are important to social anthropologists, not the "presence" of torts or contracts which are both folk and analytical concepts in another society.[18]

I consider it important that we examine in what sense the Tiv "do not understand" contract and tort, in the way that modern law understands these conceptions. I note also that they here do not differ from other tribal peoples, or from the English until comparatively recent centuries. What then is this Tiv notion of debt? I have searched the book for explanatory passages. Bohannan says [19] the scribe, working in a court set up by the British, classifies cases under the heads debt, marriage, and appeal (p. 71). His records seemingly show many cases as ordering the payment of simple debts, which in reality arose out of more complex relationships with a "best friend," with a witness who had been paid to give evidence (p. 40),[20] with an intermediary in a pawning transaction, and so forth. The court then inquires into a series of obligations and claims between the parties (pp. 106 f.). This statement brings out only that we are not here dealing with a society in which one person lends goods to a completely unrelated person.

More significant is a passage on the rule of self-help. Tiv can take things from certain kin without permission, though it is more polite to ask for them (pp. 25, 127–28). This is not theft—it is a privilege of kinship, like the Barotse privilege examined in Chapter 5. Again it is not theft if a man takes a thing under what the Tiv call "taking for debt." He proceeds immediately with it to his home, and convenes his agnatic lineage to show it to them. He specifies to them that he has

18. Ibid.
19. Citations of pages in parentheses are again from his *Justice and Judgment*.
20. Cited above in Chap. 6, at p. 200.

taken the article "in compensation for a particular debt." His agnates will then decide whether to back him or make him return the article. The action is public; and if his agnates consider his case just, they try to convince the victim's lineage of the justice. If they "do not agree that the debt is just, or that the method of collecting it was correctly resorted to, they will withhold their support," whereupon the owner can take the article back. Tiv cases of apparent theft may therefore turn into inquiries whether the appropriation of goods was justified by a prior debt to the taker or one of his kinsmen (pp. 128–29). Many appropriations of goods are then part of a chain of debts.

Debts in the sense of obligations to provide a woman in marriage, or goods, dominate relations between kin and in-laws. Breaches of obligations to these persons also set up debts. A man was advised by the Tiv judges to give his father-in-law a conciliatory gift because he had, in their eyes, maltreated his wife by not giving her children and then beating the children whom she bore by other men, and because he had insulted his father-in-law by bringing him to court "when actually he himself was at fault. The gift was a recognition of wrong and a basis for re-establishing the relationship. It was atonement, but not what a Tiv would call punishment or penalty." Note that the court only suggested the gift be made, and did not care whether or not it was (pp. 99, 79, 132). Another man was ordered by the court to pay a small sum of money for what was held to be an unwarranted assault on a woman (pp. 131–32). Bohannan comments (p. 132) on these two cases that:

> Reimbursement for "damages" centres on the notion of *wam*. *Wam*'ing a person means to make him a gift, thereby erasing a fault by compensation. If the gift is accepted, it serves both as an apology on the part of the offender and as a token of forgiveness on the part of the injured person. Sometimes a person himself makes the offer to *wam* another; but more often one of them forces an arbitration of their differences.

Relevant also are Tiv ideas about fines. A man is held responsible for his sister's son's offenses if the nephew is living with him, although this is an agnatic society. A sister's son of a local man was fined for beating a woman who alleged she caught him stealing cassava from her field, and his uncle too was fined. Bohannan says "both paid their fines because they knew they were wrong, but, more importantly, because

they knew that their relationships with their neighbours would continue to be strained until they made some sort of move to admit that
they were wrong." The fines paid here, Bohannan continues, "were
aligned with the idea of *tia,* which is usually translated inaccurately as
'fine.' *Tia* is an animal which Tiv bring to the judges or arbitrators
of their cases in order that the animal may be butchered when the case
is settled." Traditionally it was provided by the plaintiff, not by the
man who lost the case. The entire community shared the meat, "in
recognition of the fact that one has had one's affairs and relationships
renovated and harmony now reigns." A man similarly supplies a tia
beast for slaughter if he takes his wife to her home for a ceremony to
be performed on her behalf, both as "payment for services and, at the
same time, indication of the 'repaired' relationship." If a man summons the elders to arrange a séance to investigate mystical dangers he
sometimes provides a tia beast. Bohannan states that Tiv have, "without signal success, tried to bring fines into line with their ideas of *tia*"
(pp. 66–67). That is, they have presumably regarded levying a fine
and taking it for the Native Treasury as a payment to the community
for its trouble and as a symbol of readjustment of relationships within
the community.

These several quotations, embodying though they do highly skilled
research and analysis, still fail to fix what Bohannan means when he
says the Tiv classify on the notion of debt. This notion becomes clear
only when we turn back to his initial analysis of kinship, and more
particularly of marriage—since in a book on justice and judgment it is
the relationships out of which most disputes arise that are most fully
analyzed.

Marriage is "one of the most disturbed areas of Tiv life." [21] The
Tiv used to practice exchange marriage, in which if a woman was
given in one marriage, her husband had to return a woman to her
group. Tiv believed that "the only commodity decently exchangeable
for the fertility of one woman was that of another." Their social
system was deeply involved in these exchanges. The British Government forbade them, and marriage payments were instituted in their
place. Nevertheless, men have a great interest in the women over
whose marriage their agnatic group has control. The male members of
a small designated group of closely related agnates distribute the
women of their group as marriage wards among themselves, in as

21. Bohannan, *Justice and Judgment among the Tiv* (1957), pp. 72 f.

equitable a manner as possible. The guardian receives the marriage payment for his ward and can use it for his own marriage or that of a male dependent. Bohannan comments:

> The result of the abolition of exchange marriages has been that two formerly enmeshed structures are now rendered discrete. In a social system characterized by marriage ratified by bridewealth [marriage payment] one can see a kinship structure which has its nodes at individual marriages. There is, in addition, a network of debt relationships which is more or less coterminous with the network of marriage and kinship relationships, but which has its nodes in the individual contracts between women's guardians and their husbands. This logical separation was not possible under the system of exchange marriage, in which debts did indeed exist, but the debts themselves could be seen as potential future links in the kinship system, not a special system which stood outside it. In the exchange system, the debt owed was a woman—ward to one man, wife to the other. The debt one assumed at marriage was discharged when one's wife's guardian married one's own ward . . . The debt aspect of marriage is summed up in the Tiv notion *kem*. One says, "I *kem* my wife from her guardian." *Kem* means "to accumulate" and its only other common usage is in "accumulating a farm"—that is, gradually over the years getting more and more seed yams so that one can have a bigger and bigger farm. The *kem* relationship of debt between a man and his wife's guardian is never broken, because *kem* is perpetual, the debt can never be fully paid. I [Bohannan] translate *kem* "to make payments." [22]

Debts over women to kinsmen and in-laws are segregated; if a guardian's kinsman takes money for his ward, the matter becomes a debt among kinsmen which does not concern the husband. [23]

Here is the matrix for the Tiv notion of *injo*—translated by Bohannan as debt—which he finds in Tiv relationships of all kinds. It is a particular obligation set in a complex network of status relationships, depending on one another, and constituting the main involvement of man or woman for most purposes. The obligation is stated in material

22. Ibid., p. 72.
23. Ibid., p. 80.

form—a woman, goods transferred at marriage. Payment is made to create a reverse obligation: one accumulates obligations that will "bear," as one accumulates a farm that will yield fruit. These debts over women are also important bonds of cooperation, as well as sources of hostility, between the men of the agnatic groups which act as productive units and political sections. From this combination of co-operation and hostility originate mystical fears and ties: séances to detect mystical causes of misfortune frequently involve "debts and marriage wards." [24] The two sets of injo which center on a woman—those involved in allotting her to a guardian kinsman, and those involved in her marriage to an outsider—are kept distinct.

The concept of injo seems then to be extended, out of these dominant relationships, to relationships arising from both transactions and injuries. This can only mean that the payments entailed in these relationships, the property elements, are considered as if they arise from obligations in a quasi-status relationship; Bohannan does not discuss this point. His only relevant discussion is on putting livestock out to be herded under agistment. Tiv do not keep their own livestock at home, for then "it is subject to the legitimate claims of one's kinsmen." Livestock and especially goats are therefore placed with one's friends or distant kinsmen, and one gets livestock for oneself from them. One can then say truthfully that all the goats in one's own compound belong to someone else. The caretaker's reward is that he receives one kid in three. A "very complicated debt structure" results, which is a fertile source of litigation. Bohannan does not here discuss the nature of the relationship established between owner and caretaker or whether it involves other obligations.

Tiv *injo,* the concept of material obligations in status or quasi-status relationships, is thus similar to what the Barotse call *bung'a,* ownership, and the Kachin, *hka.* It reflects the close involvement of property rights within status relationships. Women come into this reckoning, partly as the focus under exogamy for the extension of quasi-kinship bonds, and partly because in the end Tiv considered that all exchanges of goods should drive toward accumulating the property which can be exchanged for wives.[25] Malinowski similarly stated of the law of

24. Ibid., p. 166, and following sections.
25. See Bohannan, "Some Principles of Exchange and Investment among the Tiv" (1955). See also Goody, *Death, Property and the Ancestors* (1962), pp. 100 f.

Oceania that reciprocal obligations within the system produced a network of debts.[26]

It is not therefore correct to say that the Tiv do not think in terms of contract and injury (tort). Bohannan himself writes:

> Like the term "law" itself, "contract" must be given two definitions: one in European law, the other in comparative jurisprudence. I am interested in explaining the Tiv notion, in which a word like "contract" does not enter. If, later, we want to compare the Tiv notion either with contract in English law or with some more generalized notion of contract used by comparative jurists, it would no doubt be illuminating. I am not saying that Tiv do not "have" contract; I am merely saying that they have it like M. Jourdain spoke prose.[27]

But it seems that what Tiv do is emphasize the property strand in relationships of kinship and in-lawship, and in assessing recompense for default in these or injury by an "outsider." This common element they seem to call injo, and Bohannan translates it as debt. Unfortunately, Bohannan apparently could not cite cases to show that in transactions it is not agreement that is emphasized but property, under the title of debt, as among the Barotse. But my recapitulation and re-analysis of the treatment by these authors of debt among Kachin and Tiv does suggest that the Barotse situation is typical of tribal society.

Clearly then the description of a folk system of legal ideas as advised by Bohannan is the first step only in analysis. Thereafter we must try to relate the particularities of a folk system to other elements in the social system. This necessarily involves comparison of sets of legal ideas in different societies and cognizance, where we have historical data, of the development of particular sets of legal ideas. To emphasize this point I interrupt my discussion of debt to refer back to Bohannan's insistence that in classifying suits under debt, and not by their tortious or contractual origin, Tiv jurisprudence differs radically from Western jurisprudence. I have already cited authorities to show that early actions in English, and possibly in Roman, Near Eastern, and Chinese law, were actions in debt. I now refer to the distinction of contractual as against delictual or tortious liability in Roman and

26. In his "Introduction" to Hogbin, *Law and Order in Polynesia* (1934), pp. xxxiv–v.
27. Bohannan, *Justice and Judgment among the Tiv* (1957), pp. 104–05.

English law. I shudder at the temerity of my compressions of deeply involved developments, and plead that I am making them only to indicate the dangers of Bohannan's type of cultural solipsism.

In his *Historical Introduction to Roman Law* (1939), Jolowicz wrote:

> *Contractus* is simply the verbal noun derived from *contrahere* (literally, "to tie"), and it is used elliptically for *contractus negotii* or *obligationis*, whether what we call contract was involved or not. Logically there was no reason why it should not be used of obligations contracted by delict, but usage seems to have confined the word to *negotia* (transactions), in opposition to delict. At the end of the republic indeed terminology had not got even as far as this, for, though Cicero uses the word *contrahere*, he does not use the noun. Still less was there any classification of obligations into those arising from contract and delict, or of contracts according to their different methods of formation. . . . In the more detailed discussion which follows, the usual classification under contract and delict will be preserved for the sake of convenience, but it must be remembered that the terminology is in advance of the time of which we are speaking, and that contract often grows up out of delict. [pp. 285–86]

Only in post-classical Roman law was agreement itself recognized as giving rise to an obligation, and a "general rule . . . substituted for the different treatment of individual cases in the classical law" (pp. 529–30). Moreover, by the time of the classical law:

> As intention is required for contract, so the mental element of guilt is required for delict, and a place has to be found for some cases of liability from which this is or may be absent. [p. 531]

Roman substantive law remained secreted in the interstices of procedure (Maine) for many centuries, but obligations arising from contract and from delict were beginning to be separated, though no general theory of contract (or delict) emerged:

> So far were the Byzantines from developing an independent theory of contract, that it is they especially who use the word in an extended sense so as to include *negotiorum gestio* and *tutela*. The doctrine of obligations *quasi ex contractu* and *quasi ex delicto*

owes nothing to the schools of law; it has no value and is the result of hasty adaptation by the compilers of classical texts. [p. 535]

But the distinction had now emerged.

Similarly, the development of English doctrines on contract and tort is markedly influenced, like the Roman, by the nature of remedies and their writs. Again I summarize very complex developments, for my immediate purposes only. I cite from the authority of Winfield's *The Province of the Law of Torts* (1931: pp. 20 f.). In considering Finch's book on the practice of law, published in 1613 in French and in 1627 in English, Winfield finds no clear marking off of torts, as now understood, from crimes, breaches of contract, breaches of bailment and breaches of trust. Contract was then in a phase of rapid growth. The confusions in the book, he says, emphasize "the great difficulty that the lawyers of that era had in perceiving the difference of contract from tort" (p. 23). Blackstone improved on this, but English law was "not yet ripe enough" for a sharp difference to be drawn between tort on the one hand, and breach of trust, breach of contract, and breach of bailment on the other hand, though civil injuries and crimes were by that time distinguishable "with tolerable clearness." Blackstone still treated contract in a scattered manner, so that it appeared under "Rights of Things" and also under "Private Wrongs"; but contractual obligation was detachable from obligation arising from tort by being treated as a *chose in action* or species of property (p. 27). Nevertheless the fact of agreement marked it off from tortious liability. It is only in the nineteenth century, as forms of action became less decisive and schools of jurisprudence were established, that these points were substantially clarified.

It seems that the almost clear distinction of contracts and torts, not fully worked out even in Justinian's jurisprudence, begins to be achieved only in the law of industrial societies. It is then not surprising that the Tiv did not make this distinction; and we can attempt to explain their failure to do so by comparing the social conditions in which their law, like the law of other societies, operated. In Tiv law, as we have seen for the Barotse, procedure for action was simple, and forms of action did not themselves restrict suits. I suggest it was the formalism of procedure, which developed when writing in the hands of professional lawyers made this possible, that for so long prevented the liberation of legal ideas from out-of-date classifications.

I have tried to show, I hope successfully, that what Bohannan sees as the folk system of the Tiv is widely distributed in tribal law; and Holmes, Maitland, Seagle, and many other jurists have made the point about early European law. Clearly we must not force tribal law into a Procrustean bed of Western jurisprudential concepts, but we may with care use those refined concepts for comparison and analysis. The alternative is to invent a new terminology. I am not concerned with this methodological problem; I am concerned here only to put forward a hypothesis to explain the wide distribution of this idea of "debt" in societies dominated by status. Before I pursue this analysis, I give further examples to show how the high significance of debt in multiplex status relations can persist in rural areas within a commercial, industrial economy.

In the 1930s Arensberg and Kimball studied the small farmers of County Clare, Eire. These farmers live off the land and sell their surplus products for certain necessities which they must obtain from shops. The farms are worked by families, ideally a couple and their children, but in the absence of children other kinsmen or kinswomen are called in. Farming families are related to one another in a network of kinship ties which also cover the villages and small towns of the county. Since the farms are small and relatively poor, only one son and one daughter in each family can marry. The son who is to inherit the farm is also the one who marries, and his bride brings (1936) a dowry of £250 to £350, roughly equivalent to the value of a farm. The parents then retire and hand over the farm to the new couple, and a condition that they will support the parents is contained in the marriage deed.

Shopkeepers' families in the small towns run on a similar principle. Here again one son or son-in-law succeeds to the shop. Shopkeepers' families do not intermarry so much with one another as into the farmers, thus acquiring customers. Or a farmer's younger son is bought into apprenticeship in a shop. Connections between townsmen and farmers are expressed and maintained, and sometimes set up, by debt. The countryman is always in debt to his shopkeeper kinsman, since he requires goods in advance of harvest or sale of stock. This permanent state of indebtedness is part of their relationship. If a countryman pays his debt to a shopkeeper, this is a sign that he is going to change both his shop and his social relationship. The debt, like the dowry when a girl marries into a farm, is a measure of status: it signifies acceptance of the network of social obligations and one's own place in that network, which links the whole countryside. Debts must be owed in only a limited number of places; if they are placed too widely, the system is being abused and shopkeepers will call them in. But, if properly handled, debts establish a firm relationship which passes down the generations from father to son.[28] We must, of course, see this particular set of relationships against the background of the world-wide problem of rural indebtedness for small farmers; someone in the wider economic system in fact carries the debt for the shopkeeper. Yet looked at within the countryside itself, here is a remarkable instance of how debt can survive as a dominant mode of establishing and maintaining social relations in a commercial age. Nor do I doubt that large stores in towns are pleased to hold unrelated customers who maintain some kind of debt in their accounts—like Kachins and men of County Clare—as earnest that they will remain customers.

Debt may operate in this way, with some unpaid amount left, or more than was due being paid to establish indebtedness the other way. Alternatively, it may be a long series of more or less balancing payments, such as is reported by Frankenberg from a Welsh village, where "getting something for nothing from another villager is not an achievement, [but] is a disgrace." He describes how even sisters feel it necessary to make return to each other, and how reluctant people are to accept the smallest favors. Here the wife of a villager who did local building jobs divided her trade among the shopkeepers. But we still lack information to indicate which circumstances will evoke which pattern. It does seem clear that wherever we have pockets of multiplex relationships in modern society, the whole problem of material indebtedness comes to the forefront, as it does in tribal society. It is clear from Frankenberg's report that material obligation, and discharge of that obligation, are important to his Welsh villagers. What they fear is acquiring debts they cannot hope to discharge.[29]

I am aware of the fact that obligations in all personal relations in modern society are expressed in the form of material gifts, and redress for small offenses is similarly made. The offer of a cigarette or drink,

28. Arensberg, *The Irish Countryman* (1937), Chap. 5.
29. *Village on the Border* (1957), pp. 105 f.

the invitation to take a meal or to attend an entertainment, are the very fabric of friendship. A token after unintended offense is offered. The more intensive the friendship, indeed, the greater may come to be the significance of these small material exchanges. It may come to the point that neither party pays for himself in saloon or restaurant; each must constantly entertain the other. This duplicates, in my opinion, the high moral significance of goods in tribal society. Among the Kachin, in Leach's words, "the immaterial *hka*" is paid by the ritual *hpaga*.

In conclusion I recapitulate some of my earlier accounts of Barotse law to bring out descriptively the elements which I believe are relevant to the emphasis placed on the notion of debt.

The conscious aim of the court in trying to settle disputes between kin is to apply the law so that litigants may continue to live together and that their relationship, as a defined set of mutual obligations, may endure. To achieve this aim the court must evaluate ethically their behavior to each other as well as to other persons linked in the same system of relationships, and must support those who have done well and rebuke into better behavior those who have done ill. But the court has also to give judgment on a specific demand, as for example whether plaintiff or defendant has the right to a particular garden. Directions about the property are handed down in the midst of sermons on parental, filial, and fraternal love.

Sometimes the person who possesses the right to the property is the person who has done ill. The court, as we have seen, does not shirk the task by saying "this is a court of law and not a court of morals." It attempts a reconciliation of law and justice. The reconciliation of law and justice is strictly limited by the system of law which the court should apply. Where a wife sues for and is granted a divorce on the grounds that her husband has wronged her, the court cannot compel him to give her goods other than half their crops; it can only plead with him to do so.[30] Where a superior in a kin relationship, in a village, or in a political unit has done wrong to a junior, the court similarly cannot always force him to do right, and it cannot always deprive him of the rights of his position. This is clearly illustrated in the case of the headman's fish dams in Chapters 1 and 4. When the

30. See "The Case of the Ungenerous Husband," in my *Judicial Process among the Barotse* (1955), p. 172.

headman forbade his sisters' sons to work his fish dams unless they joined his village, the court disapproved of this as unjust ("they have not done wrong," said one judge). But only a solitary judge held that the dams now belonged to the nephews and were lost to the headman. The senior sitting judge said, "We cannot change the law against Mahalihali" (the headman), and this was felt by most judges. They contented themselves with imprecise statements that he ought to allow his nephews to fish. For to have changed the law against Mahalihali and to have allowed his nephews the right to hold the dams or fish them without his permission would have altered principles on which the whole structure is erected: land in a village attaches to the title of its headman, and all his villagers have enforceable rights to sufficient of this land for their sustenance. Other kin have moral claims to use the land if there is more than the villagers can use, but they cannot move title to what they use into another village. The property rights of a corporation sole must not be tampered with by judicial action (the incumbent may himself give some away) or the consequences would be incalculable. In this case, had the ruling that the headman had lost his rights over the dams been adopted by the court, other sisters' sons working their maternal uncles' land while living with their fathers, or sons residing at their mothers' villages but working their fathers' land, could have brought suits for independent holding. Headmen would have hesitated to lend land to kin living elsewhere. The whole of Lozi social structure, as a permanent arrangement of headmen's titles in relation to land distribution, would have been shattered. It was left to the experienced and wise head of the court to find a solution that would not tamper with the law but would see that justice was done: the court would leave the position of the headmanship, as a *universitas juris,* untouched, but would place in the position an individual who would discharge his varied obligations to dispose of the property of the position more generously. The organization of status relationships must be maintained: property is referred to, and interdependent with, this organization.

The judgments in this case illustrate a significant aspect of Barotse law. Many of its legal rules are imprecisely formulated. When one questions informants, or the court itself on cases stated, or when the Barotse discuss legal problems, the answer is often on the moral issue involved, as: "People would not sue," or, "I cannot stop my married daughter working on my land." Legal issues and moral issues are con-

stantly confounded, and a man's rights to his legal dues may depend
on his fulfilling his moral obligations sensibly and uprightly. But
though Barotse status relationships involve this high moral element,
there must be a measure for assessing fulfillment. This fulfillment is
seen in the constant discharge of obligation, the rendering of service
and of material help—i.e. the discharge of debt. Somewhat paradoxically, the very high emphasis on morality, in a society with limited
goods, puts great emphasis on material discharge of obligation and
makes failure to render it a wrong.

This situation reflects the fact that, in these undifferentiated relationships, serving manifold interests, the Law of Persons and the Law
of Property are confounded. The dominant rights, which the king and
other rulers and headmen have in the land and other property of the
groups which they control, are essential constituents of their relations
with their fellows. I do not wish to give the impression either that
property is an appendage to social relationships or that social relationships are built solely on property. In some relationships, rights to property accrue from kinship status; in others, transfers of property establish the relationships themselves. Throughout, property relations and
status relationships are fundamental attributes of each other; the Barotse state this quite explicitly. The king's ownership of the land, the
headman's control of the village's estate, are stated by the Barotse and
are seen by the outsider to be basic to their relations with their subordinates. Rights of husband and wife to the property of the marriage
are central to the marital relationship. My argument has been that in
the Barotse system property rights over land, things, titles, and persons inhere in social positions which are linked together by general
definition in complex arrangements, and that therefore the vastly
greater part of the Barotse law of property is also the Barotse law of
persons. Property is an essential nexus in all social relations and the
relationships cannot be defined without reference to it. Hence the
rendering of property—the paying of material debts—dominates the
most important relationships of Barotse law.

I have tried to show in my analysis of the Law of Transactions and
the Law of Wrongs that these same concepts are extended to cover
relationships with "strangers." Transfers of property to establish a
debt are necessary to make an agreement enforceable at law. An injury sets up a debt, which has to be redeemed, since either it is in
breach of status relation, or it tends to found an absolute liability.

Moreover, as transactions between strangers tend to be expanded to the pattern of kinship relationships, even a wrong committed by a man on a stranger may be similarly expanded by mystical beliefs. All relations become quasi-status in character.

For reasons which I cannot here attempt to examine, this bias of the law persisted in the history of Europe long after society had ceased to be dominated by kinship relationships. But status, though of a different kind, was still important. Trade had expanded far beyond the trade of the tribes with which I have been dealing, but most commodities were still employed in status relations. Hence the notion of debt prevailed. Thus a lord in the Middle Ages, claiming for the services due from his tenant, took action by distress: an extrajudicial levy on the tenant's movables not for sale, but as a gage. Noyes considered that "It is not a means whereby the distrainor can satisfy the debt [sic] that is due to him," but a method of constraining the defaulting tenant. To me, with all respect, it seems the old notion that a high moral duty appears in material form as a "debt." [31]

Legal ideas also outlive the situation that breeds them, and the restricting influence of set forms of action, with writing and a class of lawyers, may have helped preserve them. Stone stressed the importance of historical anomalies, "the contemporaneity of the non-contemporaneous." [32] Ehrlich discussed the late persistence of the idea of *Schuld* in the history of contract.[33] But new developments, as in the later contracts in Rome, or actions other than that in debt in England, developed alongside the old legal forms. They indicated a movement away from a situation where the law was mainly interested in commodities insofar as they conserved pre-established status relationships or established new status relationships. Commodities were no longer of primary value in discharging or creating debts in linked series between persons of linked status. Commodities began to develop an autonomous existence, entirely independent of their significance in multiplex status relations. There is a kind of paradox here. For as commodities in a more highly differentiated society began to form an autonomous system, and themselves increasingly drew people into impersonal, restricted, ephemeral relationships, the commodities lost some

31. Noyes, *The Institution of Property* (1936), p. 259.

32. *The Province and Function of Law* (1947), p. 479.

33. *Fundamental Principles of the Sociology of Law* (1913), pp. 104 f. Note that in so far as etymological connections show anything about social thought, Schuld = debt; schuldig = guilty; unschuldig = innocent (in Afrikaans, skuld, skuldig, onskuldig, respectively).

of their symbolic value. The emphasis on material obligation lessened: the notion of debt ceased to dominate the law. The law was still concerned with adjustment of claims to commodities, but it envisaged these as arising from differentiated forms of ownership, contract, and injury, and not from debt.[34]

I have suggested throughout that when we analyze Barotse law, or perhaps any tribal legal system, we find that every doctrine is influenced by the fact that the society is dominantly organized around fixed, permanent, and multiplex status relationships. This point was fundamental in Sir Henry Maine's approach, but I hope my treatment of Barotse law has filled in some of the details. I have described how this situation influences ideas of constitutional powers, and how land tenure is involved throughout in status relationships. Indeed land among the Barotse plays a role in these relationships which is sharply different from the role of chattels. Land is the most general utility of the society, but in addition the whole social structure is stabilized through time and change about positions on the land. Hence the Barotse judges defend this structure of landholding; but they distinguish between the positions and their incumbents. If an incumbent defaults in other duties of his station, he can be expelled from the position. The structure of positions is not thereby affected.

Chattels establish more ephemeral links between the personnel of these stabilized positions. Occupants of several statuses may hold rights at the same time in a piece of land or in a chattel. All these rights are described by one term, "ownership." Here Barotse jurisprudence has not refined or elaborated its terminology. The complex vocabulary of this jurisprudence lies in defining social positions—status—and in defining different kinds of property. And since the Barotse are interested in property insofar as it knits together people in different status relationships, they tend to stress obligations arising out of ownership of property rather than rights in it. But property is an essential element in constituting and maintaining these relations: the Law of Persons, the Law of Things, and the Law of Obligations are inextricably involved in one another.

I have tried to show how this general background to Barotse law,

34. It is appropriate that I here acknowledge, at the end of this speculative summary, the stimulus I have received from Seagle's *The Quest for Law* (1941) and Stone's *The Province and Function of Law* (1947). I need hardly add that neither is responsible for my temerity or my errors.

the way it is rooted in obligations between persons of set status, affects their interpretation of the relatively few transactions they have. As kinship relationships are each distinct, so each form of transaction is specific, and there is no general theory of agreement. The stress of contractual law, as in status relationships, is on obligation: the rule is *caveat vendor,* and not *caveat emptor.* Finally, since ownership of obligations from others, expressed in claims on things, plays a domi- nant role in the law, no obligation is established by bare promises or executory contracts. Some property must pass or be created to estab- lish obligations; in Maine's words, contracts are conveyances. The same situation affects conceptions of wrong and injury, of responsi- bility and liability, and of obligation and debt.

I hope my anthropological colleagues will derive some understand- ing of the legal systems they have studied from my attempt to inter- pret Barotse law in terms of the problems which jurists have set. Correspondingly, I hope lawyers may feel that my attempt as an anthropologist to understand the ideas of jurisprudence in one African society throws some light on the problems of inadequately recorded early systems of law. If I have achieved these aims in the least, I shall feel well repaid.

BIBLIOGRAPHY

Achebe, C., *Things Fall Apart*, London, Heinemann, 1958.

Allan, W., *The African Husbandman*, Edinburgh, Oliver and Boyd, 1965.

———, M. Gluckman, D. U. Peters, and C. G. Trapnell, *Land-holding and Land Usage among the Plateau Tonga*, Rhodes-Livingstone Paper No. 14, 1948.

Andrzejewski, S., *Military Organization and Society*, London, Routledge and Kegan Paul, 1953.

Arensberg, C., *The Irish Countryman*, Cambridge, Harvard University Press, 1937.

———, and S. T. Kimball, *Family and Community in Ireland*, Cambridge, Harvard University Press, 1940.

Barnes, J. A., *Marriage in a Changing Society*, Rhodes-Livingstone Paper No. 20, 1951.

———, *Politics in a Changing Society*, Capetown, Oxford University Press (transferred Manchester University Press) for the Rhodes-Livingstone Institute, 1954.

———, "Seven Types of Segmentation," *Rhodes-Livingstone Journal*, 17 (1955), 1–22.

Barton, R. F., *Ifugao Law*, University of California Publications in American Archaeology and Ethnology, 15, 1919.

———, *The Kalingas* (posthumously published, ed. by E. A. Hoebel), Chicago, University of Chicago Press, 1949.

Bernardi, B., *The Mugwe, A Failing Prophet*, London, Oxford University Press for the International African Institute, 1959.

Biebuyck, D., ed., *African Agrarian Systems*, Oxford University Press for the International African Institute, 1963.

Bloch, M., *Feudal Society*, trans. from the French (*La Société féodale*, 1939–40), by L. A. Manyon, London, Routledge and Kegan Paul, 1961.

Bohannan, P. J., *Tiv Farm and Settlement*, London, H.M.S. Office, 1954.

———, "Some Principles of Exchange and Investment among the Tiv," *American Anthropologist*, 57 (1955), 60–70.

———, *Justice and Judgment among the Tiv*, London, Oxford University Press, 1957.

Brooke, N. T., "Some Legal Aspects of Land Tenure in Nigeria," *African Studies* (1946), pp. 211–20.

Busia, K. A., *The Position of the Chief in the Modern Political System of Ashanti*, London, Oxford University Press for the International African Institute, 1951.

Cardozo, B. N., *The Nature of the Judicial Process*, New Haven, Yale University Press, 1921.

Cheshire, G. C., *The Modern Law of Real Property*, 9th ed., London, Butterworth, 1962.

Chubb, L. T., *Ibo Land Tenure*, Ibadan, Ibadan University Press, 1961.

Cohn, N., *The Pursuit of the Millennium*, London, Secker and Warburg, 1957.

Coillard, F., *On the Threshold of Central Africa*, London, Hodder and Stoughton, 1904.

Colson, E., "The Role of Cattle among the Plateau Tonga," *Rhodes-Livingstone Journal*, 11 (1951), 10–46; reprinted in *The Plateau Tonga of Northern Rhodesia*, Manchester, Manchester University Press for the Rhodes-Livingstone Institute, 1962.

————, *Marriage and the Family among the Plateau Tonga of Northern Rhodesia*, Manchester, Manchester University Press for the Rhodes-Livingstone Institute, 1958.

————, *The Social Organization of the Gwembe Tonga*, Manchester, Manchester University Press for the Rhodes-Livingstone Institute, 1960.

————, *The Plateau Tonga of Northern Rhodesia: Social and Religious Studies*, Manchester, Manchester University Press; New York, Humanities Press, 1962.

————, and M. Gluckman, eds., *Seven Tribes of British Central Africa*, 1951; 2d imp., Manchester, Manchester University Press; New York, Humanities Press, 1959.

Cory, H., *Sukuma Law and Custom*, London, Oxford University Press for the International African Institute, 1953.

Cunnison, I., *History on the Luapula*, Rhodes-Livingstone Paper No. 21, 1951.

————, *The Luapula Peoples of Northern Rhodesia: Custom and History in Tribal Politics*, Manchester, Manchester University Press for the Rhodes-Livingstone Institute; New York, Humanities Press, 1959.

Curtis, C. P., *It's Your Law*, Cambridge, Harvard University Press, 1954.

Danquah, J. B., *Akan Laws and Customs and the Akim Abuakwa Constitution*, London, Routledge, 1928.

Diamond, A. S., *Primitive Law*, London, Watts, 1935.

Dobb, M., *Studies in the Development of Capitalism*, London, Routledge and Kegan Paul, 1946; 5th imp. 1951.

Dowling, N. T., *Cases on Constitutional Law*, 5th ed., Brooklyn, Foundation Press, 1954.

Dundas, C., "Native Laws of Some Bantu Tribes of East Africa," *Journal of the Royal Anthropological Institute*, 51 (1921), 217–78.

Durkheim, E., *De la Division du travail social*, Paris, Alcan, 1893, trans. as *The Division of Labour in Society* by G. Simpson; Glencoe, Ill., Free Press, 1933.

Ehrlich, E., *Grundlegung der Soziologie des Rechts* (1913), trans. as *Fundamental Principles of the Sociology of Law* by W. L. Moll; Cambridge, Harvard University Press, 1936.

Elias, T. O., *Nigerian Land Law and Custom*, London, Routledge and Kegan Paul, 1951.

———, *The Nature of African Customary Law*, Manchester, Manchester University Press, 1956.

Ellis, T. P., *Welsh Tribal Law and Custom in the Middle Ages*, Oxford, Clarendon Press, 1926.

Epstein, A. L., *The Administration of Justice and the Urban African*, London, H.M.S. Office, 1953.

———, *Juridical Techniques and the Judicial Process*, Rhodes-Livingstone Paper No. 23, Manchester, Manchester University Press, 1954.

Evans-Pritchard, E. E., *Witchcraft, Oracles and Magic among the Azande of the Anglo-Egyptian Sudan*, Oxford, Clarendon Press, 1937.

———, *The Nuer*, Oxford, Clarendon Press, 1940.

———, "The Nuer of the Anglo-Egyptian Sudan," in *African Political Systems*, ed. M. Fortes and E. E. Evans-Pritchard, London; Oxford University Press for the International African Institute, 1940.

———, *The Political System of the Anuak of the Anglo-Egyptian Sudan*, London, Percy Lund, Humphries, for the London School of Economics and Political Science, 1940.

———, "Further Observations on the Political System of the Anuak," *Sudan Notes and Records*, 27 (1947), 62–97.

———, *Kinship and Marriage among the Nuer*, Oxford, Clarendon, 1951.

———, *The Divine Kingship of the Shilluk of the Anglo-Egyptian Sudan*, Frazer Lecture 1948, Cambridge, University Press, 1948; republished in his *Essays in Social Anthropology*, London, Faber and Faber, 1962.

Fagan, H., and R. H. Hilton, *The English Rising of 1381*, London, Lawrence and Wishart, 1950.

Fauconnet, P., *La Responsabilité*, Paris, Librairie Felix Alcan, 2d ed. (1928).

Fifoot, C. H. S., *English Law and Its Background*, London, Bell, 1932.

Firth, R., *We, The Tikopia*, London, Allen and Unwin, 1936.

———, *Primitive Polynesian Economy*, London, Routledge, 1939.

———, *Social Change in Tikopia*, London, Allen and Unwin, 1959.

Forde, C. D. "Ward Organisation among the Yakö," *Africa*, 20 (1950), 276.

———, "Death and Succession: An Analysis of Yakö Mortuary Ritual," in *Essays on the Ritual of Social Relations*, ed. M. Gluckman; Manchester, Manchester University Press, 1962.

Forde, C. D., *Yakö Studies,* London, Oxford University Press for the International African Institute, 1964.

———, ed., *African Worlds,* London, Oxford University Press for the International African Institute, 1954.

———, *The Dynamics of Clanship among the Tallensi,* London, Oxford University Press for the International African Institute, 1945.

Fortes, M., *The Web of Kinship among the Tallensi,* London, Oxford University Press for the International African Institute, 1949.

———, "Analysis and Description in Social Anthropology," Presidential Address to Anthropology Section of the British Association for the Advancement of Science, in *The Advancement of Science,* No. 38 (Sept. 1953), pp. 1–11.

———, and E. E. Evans-Pritchard, ed., *African Political Systems,* London, Oxford University Press for the International African Institute, 1940.

Frankenberg, R. J., *Village on the Border,* London, Cohen and West, 1957.

Gann, L. H., "The End of the Slave Trade in British Central Africa: 1889–1912," *Rhodes-Livingstone Journal: Human Problems in British Central Africa,* 16 (1954), pp. 27–51.

———, *The Birth of a Plural Society: Northern Rhodesia 1894–1914,* Manchester, Manchester University Press for the Rhodes-Livingstone Institute, 1958.

Gibbs, J. L., Jr., "The Kpelle Moot: A Therapeutic Model for the Informal Settlement of Disputes," *Africa* 33 (1963), 1–11.

Gibson, G. D., "Double Descent and its Correlates among the Herero of Ngamiland," *American Anthropologist,* 58 (1956), 109–39.

Gluckman, M., *Economy of the Central Barotse Plain,* Rhodes-Livingstone Paper No. 7, 1941.

———, *Administrative Organization of the Barotse Native Authorities,* Rhodes-Livingstone Communications No. 1, 1943.

———, *Essays on Lozi Land and Royal Property,* Rhodes-Livingstone Paper No. 10, Livingstone, Northern Rhodesia, Rhodes-Livingstone Institute, 1943.

———, "A Lozi Price Control Debate," *South African Journal of Economics,* 11 (3) (Sept. 1943); summarized in *Colonial Review* (March 1944).

———, "Kinship and Marriage among the Lozi of Northern Rhodesia and the Zulu of Natal," in *African Systems of Kinship and Marriage,* ed. A. R. Radcliffe-Brown and C. D. Forde; London, Oxford University Press for the International African Institute, 1950.

———, "The Lozi of Barotseland in North-Western Rhodesia" in Colson and Gluckman, eds. (see above).

———, *Custom and Conflict in Africa,* Oxford, Blackwell; Glencoe, Ill., Free Press, 1955.

————, *The Judicial Process among the Barotse of Northern Rhodesia*, Manchester, Manchester University Press for the Rhodes-Livingstone Institute; New York, Humanities Press, 1955.

————, "African Jurisprudence," Presidential Address to the Sociology Section of the British Association for the Advancement of Science, in *The Advancement of Science*, No. 74 (Nov. 1961).

————, "Anthropological Problems arising from the African Industrial Revolution," in *Social Change in Africa*, ed. A. W. Southall, London, Oxford University Press for the International African Institute, 1961.

————, *Order and Rebellion in Tribal Africa*, London, Cohen and West; Glencoe, Ill., Free Press, 1963.

————, *Politics, Law and Ritual in Tribal Society: Some Problems in Social Anthropology*, Oxford, Blackwell; Chicago, Aldine; New York, New American Library of World Literature–Mentor Library, 1965.

————, ed., *Essays on the Ritual of Social Relations*, Manchester, Manchester University Press; New York, Humanities Press, 1962.

————, J. C. Mitchell, and J. A. Barnes, "The Village Headman in British Central Africa," *Africa*, 19 (2) (1949), 89–106, reprinted in M. Gluckman, *Order and Rebellion in Tribal Africa*, London, Cohen and West; Glenco Ill., Free Press, 1963.

Goodenough, W. H., *Property, Kin and Community on Truk*, Yale University Publications in Anthropology No. 46, 1951.

Goody, J., "Fields of Social Control among the LoDagaba," *Journal of the Royal Anthropological Institute*, 87 (1) (1957), 75–104.

————, "The Classification of Double Descent Systems," *Current Anthropology*, 2 (2) (1961), 61–88.

————, *Death, Property and the Ancestors*, Stanford, Stanford University Press, 1962.

Green, M. M., *Land Tenure in an Ibo Village in South-Eastern Nigeria*, London, Percy Lund, Humphries, for London School of Economics and Political Science, Monographs on Social Anthropology No. 6, 1941.

Griaule, M., and G. Dieterlen, "The Dogon of the French Sudan," in *African Worlds*, ed. C. D. Forde (see above).

Grinnell, G. B. *The Fighting Cheyennes*, New York, Scribner, 1915; Norman, Oklahoma University Press, 1958.

————, *The Cheyenne Indians*, New Haven, Yale University Press, 1923.

Gulliver, P. H., *Social Control in an African Society*, London, Routledge and Kegan Paul, 1963.

Hailey, Lord, *An African Survey*, London, Oxford University Press, 1938.

Halsbury, H. S. G. (1st Earl), *Laws of England*, 2d ed., London, Butterworth, 1931–42.

Hamilton, W. H., "The Ancient Maxim Caveat Emptor," *Yale Law Journal*, 40 (8) (June 1931), 1133–87.

Harris, R., "The Political Significance of Double Unilineal Descent," *Journal of the Royal Anthropological Institute*, 90 (1) (1962), 86–101.

Hart, H. L. A., *The Concept of Law*, Oxford, Clarendon Press, 1961.

Herskovits, M., *Dahomey, an Ancient West African Kingdom*, New York, Augustin, 1938.

——, *Economic Anthropology*, New York, Knopf, 1952.

Hertz, R., *Death and the Right Hand*, trans. by R. and C. Needham, London, Cohen and West, 1960, from "Contribution à une étude sur la représentation collective de la mort," *L'Annee sociologique*, 10 (1907), 89–113, and "La préeminence de la main droite: Essai sur la polarité religieuse," *Revue philosophique*, 58 (1909), 553–80.

Hoebel, E. A., *The Political Organization and Law-ways of the Comanche Indians*, American Anthropological Association, Memoir 54; Contribution from the Santa Fe Laboratory of Anthropology, 4 (1940).

——, *The Law of Primitive Man*, Cambridge, Harvard University Press, 1954.

Hogbin, I., *Law and Order in Polynesia*, London, Christophers; New York, Harcourt, Brace, 1934.

——, *Experiments in Civilization*, London, Routledge, 1939.

——, *Transformation Scene*, London, Routledge and Kegan Paul, 1951.

Holdsworth, W. S., *A History of English Law*, 3d ed., London, Methuen, 1923, vol. 2.

Holleman, J. F., "Die Zulu Isigodi," *Bantu Studies*, 15 (June and Sept. 1941), Part 2, 91–118; Part 3, 245–76 (published also separately: Johannesburg, University of the Witwatersrand Press).

——, *The Pattern of Hera Kinship*, Rhodes-Livingstone Paper No. 17, 1949.

——, *Shona Customary Law*, Cape Town and London, Oxford University Press, for the Rhodes-Livingstone Institute and the Beit Trust, 1952.

Holmes, O. W., Jr., *The Common Law*, Boston, Little, Brown, 1881.

Homans, G. C., *English Villagers in the Thirteenth Century*, New York, Russell and Russell, 1941, 1960.

Howell, P. P., *A Manual of Nuer Law*, London, Oxford University Press for the International African Institute, 1954.

Jalla, A., *Dictionary of the Lozi Language, 1, Lozi-English*, London, United Society for Christian Literature, 1936.

Jaspan, M. A., "A Sociological Case Study: Communal Hostility to Imposed Social Change in South Africa," in *Approaches to Community Development*, Phillips Ruopp, ed., The Hague, van Hoeve, 1953, pp. 97–120.

Jolliffe, J. E. A., *The Constitutional History of Mediaeval England, from the English Settlement to 1485*, London, Adam and Charles Black, 1937.

Jolowicz, H. F., *Historical Introduction to the Study of Roman Law*, rev. ed., Cambridge, University Press, 1939.

Kenny, C. S., *Outlines of Criminal Law*, Cambridge, Cambridge University Press, 1929.

Kern, F., *Kingship and Law in the Middle Ages*, trans. from *Gottesgnadentum und Widerstandsrecht im früheren Mittelalter. Zum Entwicklungsgeschichte der Monarchie* (Leipzig, 1914) by S. B. Chimes, Oxford, Blackwell, 1939.

Kroeber, A. L., "Law of the Yurok Indians," *Atti del Congresso-Internazionale degli Americanisti*, Rome, Sept. 1926; Rome, Riccardo Garroni, 1928, pp. 511–16.

Kuper, H., *An African Aristocracy: Rank among the Swazi*, London, Oxford University Press for the International African Institute, 1947.

Leach, E. R., *Political Systems of Highland Burma*, London, Bell, 1954.

——, "Aspects of Bridewealth and Marriage Stability among the Kachin and Lakher," in *Rethinking Anthropology*, London, Athlone Press, London School of Economics Monographs on Social Anthropology No. 22, 1961.

——, *Pul Eliya: A Village in Ceylon*, Cambridge, Cambridge University Press, 1961.

Lévi-Strauss, C., *Les Structures élémentaires de la parenté*, Paris, Presses Universitaires, 1949.

Lewis, I. M., "Clanship and Contract in Northern Somaliland," *Africa, 29* (1959), 274–93.

Lindblom, G., *The Akamba*, Uppsala, University of Uppsala, 1920.

Lips, J. E., "Naskapi Law: Law and Order in a Hunting Society," *Trans. American Philosophical Society, 37*, part 4 (1947).

Llewellyn, K. N., and E. A. Hoebel, *The Cheyenne Way*, Norman, University of Oklahoma Press, 1941.

Lloyd, P. C., *Yoruba Land Law*, London, Oxford University Press for the Nigerian Institute of Social and Economic Research, 1962.

Low, D. A., and R. C. Pratt, *Buganda and British Overrule*, London, Oxford University Press for the East African Institute of Social Research, 1960.

Lowie, R. H., *Primitive Society*, London, Routledge, 1921.

Maine, H. S., *Ancient Law*, London, Murray, 1861 (1909 ed.: Pollock's notes).

Mair, L. P., *An African People in the Twentieth Century* (on Baganda), London, Routledge, 1934.

Maitland, F. W., *The Constitutional History of England*, Cambridge, Cambridge University Press, 1908.

——, *The Collected Papers of Frederic William Maitland*, Cambridge, Cambridge University Press, 1911.

Malinowski, B., *Argonauts of the Western Pacific*, London, Routledge, 1922.

———, *Crime and Custom in Savage Society*, London, Kegan Paul, Trench and Trubner, 1926.

———, *Myth in Primitive Psychology*, London, Kegan Paul, Trench and Trubner, 1926; reprinted in B. Malinowski, *Magic, Science and Religion, and Other Essays*, Glencoe, Ill., Free Press.

———, *Coral Gardens and Their Magic*, London, Allen and Unwin, 1935.

Manning, B. L., "England: Edward III and Richard II," chap. 15 of *Cambridge Mediaeval History*, Cambridge University Press, 7 (1932), 434–85.

Maquet, J. J., *The Premise of Inequality in Ruanda*, London, Oxford University Press for the International African Institute, 1961.

Mauss, M., *Essai sur le don, forme archaique de l'échange*, Paris, Presses Universitaires, 1925; trans. by I. Cunnison as *The Gift: Forms and Functions of Exchange in Archaic Societies*, London, Cohen and West, 1954.

Meek, C. K., *Law and Authority in a Nigerian Tribe*, London, Oxford University Press, 1937.

———, *Land Law and Custom in the Colonies*, 2d ed., London, Oxford University Press, 1949.

Meggitt, M. J., *Desert People. A Study of the Walbiri Aborigines of Central Australia*, London and Sydney, Angus and Robertson, 1962.

———, *The Lineage System of the Mae Enga of the New Guinea Highlands*, Edinburgh, Oliver and Boyd, 1965.

Mills, M. E. E., and M. Wilson, *Keiskammahoek Rural Survey*, Vol. 4: *Land Tenure*, Pietermaritzburg, Shuter and Shooter, 1952.

Miner, H., *The Primitive City of Timbuctoo*, Princeton, Princeton University Press for the American Philosophical Society, 1953.

Mitchell, J. C., "The Political Organization of the Yao of Southern Nyasaland," *African Studies*, 8 (3) (Sept. 1949), 141–59.

———, "Land Tenure and Agriculture among the Machinga Yao," *Rhodes-Livingstone Journal: Human Problems in British Africa*, 10 (1950), 1–13.

———, *The Yao Village*, Manchester, Manchester University Press for the Rhodes-Livingstone Institute, 1956.

Murdock, G. P., and W. P. Goodenough, "Social Organization of Truk," *Southwestern Journal of Anthropology*, 3 (1947), 331–43.

Murray, J. H., ed., *A New English Dictionary on Historical Principles*, Oxford, Clarendon Press, 1901.

Nadel, S. F., *A Black Byzantium: The Kingdom of the Nupe of Nigeria*, London, Oxford University for the International African Institute, 1942.

———, *The Nuba*, London, Oxford University Press, 1947.

Needham, R., "The Left Hand of the Mugwe: An Analytical Note on the Structure of Meru Symbolism," *Africa*, 30 (1) (1960), 20–33.

Noyes, C. R., *The Institution of Property*, New York, Longmans Green; London, Humphrey Milford, 1936.

Oberg, K., "The Kingdom of Ankole in Uganda," in *African Political Systems*, ed. Fortes and Evans-Pritchard; London, Oxford University Press for the International African Institute, 1940.

Obi, S. N. C., *The Ibo Law of Property*, London, Butterworth, 1963.

Oliver, D. L., *A Solomon Island Society: Kinship and Leadership among the Siuai of Bougainville*, Cambridge, Mass., Harvard University Press, 1955.

Parsons, T., *The Social System*, London, Tavistock, 1952.

Peristiany, J. G., "Pokot Sanctions and Structure," *Africa*, 24 (1) (Jan. 1954), 17–25.

Plucknett, T. F. T., *A Concise History of Common Law*, 5th ed., London, Butterworth, 1956.

Pollock, F., and F. W. Maitland, *The History of English Law before the Time of Edward I*, 2d ed., Cambridge, Cambridge University Press, 1923 (citations are by page references in 2d ed.).

Pospisil, L., *Kapauku Papuans and Their Law*, Yale University Publications in Anthropology No. 54 (1958).

Potter, M., *An Historical Introduction to English Law and its Institutions*, London, Sweet and Maxwell, 1932.

Radcliffe-Brown, A. R., "Patrilineal and Matrilineal Succession," *Iowa Law Review* (1935); reprinted in his *Structure and Function in Primitive Society* (see below).

———, *Structure and Function in Primitive Society*, London, Cohen and West, 1952.

Rattray, R. S., *Ashanti*, Oxford, Clarendon Press, 1923.

———, *Ashanti Law and Constitution*, Oxford, Clarendon Press, 1929.

Richards, A. I., "Mother-right in Central Africa," in *Essays Presented to C. G. Seligman*, ed. E. E. Evans-Pritchard, R. Firth, B. Malinowski, and I. Schapera; London, Kegan Paul, Trench, Trubner, 1933.

———, *Land, Labour and Diet in Northern Rhodesia*, London, Oxford University Press for the International African Institute, 1939.

———, "Social Mechanisms for the Transfer of Political Rights in Some African Tribes," Presidential Address, *Journal of the Royal Anthropological Institute*, 90 (1960), 175–90.

——— (ed.), *East African Chiefs*, London, Faber and Faber, 1960.

Richardson, J., *Law and Status among the Kiowa Indians*, American Ethnological Society, Monograph 1, 1940.

Rostow, E. V., *Planning for Freedom: The Public Law of American Capitalism*, W. W. Cook Foundation Lectures, Series 9, 1958, New Haven, Yale University Press, 1959.

Salmond, J., *Jurisprudence,* 1st ed., London, Stevens and Haynes, 1902.

Schapera, I., *A Handbook of Tswana Law and Custom,* London, Oxford University Press for the International African Institute, 1938.

————, *Native Land Tenure in the Bechuanaland Protectorate,* Lovedale, South Africa, Lovedale Press, 1943.

————, "The Sin of Cain," *Journal of the Royal Anthropological Institute,* 85 (1955), 33–43.

————, "Witchcraft beyond Reasonable Doubt" (on Bechuana, Tswana), *Man,* 55 (80) (May 1955), 72.

————, *Government and Politics in Tribal Societies,* London, Watts, 1956.

Schneider, D. M., "Double Descent on Yap," *Journal of the Polynesian Society,* 71 (1) (1962), 1–24.

————, and K. Gough, eds., *Matrilineal Kinship,* Cambridge, Cambridge University Press; Berkeley and Los Angeles, University of California Press, 1961.

Seagle, W., *The Quest for Law,* 2d ed., New York, Knopf, 1941, republished as *The History of Law,* New York, Tudor, 1946.

Sheddick, V. G., *Land Tenure in Basutoland,* London, H.M.S. Office, 1956.

Shenton, D. M. (Lady), "English History (up to the Tudor Age)," in 5, *Chambers's Encyclopaedia,* 240–56; London, Newnes, 1959.

Smith, M. G., *Government in Zazzau,* London, Oxford University Press for the International African Institute, 1960.

Smith, W., and J. M. Roberts, *Zuni Law: a Field of Values,* Peabody Museum of American Archaeology and Ethnology, Harvard University, 43 (1), 1954.

Spencer, R. H., *The North Alaskan Eskimo: A Study in Ecology and Society,* Smithsonian Institution Bureau of American Ethnology, Bulletin 171, Washington, U.S. Gov. Printing Office, 1959.

Stirke, D. W., *Barotseland: Eight Years among the Barotse,* London, Bale, Sons and Danielson (n.d.) [? 1922].

Stone, J., *The Province and Function of Law,* London, Stevens, 1947.

Ter Haar, B., *Beginselen en Stelsel van het Adatrecht,* Groningen and Batavia, Wolters, 1939; trans. by E. A. Hoebel and A. A. Schiller as *Adat Law in Indonesia,* New York, Institute of Pacific Relations, 1948.

Thomas, W. I., and F. Znaniecki, *The Polish Peasant in Europe and America,* Boston, Badger, 1918/20.

Trevelyan, G. M., *English Social History, A Survey of Six Centuries, Chaucer to Queen Victoria,* New York, Longmans, Green, 1942.

Turner, V. W., *Schism and Continuity in an African Society: A Study of Ndembu Village Life,* Manchester, Manchester University Press for the Rhodes-Livingstone Institute, 1957.

————, "Three Symbols of *Passage* in Ndembu Circumcision Rituals," in

Essays on the Ritual of Social Relations, ed. M. Gluckman; Manchester, Manchester University Press, 1962.

———, "Symbols in Ndembu Ritual," in *Closed Systems and Open Minds,* ed. M. Gluckman; Edinburgh, Oliver and Boyd, 1964.

Uberoi, J. P. S., *Politics of the Kula Ring: An Analysis of the Findings of Bronislaw Malinowski,* Manchester, Manchester University Press; New York, Humanities Press 1962.

Vedder, H., *South-West Africa in Early Times,* London, Oxford University Press, 1938.

Vinogradoff, P., *Outlines of Historical Jurisprudence,* London, Oxford University Press, 1920.

———, *The Collected Papers of Paul Vinogradoff,* with a Memoir by the Right Hon. H. A. L. Fisher, 2 vols., Oxford, Clarendon Press, 1928.

Wallace-Hadrill, J. M., "The Bloodfeud of the Franks," *Bulletin of the John Rylands Library,* 41 (2) (March 1959), 459–87.

Watson, W., *Tribal Cohesion in a Money Economy,* Manchester, Manchester University Press for the Rhodes-Livingstone Institute; New York, Humanities Press, 1958.

Wessels, J. H., *History of Roman-Dutch Law,* Grahamstown, African Book Co., 1908.

Westbeech, G., "The Diaries of George Westbeech" in *Trade and Travel in Early Barotseland,* ed. E. C. Tabler; London, Chatto and Windus for the Rhodes-Livingstone Museum, 1963.

Wile, I. S., *Handedness: Right and Left,* Toronto, Longmans, 1934.

Williams, G. L., "Language and the Law," *Law Quarterly Review,* 61 (1945), 71–86, 179–95, 293–303, 384–406; and 62 (1946), 387–406.

Wilson, G., *The Land Rights of Individuals among the Nyakyusa,* Rhodes-Livingstone Paper No. 1, 1938.

Wilson, M., "Effects on the Xhosa and Nyakyusa of Scarcity of Land," in *African Agrarian Systems,* ed. D. Biebuyck; London, Oxford University Press for the International African Institute, 1963, pp. 374–91.

Winfield, P. H., *The Province of the Law of Tort,* Cambridge, Cambridge University Press, 1931.

———, "The Myth of Absolute Liability," *Law Quarterly Review,* 42 (1926), 37–51.

INDEX

Abduction, 194

Absolute liability. *See* Liability, absolute

Absorbent legal concepts, 24

Accident: responsibility for, 205; Nuer compensation for, 207; and homicide, 212; among Barotse and Kamba, 233

Accusation: fined, 178; false, damages for, 231; per se damaging, 238; of witchcraft, 238

Achebe, C., 210

Action: and intention, 207; in debt, 262 f.

Act of Settlement, 59

Acts of God: and Barotse, 188, 232; and N. Rhodesian tribes, 188

Address, 138

Administration: divisions of, 41–42; affairs of, 44; and political system, 63; and rebellion, 63 f.; re-establishment system, 69; kings', of land, 144. *See also* Estates

Adultery: and Urban African Courts, 193; and higher fines, 194; and Nuer, 219–20; and redress, 220; and Barotse, 228 f.

Africa, African: polities, segmentation and conflict in, 49 ff.; morphological arrangement of states, 68 f.; land rights, 76; alienation of land in, 99; cash cropping in, 99; succession in, 123 f.; and English law, 234 f.; and Urban Courts, 244–45

Agency, 179, 187–89; in Ifugao, 198

Agistment: described, 161; case on, 184 f.; and property, 186–87; and Tiv, 261. *See also* Herding

Agreement, 182, 194; and property exchange, 177; bare, 182

Akan, 196

Ambush: and Nuer, 208; and English law, 216 f.; foresteal, 219

Andrezejewski, S., 50 n.

Anglo-Saxons: chattels and kindreds, 133; and Barotse law, 166; vengeance groupings, 214

Animals, 195 f.

Anuak, 47

Appeals, 62 f.

Arensberg, C., and S. T. Kimball, 249, 265–66

Aristotle, 49

Armies, 63, 66. *See also* Weapons

Ashanti, 3

Assembly, Barotse national: to try Ngambela, 36–37; to debate British protection, 45

Australian Aborigines, 221–23

Baganda: treason law, 60; "politics of the capital," 68; land tenure, 109

Barnes, J. A., 127

Barons, English, 71 f.

Barotse: defined, xvii–xviii, 27; movements of with flood, 65–66

  continuity: and king's land rights, 82 f.; and villages, 117 f.; within change, 120 f.; and corporate units, 128 f.; and spatial position, 128 f., 137; structural, 130

  contract: uberrimae fidei, 175; executory transactions, 180; laws of, 180 f.; doctrine of fair price, 192

  courts and law: procedures, 4, 9–11, 13 f.; rules, 17; and mulao, 18; and natural law, 18; and reasonable man, 20 f.; hierarchy of concepts, 23; settlements, 62; and legal propositions, 103 f.; and morality and rights, 267–69

  debt: concept of, 245; and personal relations, 267

  injuries: and legend about theft, 7; and motivational theory, 18; compensation, 211

  land tenure, 14 f., 82 f.; and king's rights, 79 f.; and communal labor, 108

  ownership, 101 f.; and village land rights,

Storrs Lectures